The Good News for the Liturgical Community
Cycle B

The Good News for the Liturgical Community
Cycle B

Valentino Del Mazza, S.D.B.

St. Paul Editions

IMPRIMI POTEST:
Rev. D. Eugenio Valentini, S.D.B.

NIHIL OBSTAT:
Rev. Richard V. Lawlor
Censor Deputatus

IMPRIMATUR:
+ Humberto Cardinal Medeiros
    Archbishop of Boston

Observations regarding the quotations used in the text:

The Bible text in this publication is from the *Revised Standard Version Bible* (modified form), *Catholic Edition*, copyrighted © 1965 and 1966 by the Division of Christian Education of the National Council of the Churches of Christ in the U.S.A., and is used by permission.

Excerpts from addresses of Pope Paul VI and Pope John Paul II have been taken with permission from the texts published in the weekly English editions of *L'Osservatore Romano*, the official publication of Vatican City.

Excerpts from the documents of Vatican Council II have been taken from the N.C. translations appearing in *The Sixteen Documents of Vatican II*, St. Paul Editions.

Library of Congress Cataloging in Publication Data

Del Mazza, Valentino.
    The good news for the liturgical assembly.

    Translation of La buona novella per l'assemblea liturgica.
    1. Church year—Meditations.
BX2170.C55   [D4413]   242'.3   80-10138

ISBN 0-8198-3004-6 cloth
ISBN 0-8198-3005-4 paper

Copyright © 1980, by the Daughters of St. Paul

Printed in the U.S.A. by the Daughters of St. Paul
50 St. Paul's Ave., Boston, MA 02130

The Daughters of St. Paul are an international congregation of religious women serving the Church with the communications media.

To my Catholic friends in America

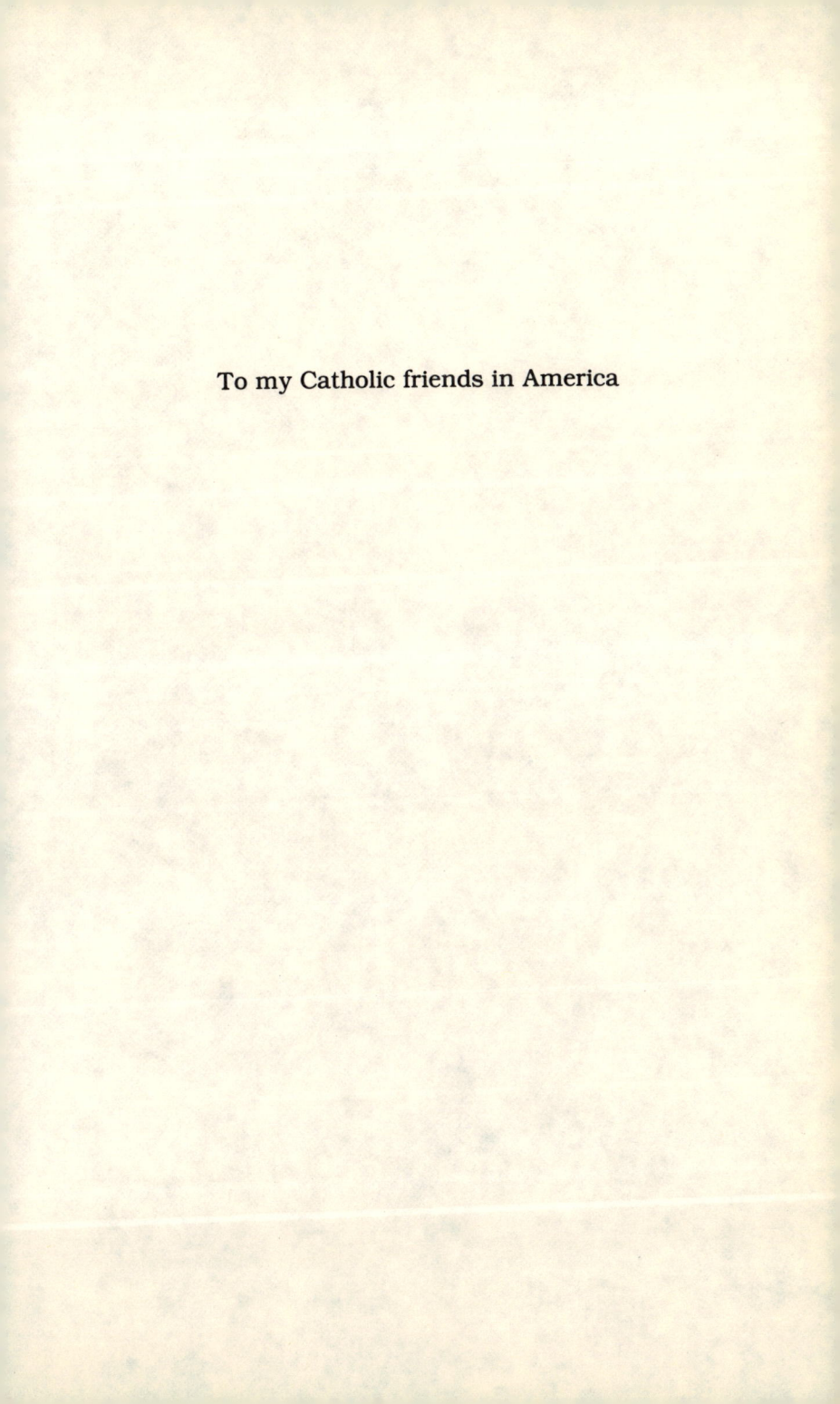

Contents

Preface	13
Advent	15
Christmas Season	30
Lenten Season	50
Easter Season	73
Ordinary Time	119

Preface

The publication in the United States of America of Father Valentino Del Mazza's book *The Good News for the Liturgical Community* will make available to American Catholics the many perceptive insights which he has gleaned from the Sunday Scripture readings in cycle "B" of the *Lectionary*. Here Father Del Mazza presents his biblical and doctrinal reflections in a clear, straightforward manner. His meditations contain many noteworthy citations of the words of the last Popes, the documents of the Second Vatican Council, and the writings of St. Augustine and other significant authors as well. Each of his reflections is followed by some brief suggestions of the pastoral dimensions of the message.

I am hopeful that the content of this volume will bear much fruit in the lives of those who will read it carefully and explore the implications of their Christian heritage ever more profoundly.

Rev. Msgr. Harold P. Darcy
Rector
Pontifical North American College
Rome

Feast of St. Charles Borromeo, 1978

FIRST SUNDAY OF ADVENT:

Man and the Love of God

Readings: Isaiah 63:16-17, 19; 64:2-7
1 Corinthians 1:3-9
Mark 13:33-37

In her first liturgy of the word for Advent, the Church, rendered more beautiful and winning by her liturgical changes, breaks forth into a cry of hope in the name of all mankind: "Return, for the sake of your servants" (First Reading). This call permeates all of Advent and points out, with sober intensity, the essential vocation of man: to attain profound, joyous union with God. In Christ all creation has a theocentric movement (cf. Constitution on the Church, 36). "The first orientation of life, the central axis to which my humanism is geared, remains the theological one. The commandment that surpasses and synthesizes all the others is always the one that bids us love God (cf. Matthew 22:37; Deuteronomy 9:5).... My position with regard to God is the most precious and most important thing. The hierarchy of my duties keeps the first level for God: 'I am the Lord your God' (Exodus 20:2). Christ will repeat it: 'But seek first his kingdom' (Matthew 6:33)....our practical conception of life must reserve the first place for God,...and not just an honorary first place, purely formal, or ritual, but also logical and functional" (Paul VI, July 26, 1972).

But why must we listen to and answer God's call? To honor God is "the key to interpret real life, the supreme good fortune, the highest good, the prime degree of real existence" (Paul VI, *ibid.*).

Man is a microcosm; his very makeup implies universal interaction. In the concrete, he is imbued with a consciousness of things around him, of himself, of others, and of God. With his body he is bound to earth, but with his spirit he is aware of values and is borne upwards beyond himself. Indeed, transcending all relations with the world and with persons, every human being carries within himself the call to union with God, and it is precisely in this union that he finds his perfection (cf. Wisdom 15:3).

It is a fundamental principle that lower beings serve higher ones: the body exists for the soul in its two essential elements, intellect and will, and for the supernatural. The saintly fifteenth-century archbishop of Florence, Antonio Pierozzi, put it as follows: "Material things have been created by God for our body, the body for the intellect, and this in turn for the will; but the will, the focal point of the person, tends to perfection; it is a pilgrim journeying towards God." "You have granted us union with yourself, Lord, not because you need us, but because we need you" (Fourth ode of Solomon). And St. Augustine sums it all up when he says: "To seek You, Lord, is to seek myself, to find You is to find myself, to possess You is to possess myself."

To be at the beck and call of *Love* means to enjoy peace of mind. What is unhappiness? It is a relationship with nothingness; it reveals our metaphysical need not just of something, but of Someone. Deliberate acceptance of false ideas and tenets has a negative impact on the soul. One cause of our neurosis may well be regation, the rejection and struggle against the idea and the life of God. Pascal speaks of the two extremes in man, the infinite and the zero: wretchedness and grandeur—the former because of man's infinite distance from his Creator, the latter because of man's kinship with God, for he has been created in God's image. The clinical record of each one of us may well read: "Disease: infinity," the yearning for the infinite. When all is said and done, human tensions are really eschatological tensions. "Man needs the infinite just as much as he needs the planet on which he is walking." When he knowingly rejects this vertical calling and substitutes a horizontalism that is exclusively worldly and pagan, his very being is thwarted.

To meet God face to face, to participate in loving dialogue with him—this is real nobility of soul. A man's worth is gauged in terms of what he goes in search of. Our age is measured not by our years but by our ideals. To go questing for God, to be possessed by Him is the most wonderful adventure possible for a human being. Some people build their lives around enjoyment; others seek possessions; still others, action as such. But the genuine Christian, one who is not merely Christian in name, seeks God first and foremost. The first page of the Bible portrays the ideal man: he rules over nature; he helps his fellowman; but he does all things in view of a vital union with the Most High. This is where true nobility is to be found; this is indeed genuine character. "God is not greater because you honor Him, but you are greater if you serve Him" (St. Augustine).

It is God who takes the initiative in this wonderful meeting between God and man. God is faithful (Second Reading). This means that God will never tire of bestowing His infinite love upon us; He is leading us "with the mercy and righteousness that come from him" (Baruch 5:9). He does not lose patience with us, even in the face of our constant betrayals (cf. Decree on Ecumenism, 1). As long as God does not cease to be infinitely good and we do not become infinitely evil (both of which are impossible), there will always be the possibility of dialogue and understanding. For God has pledged Himself to be faithful to His covenant of love with us. His infinite goodness will always envelop us as the sea envelops its reefs, for "the gifts and the call of God are irrevocable" (Romans 11:29).

PASTORAL REFLECTIONS

1. The liturgy is the meeting place between God's goodness and our wretchedness. And what is Advent? The special time in which God's fidelity to His people is underlined. It is the annual renewal of *God's offer of eternal friendship* through Jesus Christ, in whom we have been "richly endowed with every gift" (Second Reading).

2. In the face of this prospect of divine intimacy, see what *our responsibility* is: to accept or to reject it. The Gospel of St. Mark (Third Reading) invites us to be on guard, to await the love of God, which becomes more urgent as Christmas draws near. And to shake us out of our lethargy we are reminded of the final day of reckoning. History is often the result of circumstances. It is for us to lay hold of and make fruitful this acceptable time so that our autobiography may become divine history.

3. Undoubtedly all this is very simple to say but difficult to do. For this reason, in addition to watchfulness, we need *prayer*. It is not virtue that creates prayer, but prayer that gives birth to virtue. It is prayer which develops in us a sense of the divine, which gives us hope, strength, salvation. It is in prayer that the human *I* encounters the divine *You*. Prayer is like music: it pierces the heavens.

SECOND SUNDAY OF ADVENT:

Justice and Religion

Readings: Isaiah 40:1-5, 9-11
2 Peter 3:8-14
Mark 1:1-8

Isaiah, son of Amos, the poet among the prophets, foretold the triumphant coming of the Messiah and invited his people to prepare a worthy highway for Him: "Make straight in the desert a highway for our God"

(First Reading). Eight centuries later, the Baptist echoed this message shortly before the official entry of the Messiah: "Prepare the way of the Lord, make his paths straight" (Third Reading). And the apostle Peter gives a pastoral slant to the moral importance of this waiting and preparation for the Messiah, inviting us to collaborate in the formation of "new heavens and a new earth in which righteousness dwells" (Second Reading).

It would be profitable at this point to review the spiritual content of our justice. The classical divisions of this cardinal virtue still bear the names of commutative or remunerative justice (economic relations between individuals), distributive justice (relations between the state and the individual), and legal justice (the duties of the citizen toward the state). Recently the expression has widened in its interpretation. Formerly, in economic relationships the dichotomous "have-give" was the decisive factor; now, on the other hand, the deciding factor in these same relationships is the personal dignity of the individual considered in the practical context of family and society: "Work is not above man or against him, but for him" (Paul VI). Another new aspect is the move from the individual to the international level. Vatican II, Pope John's *Pacem in terris,* and Pope Paul's *Populorum progressio* give us what might be called a "theoretical triangle" of these new aspects. Pope Paul's document hinges completely on the basic principles that those who possess material goods in abundance must put them at the service of others, that if there is a conflict between possession and service, the latter should prevail, and that this rule holds also between nation and nation.

It is plain that this new dimension of justice presupposes reasons much more profound than mere social and economic relations. Indeed, genuine justice is something sacred. After all, justice is based on what is right. Justice and law are external manifestations of an inherent right that belongs to man as a creature of God. They define, express, and regulate the practice of that right, which is inborn in every human being as such. This being the case, people who scream aloud for justice and then annihilate the individual by absorbing him into a totalitarian society or by suppressing his most intimate spiritual longings, actually deprive justice of its real foundation.

So far as distributive justice is concerned, we must not forget that the state has the duty to see that the whole man be developed—and man has many needs, material, spiritual, and eternal. For, in the words of Tolstoi, he is made up of "body, soul, and longing for God." If a state thinks that it has fulfilled its duty by simply providing for man's material needs, and if it neglects such things as the defense of truth, peace, and moral values, it would be guilty of injustice toward the very people it professes to help.

Legal justice too has this sacred aspect and must be practiced accordingly. The good citizen, who fears God, will certainly do his part for the efficient economy of the state and will act with objective justice. But he will go further: he will respect legitimate authority in those who hold and exercise it; he will better the whole texture of society by a virtuous and honorable life. Indeed, citizens who plan or support the introduction of ill will, divisions, double-dealing, or evil practices into a community would not only sully it and hinder its service of authority, but would destroy the very well-being and justice they profess to promote.

Commutative justice too, considered on a global level, may not dispense with this religious aspect. Man is created by God, and justice must "give to God the things that are God's" (Matthew 22:21). The ancients were so deeply aware of this ontological dependence on their Creator that they felt bound to offer sacrifice to Him because they were unable to make Him an adequate return. Indeed, an act of religion is not just a "moment of faith": it is part of the duty of commutative justice between us and God.

"Unfortunately, we are living in an age when material things, enhanced by constant technical and economic progress, possess a hitherto unheard-of attraction for man. Material comfort so engrosses man's interests, that the practice of faith and esteem for spiritual values become increasingly difficult, and the temptation to forget God is the normal thing" (Paul VI, January 5, 1972).

PASTORAL REFLECTIONS

1. We are confronted by a society that is immensely selfish, and by a neo-paganism in which nearly all actions and decisions are motivated solely by gain. We simply must imbue our Christian calling with this *religious outlook* if we want to travel untrammeled along the straight path of justice. Indeed, our personal and social destiny will be decided by our practice of this virtue or our neglect of it. The basic theme of Dostoevski's novel *The Brothers Karamazov* (and, in fact, of all his works) is the struggle between the devil and God. The battlefield is in the hearts of men, and the "apple of discord" is usually a matter of justice or injustice between man and man.

2. G.B. White says: "The greatest need of the world is the need of men: men who cannot be bought or sold; *men who are faithful and honest* in the very depth of their soul; men who are not afraid to call sin by its real name; men whose conscience is as faithful to duty as the magnetic needle is to the north pole; men who will stand firm for justice even if the heavens should fall."

3. Granted that *it is not easy to be just.* Holy Scripture cries out in wonderment when a just man is found:
Blessed is the rich man who is found blameless,
   and who does not go after gold.
Who is he? And we will call him blessed,
   for he has done wonderful things among his people.
Who has been tested by it and been found perfect?
   Let it be for him a ground for boasting.

Who has had the power to transgress and did not transgress,
> and to do evil and did not do it?
>> (Sirach 31:8-10)

But it is a necessary virtue, a condition for authentic Christian living; it is the road to Christ's kingdom (cf. Constitution on the Church, 36), along which God continues to mingle with men and to be an integral part of our history (cf. Luke 19:5-9).

THIRD SUNDAY OF ADVENT:

Christian Joy

> Readings: Isaiah 61:1-2, 10-11
> 1 Thessalonians 5:16-24
> John 1:6-8, 19-28

Self-examination makes it clear that we were created for happiness. Pascal maintains that "all men are in search of happiness, even if they hang themselves." The purpose of our whole being is happiness; it is just as necessary for us as oxygen is for our lungs or blood for our bodies. Yet somehow this happiness seems to escape us, like water running through our fingers. Is the reason some psychological imbalance or possibly a malfunctioning of glands? At any rate, there is no doubt that much of the blame may be laid at the door of modern society, which seems organized simply to poison or to dry up the pure springs whence flows our happiness, our joy.

We have to accept most of the blame ourselves, however, for we go searching for joy where it is not to be found. On this third Sunday of Advent, the liturgy sets us on the right path and presents us with a number of excellent formulas for finding and preserving joy, that will-o'-the-wisp for the pagan, but the great secret of the Christian.

To live in joy it is essential to be in the state of grace.
> I will greatly rejoice in the Lord,
>> my soul shall exult in my God;

For he has clothed me with the garments of salvation,
he has covered me with the robe of righteousness.

(First Reading)

Man lives his life on three levels: body, spirit, and supernature or grace. By the law of psychosomatic solidarity, when something goes wrong in one part of our organism, our whole being suffers. On the other hand, when man, besides developing himself physiologically and psychologically, also tries to live in the state of grace, then every essential part of his being functions efficiently, and he experiences the joy of perennial youth.

Furthermore, grace means joy because it is the greatest conquest man can achieve on earth; in fact, the only infinite reality in the world is grace. In his plodding worldly wisdom, man seeks happiness by straining after riches, but it is only by grace that we can gain possession of the Measureless, the Perfect—God. Indeed, when we are in grace we already live substantially in the bliss of heaven "a true Paschal joy."

Sin means setting ourselves up as gods in opposition to God; paganism is acting the part of God without God; but to become divinized by means of God's grace—this is Christianity, this is joy. "When I am full of myself, Lord, I am sad; when I possess You, ah, there is my joy!"

It is easy enough to see that deliberate sin militates against our happiness. The sinner injures his own life. We are not really what we eat or what we have; we are first and foremost what our sins have made us. We are what we deserve to be. Sin, like "the leaden cover" (Zechariah 5:7), overwhelms us (cf. Psalms 38:5). In time sin will grind God's opponents into powder. There is a kind of "consubstantiation" between our evil acts and our wretched condition.

Sin is a sadness that makes us wretched. It brings a sense of aloneness even when we are in the midst of a crowd, a sense of being trapped even when we are well provided for; smiling always, yet conscious of the falsity of that smile. Sin brings wretchedness in its wake because deliberate fault is always accompanied by a profound sense of inferiority in the presence of good people, whom we have perhaps despised. The sinner lives in a kind of self-deception that might be called "the despair of weakness." He is of necessity cast down; in fact, Seneca calls such a one "his own executioner." Deep in the heart of the sinner the image of God is distorted, in travail, because divine rights have been violated; there is an interior voice, tormented and tormenting, that cries aloud, "You are not what you should be." The sinner is in bondage to a false self, a mere caricature of the genuine self intended by the Creator.

One of the causes of today's discord and social unrest may well be this: he who is afflicted with an interior sense of guilt tries to externalize it, and in the resultant commotion he seeks an excuse for not pledging himself to the good, for distracting himself from the qualms of his own conscience. Much of our restlessness, of our revolt against uncertainty to the point of absurdity, is not seldom the result of an interior conflict, of a deliberate divorce between moral life and life in practice. For this reason St. Paul, when he is preaching the duty of joy, uses a provocative phrase to bid us "abstain from every form of evil" (Second Reading).

Another ingredient of Christian joy is humility. The mighty yet humble John the Baptist is an excellent example of the combination of humility and joy (Third Reading). The humble person is at peace because he faces the fact that his poverty limits his field of action. He works as if everything depended on him, and awaits results as if everything depended on others as well. He knows he is "small change." Whether he is treated badly or indifferently, whether he is arguing for truth or defending justice, he is calm and happy. He does not seek the limelight. He knows his limitations, knows that he is a tiny cog in the vast mechanism of the world; and so he adapts himself intelligently to the ups and downs of life. His healthy outlook makes for contented and unruffled living. "When we trample our pride underfoot, we have nothing to fear; serenity is ours" (Pope John).

In a word, humility begets happiness precisely because it unites us to God and obtains for us His all-powerful mercy: "...(he) gives grace to the humble" (1 Peter 5:5). Humility is the door to that joyous communion with God that is offered to us as welcome guests in the kingdom of heaven (cf. Mark 10:13; Luke 15:17).

In Advent the Church, like the mystical bride, awaits her Savior. But the Messiah also awaits us, His people; above all, He wants to forgive our sins and fill us with a joy that is complete and everlasting.

PASTORAL REFLECTIONS

1. Jesus did not say to us: "Learn of me because I am the mighty Son of the Father"; He did not teach us to perform miracles or to instruct or judge others. But He urged us to imitate *His meekness and humility.* Humility and meekness are twin sisters in the house of the Lord.

2. Christ came to manifest *the goodness of the Father* and to make us believe in divine love even when we have fallen into sin. The spirit of the Gospel bids us think of and recognize in God not so much a Father who has been offended by the ingratitude of His children, as a Father who tries in every possible way to help His children and make them happy, a Father who seeks them with an untiring love as if He could not be happy without them.

3. The Lord has come expressly *to make us happy.* We ought, then, to make joy the program of our life and the method of our apostolate among others. As a preparation for eternal bliss, we must become as it were living canticles of the Gospel message, zealous apostles of joy, messengers of serenity. A woman without love or a man without ideals is inconceivable; so too a Christian without joy, the marvelous fruit of humility, is unthinkable.

FOURTH SUNDAY OF ADVENT:

The Messianic Kingdom

Readings: 2 Samuel 7:1-5, 8-11, 16
Romans 16:25-27
Luke 1:26-38

The Chosen People were possessed of one fundamental idea, which was handed down from generation to generation: God's pledge of an eternal kingdom. It was the prophet Nathan who clearly foretold this wonderful event to David, assuring him: "And your house and your kingdom shall be made sure for ever before me; your throne shall be established for ever" (First Reading). But David was merely a figure of the true king to come, the Messiah, a truth that is attested by the fact that he and his successors never at any time proclaimed themselves absolute monarchs, like gods incarnate, as did other Eastern sovereigns, notably those of Egypt and Babylon. A Jewish king was always conscious of his role as vicar, delegate, and forerunner of the one and only authentic King of Sion, the Messiah to come. Other prophets only enriched and developed the initial theme of Nathan, impressing indelibly on the hearts of the Jews the hope, the certainty of this unique, transcendental national privilege that was theirs.

The patriarch of the prophets, Isaiah, after giving assurance that God will fulfill His promise to David, sings exultantly of the permanence and fecundity of the Messianic kingdom to come. This kingdom, the prophet declares, will last forever, for at its head is one who, born of a virgin, will be its Wonder-Counselor, God-Hero, Prince of peace, filled with wisdom, strength, counsel, and majesty; He will govern all peoples. In this Messianic kingdom there will be all spiritual wealth and abundance, but the places of honor will be reserved for the poor, the outcast, and the abandoned. In view of this coming of the kingdom of God in the history of Israel, the prophet sees and describes the Temple of Jerusalem in soaring lyrics: it becomes a focal point, radiating light throughout the world like a magnificent cathedral illuminating all nations. Jerusalem, the Holy City, becomes the mystical capital of life and grace for the good of the whole universe.

The prophet Jeremiah, even as he foretells the enslavement of his people in a foreign land because of their infidelity, is full of hope as he sings of their approaching liberation through the coming of the messianic kingdom, as an avalanche moves inexorably into the valley below and becomes the foundation of a new structure even as it crumbles. Nebuchadnezar's kingdom of gold, the silver reign of the Medes and Persians, the bronze monarchy of Alexander, and finally the kingdoms of the great Macedonian's successors, the so-called Diodachi, who ruled till Rome came into power —all these, according to the explanation of Daniel, constituted the mysterious and laborious stages of preparation for the coming of the one true kingdom. The prophet Ezekiel too adds his voice in the staging of the messianic kingdom by describing its universality and interior unity.

This harmonious development of Nathan's original theme was further amplified and embellished by the so-called Minor Prophets. Hosea prophesied to the people that after their punishment would come the real kingdom of David, figure of the Messiah. Amos and Abdias express the same thought. Similarly, Zechariah hymns the praises of one of David's descendants as the offspring of a wholly spiritual age and of an indestructible kingdom. Micah, in turn, expressly prophesies and describes Bethlehem, the birthplace of the Messiah-King to come. Malachi, the last of the twelve Minor Prophets, outlines the sacrificial function of the Messiah: from the rising of the sun even to its setting, he will bring a "pure offering" for the salvation of the world and for universal gladness (Malachi 1:11).

After Malachi there is a silence of about five centuries; it is like a dramatic pause of watchful waiting for the striking of the momentous hour of the great event. And last of all the angel Gabriel is sent to Mary and says to her: "Hail, full of grace, the Lord is with you...you will conceive...the Son of the Most High; the Lord God will give to him the throne of his father David and he will reign over the house of Jacob for ever; and of his kingdom there will be no end" (Third Reading). So does the prophecy of Nathan move from the realm of prophetic description and hope into that of unending history. The Savior Himself, when He begins His apostolate, will actualize the program and the significance of this kingdom—promised, awaited, and desired for centuries: "I must preach the good news of the kingdom of God to the other cities also; for I was sent for this purpose" (Luke 4:43).

With the Incarnation, therefore, the kingdom of God definitely became part of mankind's history. To deny the royal presence of Christ in time is to place oneself on the fringes of history; it is a useless struggle that thwarts the destiny of our very existence.

On this Fourth Sunday of Advent, the Church offers us her final invitation to enter with confidence into this mystery "which was kept secret for long ages" that we may "bring about the obedience of faith—to the only wise God be glory...through Jesus Christ" (Second Reading).

PASTORAL REFLECTIONS

1. Whether we want it or not, whether we like it or not, for ages—in Europe, in America, in Oceania, in Africa, and in part of Asia—*Jesus has played a part in history and in our destiny.* Even Joseph Ernest Renan (+ 1892) had to admit: "A thousand times more alive, a thousand times more loved after His death than in the days of His sojourn on earth, Jesus Christ has become the cornerstone of humanity, so that to uproot His name would mean to shake humanity's very foundation."

2. This *dominion* of Christ is pre-eminently spiritual and can be perceived above all *through the gift of faith,* the mirror in which we can contemplate His liv-

ing image, like an inner and spatial eye, to keep within ourselves that same image and life of Christ, who by faith, as St. Paul assures us, "dwells in our hearts" (Ephesians 3:17, cf. Paul VI, November 24, 1976).

3. It is all-important that each one of us make himself *completely available to God* by imitating Mary's *fiat*: "I am the servant of the Lord. Let it be done to me as you say" (Response). Then Christmas will become much more than a beautiful commemoration of an historical event; Christmas will mean an opportunity for us to belong more closely to the kingdom of Christ, the universal kingdom of grace and peace.

CHRISTMAS:

Savior of Mankind

Readings: Isaiah 62:11-12
Titus 3:4-7
Luke 2:15-20

Christ our Savior is born. We have heard so much about Him. We have listened to His approaching footsteps as He came nearer and nearer to us. We have longed for Him, kept watch for Him, and in Him our hearts have sought all that is true and beautiful. For centuries He was the firm hope of a long line of patriarchs and prophets. Through Him and in His name the kings of the Chosen People ruled. The Israelites sang their psalms to Him. People shackled by sin and enslaved by dictators hoped in Him as their Messiah. And now at long last He appears in a crib, the gift of the Father. He is small, but there is none greater than He; He is naked, but it is He who has clothed the universe; He is poor, yet He is the Creator and Lord of heaven and earth; helpless He lies in His mother's arms, yet angel hosts adore Him. He is the prince of peace, who will continue the reign of God in time. On His Father's side, He is God; on His mother's, man. Begotten from all eternity as God, He is born in time as man. Like the Father, He is eternal life and supreme judge; as the son of Mary, He is a gift of mercy. As second Person of the Trinity, He rules the world; as brother of men, He is their mediator.

At His birth a great light appeared in the world, and His birthday is the feast of light. Let us look around.

There is progress everywhere—the discovery of sources of energy followed by technical applications. The discoveries occur at intervals, spaced over the centuries; the applications are continuous for the benefit of mankind. (Think of steam, electricity, nuclear energy and its countless applications.) In salvation history there have been two prophetic stages in energy progress: the Creation and the Incarnation. Genesis tells us (1:3) that on the first day God created light. From the point of view of science, light is the dynamic principle of every reality. Step by step God guided this energy until it reached the beauty and order of the cosmos. In the fullness of time the Son of God appeared as the light that came to enlighten every man.

In the world of men, there has been a gentle but potent force for the development and progress not only physical and horizontal, but spiritual and vertical. The Incarnate Word not merely united in Himself time and eternity, the natural and the supernatural, things visible and invisible; He was born to reunite men with God, children with their Father, the heirs with the kingdom of heaven. Light is the symbol of salvation from the night of death, of liberation from slavery—love conquering hate, grace overcoming the very shadow of sin. Light looked down, saw darkness, and said: "That is where I must go." Peace looked down, saw war, and said: "That is where I must go." Love looked down, saw hatred, and said: "That is where I must go." So the light came and grew resplendent; peace came and brought rest; love came and produced life. The Word became flesh and made His dwelling among us.

In this way a sublime and fruitful friendship was established between God and man forever. "I will be a father to him and he shall be a son to me" (1 Corinthians 17:13). That is why even today His birth exercises such a deep and powerful attraction and fascination. After twenty centuries He is still the Lord of mankind, the Lord who calls, enraptures, astonishes. Every age and every race feels His powerful attraction. The exploits of others lose their glamor and meaning and are forgotten, but the coming of Christ is as fresh and impelling as if it had occured five minutes ago. He has come into our midst to be our Savior.

History is full of momentous Christmas happenings. On Christmas Day, 496, Clovis and his three thousand warriors received Baptism at Rheims, thus making France the first nation to enter the Church. Some forty years later, on Christmas day, 537, the Emperor Justinian presided in Constantinople at the consecration of the Basilica of St. Sophia, which is dedicated to the Wisdom of the Incarnate Word. On Christmas day, 800, Charlemagne was crowned emperor of the Holy Roman Empire by Leo III. In 1223 St. Francis built the first crib at Greccio: it was a call to mankind to return to the authentic source of religion. In 1963 Paul VI, in the name of all Christians, made a pilgrimage to Bethlehem to reconfirm the Church in the fruitfulness of her ancient and divine origin.

PASTORAL REFLECTIONS

1. Today could well be *the decisive Christmas* for us. We are so much in need of the Savior, the only one who can really save us. When we are in sin, Christ is our justice; He is our way when we have strayed from the right path. In our confusion and bewilderment, He is our truth; in our anxieties, He is our comfort. In our wretchedness, He is our spiritual wealth; in our poverty, He is our grace; in our weakness, He is our strength. Christ is light in humanity's darkness, joy in discouragement, peace in sorrow, hope in death, life eternal after our sojourn in time.

2. "Brothers and sisters! Let us go to the Savior like the shepherds after the announcement. Let us open to Him, to Christ, the door of our consciousness, of our personal family, and social life. He does not come to obstruct our freedom, our activity, or our humanity. He comes to *enlighten, enlarge, and gladden* this life of

ours, which, if we consider it, really needs in every respect this mysterious infant guest, Jesus" (Paul VI, Christmas, 1971).

3. In December, 1818, strains of the melody that has captivated the whole world rang out from the village of Oberndorf, Austria: "Stille Nacht, heilige Nacht! Alles Schläft, einsam wacht...." The nations have taken this hymn to their hearts not only because of the Christmassy simplicity of Franz Gruber's music, but also because of its meaning: "Silent night, holy night! All is calm, all is bright...." In the holy couple keeping watch, we sense that He is the best part for us, we who are so much in need of song and joy. If our *happiness is* not *centered in the crib of Bethlehem,* in Christ Jesus, we may be wise, rich, powerful, even learned, but we will not be happy.

HOLY FAMILY:

Liberty and Authority in the Family

Readings: Sirach 3:2-6; 12-14
Colossians 3:12-21   Luke 2:22-40

Nowadays it seems more difficult to bring up three or four children than to govern a nation. Why? The liturgy of today tells us about the true path education should take. The first piece of advice is for children: "Whoever honors his father atones for sins, and whoever glorifies his mother is like one who lays up treasure..." (First Reading). The biblical text continues, "Whoever forsakes his father is like a blasphemer, and whoever angers his mother is cursed by the Lord" (Sirach 3:16). And in his letter to the Colossians, St. Paul gives this counsel: "Children, obey your parents in everything, for this pleases the Lord" (Second Reading). For those who have some familiarity with the things of the spirit, certain serious reflections would seem in place here.

Obedience is primarily a duty of justice. Just as the virtue of religion looks to the cult of the Godhead, the

First Principle, so the virtue of *"pietas"* (dutiful relations between parents and children) offers respect and obedience to those who collaborated with God in giving us life. Obedience is our *yes* to the order of existence and social life. Obedience is also, but secondarily, an affectionate return for the sacrifices our parents have made for us. Motherhood is the poetry of a woman's life, but it is also her martyrdom. Her love often changes to torment. The greatness of a man is found in fatherhood, but that greatness becomes daily hardship as he works, suffers, and hopes for his children. In a word, parenthood means the beginning of suffering. Even if parents have nothing else to their credit, at least they have spent their lives struggling for their children, enduring hardships of every sort for them.

Some youngsters of today work themselves into a dither about universal love; but their enthusiasm is open to doubt if they do not first love their own families. If we cannot walk on level ground, we are not likely to climb mountains. Genuine love is directed toward persons, those near us; it is not limited to ideas, projects, exotic adventures. If a man makes no effort to love those at home, it will be very difficult for him to love his finacée, his wife, other people; and it is ridiculous for a man who does not love his wife to declare that he loves his country, that he loves mankind. A further reason for respecting our parents is that this very contact with them develops in us those virtues that form the poetry of the spirit and are the laws of courtesy.

This same authority has a powerful unifying effect. Liberty without authority is license, just as authority without liberty is slavery. Novelty without tradition is mere social pedantry, just as tradition without novelty is a museum piece. Genuine education needs the give-and-take of authority and freedom. Only one who has learned to obey will know how to command. Only one who has learned to see in a command or opinion another facet of a problem will be able to take authentic action. Before becoming masters we must be disciples.

The liturgy also has some stern things to say to parents. If things go wrong, it is often largely their fault. Joseph and Mary, after taking their Son to the Temple of Jerusalem, brought Him back to Nazareth, and Jesus grew in age and wisdom (Third Reading). Genuine education aims at leading a child into the friendship of God. To foist on men ideas that are more or less valid is proselytism; but to bring men into dialogue with God is education at its best. Not to train a child to open up to spiritual things is to deprive him of full development and the real joy of living.

Every young person has his ideal to achieve. Joseph and Mary, far from separating Jesus from His program of redemption, actually assisted Him in it. Education does not mean imposing on the young person our own vocational cliché, but helping him to be himself. It is not a case of putting a psychological embargo on the personal peculiarities of a child, but rather of keeping in step with him and helping him achieve his destiny. A child is not a package brought into the world and left standing there; he is not a record card to be consulted now and again. He is the family's most precious possession and he needs constant care and spiritual attention. He is surrounded by a number of facts and happenings. Every time he comes home he is burdened with a variety of feelings, and he may be groping about uncertainly in this welter of opinions and ideas. Parents must be an intellectual buffer between the world and their children, helping them over the hurdles of heterodoxy so that they may attain self-reliance regarding life's true values.

This necessarily implies the ability and the will to make sacrifices. To choose one thing is in itself to renounce quite a number of other things. A young person must get used to resisting false values by means of a well-balanced refusal; otherwise he will not be capable of mastering his own ego. Let us not think that youth is afraid of sacrifice. If we ask little from the young, they will give nothing; if we ask much, they will give a little;

but if we ask everything, they will become heroes. It is a question of trust.

PASTORAL REFLECTIONS

1. In these matters the parents' greatest influence will come through *their own good example,* for by common agreement "the testimony of two men is true" (John 8:17). Example shows that what we preach is possible. By the very fact that they are so changeable, youngsters are inclined to imitate what they see done in the family; they carry into the world the pattern of their home life. Young people need good example. When parents exhort their children "to be good like Jesus," the children may well answer: "Certainly—when you are good like Joseph and Mary!"

2. Anxious to educate his stepson in obedience, sacrifice, love of God, and concern for the poor, George Washington became worried when he found that the boy's money-box was empty at a time when it should have been full. Inquiry showed that the boy had used his savings to help the poor. Washington considered this *his most wonderful victory:* he had conquered by dint of good example.

3. Perhaps many people will not share these simple ideas on the vexing question of education. Even so, we must accept the example of Christ who, although He was God, *submitted to Joseph and Mary.* We cannot put aside the teaching of parents so totally dedicated to their Son. Imitation of the family of Nazareth is the Christian's yardstick of all that is genuine and perfect.

MARY, MOTHER OF GOD:

Mary, Mediatrix of Salvation

Readings: Numbers 6:22-27
Galatians 4:4-7
Luke 2:16-21

In chapter VIII of the Constitution on the Church, Vatican II has very opportunely woven Mariology into the living texture of Church history. Eighteen articles of that chapter (52-69) in a marvelous crescendo describe the position of the Madonna before, during, and after the life of the Savior. Mary and Jesus walk across the stage of time holding each other's hands; all those who, like the shepherds, go to Jesus will always find with Him Mary, His Mother.

The prophecies announcing the coming of the Savior are filled with Marian allusions. Even in paradise, the "Woman" is associated with the absolute victory of the Messiah to come. Through the centuries, as the prophecies concerning the Messiah become more vivid and precise, the prophecies regarding Mary become more definite. She too is the expected of nations. Her coming, intimately united with that of Emmanuel, is clearly foretold by Isaiah (7:14). The example and gifts of the women of Hebrew antiquity—Rebecca, Judith, Anna, Miriam the sister of Moses—are nothing more than aspects or mystical types that prepared the People of God for the glorious vision of the Virgin, the most beautiful among the world's mothers. In just this way did the writers of the early Church see and praise her. In just this way did the Holy Father express himself in his homily during the Mass of the Immaculate Conception: "My brothers and sons! For a moment let us fix our thoughts on the dazzling vision of the Immaculate Conception.... An idea, a divine dream, a masterpiece of human beauty,...the divine likeness in the human countenance, invisible beauty in the physical figure...God's preferential thought for this creature of His; the intention to see in her again the original innocence of a being conceived in the image and likeness of Himself (cf. Genesis 1:26-27).... This should be the real and ideal image of the Blessed Virgin, reflected, luminous, and illuminating, in our individual souls today...as the synthesis of our admiration and devotion to the Blessed Virgin" (Paul VI, December 8, 1975).

The union between our Lady and God reached its focal point, as it were, in the moment of the Incarnation: "...when the time had fully come, God sent forth his

Son, born of woman..." (Second Reading). At that moment a creature was so intimately united to God as to become His true Mother forever. In the Old Testament the cloud represented the mysterious presence of God (Exodus 40:34-35); through the Holy Spirit the power of God will overshadow the Virgin of Nazareth so that she will become the Mother of God. In this way Mary becomes the noble dwelling place of the Trinity; she is the daughter, spouse, and mother of God. The union between our Lady and God was not limited to the physical dimension; it also penetrated Mary's whole soul. Indeed, Mary consented to the Word of God in full knowledge and utter freedom, intending, in effect, to incorporate in her *fiat* all the consequences of that word, and thus she consecrated herself wholly to God's plan of salvation.

The Virgin continued to be united with Christ during the public life of her Son, in His poverty and humiliation, in His hiddenness, in His suffering—until His death. All her actions were nothing but a dynamic response to her beloved Son. This union between Mother and Son reached its climax in the passion. At that time the two were so intimately united as to form one limitless act of loving sacrifice. On Calvary Mary descended into the very abyss of suffering with her only-begotten Son, her motherly heart at one with His sacrifice, lovingly acquiescing in the immolation of Him whom she had borne. We may say that her sorrow at the foot of the cross was so profound as to constitute a single whole with the passion of her Son. She fulfilled in her heart what God did not ultimately demand of Abraham: the sacrifice of her only Son. It was precisely through this sacrifice that Mary entered into the mystery of sacrificial Redemption as no other human being ever did. For this reason the Gospel does not speak of the appearance of the risen Christ to His Mother, for her union with Jesus in faith and love was such that it did not need to be confirmed by an exterior appearance.

But as we ponder the union and communion of our Lady with Christ, we must turn our attention particularly to the day of Pentecost, when Mary begged and joyfully received the outpouring of the Holy Spirit. God became incarnate through Mary at the moment of the Annunciation. But Christ became incarnate in the Church, still through Mary, on the day of Pentecost. In the first case our Lady united herself with the human nature of her Son; in the second, with His social, mystical nature. Paul VI, as is well known, proclaimed our Lady "Mother of the Church," declaring that she is the most important, the best, the principal chosen member of the Mystical Body of Christ (November 21, 1964). In heaven too the Virgin remains united with the pilgrim Church in time until the final encounter with Christ on the day of His Second Coming. Mary is indeed our Mother in the full sense of the word. First, she gave us the human nature of Christ. Now, throughout the ages, she continues to bestow upon us the divine nature of her Son, that is, grace (cf. Constitution on the Church, 62). In such wise, "as history grows older, our Lady becomes ever younger."

If we wished to ignore Mary, to do without her, we would not only be condemned to understand very little about the divine economy of salvation and of peace, but we would be in danger of childishly remaining outside the very life of the Church in the wretchedness of one who repudiates his own mother.

The People of God attach great importance to the position of Mary in the life of the Church. Saint Louis Grignon de Montfort puts it thus: "Where there is great love of our Lady and a deep sense of her presence, the Holy Spirit reveals Himself in a remarkable way; where there is little love of our Lady and a weak sense of her presence, the Holy Spirit is also less present." The Virgin is truly a mediatrix of our sanctity and consequently of our salvation.*

---

*Those who wish to enter more deeply into Marian themes would do well to consult *Our Lady Among Us* by Valentino Del Mazza (Boston, Mass., Daughters of St. Paul, 1977).

St. John Chrysostom summarizes the salvific role of Mary in the following eulogy: "A virgin drove us out of paradise; thanks to the intervention of another virgin, we have recovered eternal life. As we were condemned through the sin of one woman, so by the merits of another woman we have been crowned." St. Germaine of Constantinople echoes the same thought in this moving plea: "O best of women, most pure and most merciful, comfort of Christians,...shelter us under the wings of your goodness; defend us with your intercession; grant us eternal life. You are the unfailing hope of Christians.... Your gifts are countless. For no one attains salvation except through you, holiest of virgins. No one is freed from evil except through you. Who cares for mankind as you do, in conformity with your only-begotten Son?"

PASTORAL REFLECTIONS

1. Our Lady is the *greatest woman* the world has seen. She is the most perfect of creatures; Virgin and Mother, she is a woman in the fullest sense of the word: virginity always emphasizes the idea of something preserved, of interior nobility, while maternity underlines the idea of a gift for the good of one's neighbor and for the glory of God. Our Lady is in herself the marvel of marvels because of the exquisite beauty of her own soul and because of her total gift as Mother of God and our Mother. In a word, she is the fairest Mother in the world!

2. It is she who longs to *stand at our side*, to help us, and to bless us as our dear Mother. If Jesus cannot refuse Mary anything because she is His Mother, and if Mary cannot refuse us anything because we are her children, why do we not turn to her? St. Bernard says: "So great is our Lady's desire to do good to us and to help us that she is offended not only by the outrages of the wicked but also by the forgetfulness of good people who fail to ask for her help and protection."

3. "Here we must make a resolution, *a commitment.* We will take with us...the love of the Blessed Vir-

gin in every day of the year, as a 'mirror,' an example of every human and Christian virtue, as the pure and sweet woman who accompanies us on our tiring pilgrimage, as a Mother so great-hearted as to contain within her the fullness of love of Christ, her Son...and then love of mankind, of the whole Church, of each one of us..." (Paul VI, January 1, 1976).

SECOND SUNDAY AFTER CHRISTMAS:

Man and Faith

Readings: Sirach 24:1-4; 8-12
Ephesians 1:3-6; 15-18
John 1:1-10

Human history runs in two lines: one descending from the perfection of God to the needs of man, the other ascending from human lowliness to the greatness of God. These two lines meet in Christ: He is the mystical bond that brings together all reality, heavenly and earthly.

God comes to us above all as wisdom. Salvation history before Christ is a period of preparation to sensitize man for the gift of truth become a person. Divine wisdom manifested itself first in nature. We read:
"I dwelt in high places
 and my throne was in a pillar of cloud..." (First
  Reading).
The Biblical text continues:
"I grew tall like a cedar in Lebanon,
 and like a cypress on the heights of Hermon.
 I grew tall like a palm tree in Engedi,
 and like rose plants in Jericho..." (Sirach 24:13-14).
Nature is indeed the first book in which we can read the immortal workmanship of God. Just as every wave of the sea carries the light of the sun on its crest, so every created reality bears in itself the reflection of divine

wisdom. Every being is, as it were, a syllable of God. God speaks to us in the delicate flowering of the tree, in the silver tone of the streamlet, in the calm light of the moon, in the imposing strength of the forest giants. The immensity of space cries out the infinity of God. The violent storm at sea shouts of the divine power. The starry serenity of the sky proclaims the goodness of God. All creation is a silver-toned symphony in praise of the Creator's wisdom. The world of nature is a sacrament of God.

Then God spoke in words. An analysis of history inclines us to accept the opinion of St. Justin, who holds that before the Incarnation God made use of persons to clarify the relationship between truth and error. So it was that during the five centuries before Christ there was an unusual diffusion of light throughout the pagan world: we are reminded of Zoroaster in Persia, Gautama Buddha in India, Confucius and Lao Tse in China, Anaxagoras in Greece. Two centuries later the longing and striving for truth were proclaimed in a special way by the Greek philosophers Socrates, Plato, and Aristotle.

All this was a providential preparation that made for a better expectation and reception of the fullness of truth at the birth of Christ. Meanwhile, wisdom "took root in an honored people, in the portion of the Lord, who is their inheritance" (First Reading), and like a teacher telling his pupils what he wishes, God inspired certain men to communicate divine truth, the substance of His message of love. The prophets spoke in the very name of God and at His behest.

Finally, God Himself spoke directly and fully to His people through His Son. The eternal Wisdom of God, "the Word became flesh and dwelt among us; we have beheld his glory, glory as of the only Son from the Father, filled with enduring love.... For the law was given through Moses; grace and truth came through Jesus Christ" (Third Reading). Just as a thought, while remaining intact in my mind, can reveal itself at a given moment by means of my voice, so the Word of God, invisible and co-eternal with the Father and the Holy Spirit, wished to become the Word in time, Truth incarnate, visible. The Incarnation is the descent of perfect Reason into time, the only form in which Truth identifies itself with Person: "I am...the truth" (John 14:6); "I am the light" (John 8:12).

And now let us trace the ascending line. Man was made for truth. Just as a seed by an innate tendency works its way from darkness to the light of day, so the soul, in accordance with its own nature, strives for truth, which comes to it as a gift from on high. Our reasoning process is a leaping from notion to notion in order to arrive at the fullness of truth—not a mathematical or literary truth, but a truth that is alive, certain, and uplifting. But this truth is outside us. As a wave spreads out and then breaks on the sand of the seashore, so human reason strives to approach its weighty problems only to be stopped by their immensity. We are mysteries to ourselves: the more our little knowledge increases, the greater becomes the mystery of what we do not know. Of ourselves, we cannot understand either life or death. And yet in this lies the drama of our existence, in this lies our nobility. What distinguishes man from beast is precisely this power to ponder the problem of existence. No matter where a man was born or where he lives, as soon as he reaches the age of reason, he asks himself questions, at least implicitly. The function of intelligence is to "read into" events and to lay hold of their interior meaning. But to avoid errors, to understand better the reason for everything, man needs the help of supreme Truth, of Christ, the Light of our minds, the Truth for our intellect, the one and only Teacher of real knowledge. The man who does not accept Christ, supreme, eternal Truth, may know this or that from a scientific point of view, but he can never penetrate the ultimate truth of life; he may be able to work out some existential problem, but he can never control the ultimate outcome of that problem. The person without faith is like a man who knows all about the eye but has never seen a face; his very ideas remain empty, divorced from reality. He who accepts revelation may still be searching, but he who rejects it is always searching, searching everything. The divine word is truth (John 17:17), the only thing that makes us truly and interiorly free (John 8:32), "who has blessed us in Christ with every spiritual blessing...that we should be holy and blameless before him" (Second Reading).

PASTORAL REFLECTIONS

1. If God has spoken to us, we must *listen* to Him, first and foremost, because the Gospel is the moral truth that saves us. Here, in the Gospel, is the truth we must receive and live; here is the light by which we must be enlightened and which we must enkindle. Here is all the love we must have among our brothers and for our brothers. Here, in the Gospel, is the way that we ought to walk, the peace that we ought to speak, and all the joy that we ought to have in our own hearts and that we ought to manifest externally in song.

2. It is very important for the Christian to come into contact with the Gospel, for in this way he can form *a personal friendship with Jesus Christ, with His very Person.* There are three types of knowledge: knowledge of events, as when we know a happening of the day; professional knowledge, such as a person has who knows his craft well; and vital knowledge, which manifests itself in a conscious relationship between person and Person. The third type of knowledge is the only authentic one—it is love, it is life, it is sanctity: "And this is eternal life, that they know you the only true God, and Jesus Christ whom you have sent" (John 17:3).

3. We ought to *communicate this light of truth* to our fellow men through the apostolate. The needs of man are not merely economic or earthly: "Man shall not live by bread alone, but by every word that proceeds from the mouth of God" (Matthew 4:4). Man has a higher destiny; he needs the heavenly food of the Word

of God, without which his true stature would be dwarfed and his true salvation prejudiced. In the Constitution on the Church in the Modern World, Vatican II teaches that precisely through the Word of God evangelization and human advancement can become two complementary aspects of our activity without danger that one will prevail at the expense of the other (cf. Pope Paul VI, September 22, 1976).

EPIPHANY:

The Manifestation of the Lord

Readings: Isaiah 60:1-6
Ephesians 3:2-3, 5-16
Matthew 2:1-12

The world was waiting for the Savior. We might say that all religions were ever straining toward a God made man, through whose mediation sin would be defeated and a new birth inaugurated. China awaited the Messiah in the person of Kiunt-se, a shepherd-king who would rule the world. In 600 B.C. Confucius, repeating an ancient Chinese tradition, declared that the Holy One would arise west of China. Japan, Siam, and Tibet—all following the doctrine of Fo—likewise expected a heavenly being to repair the injury done to man by sin. The Hindus sang of the incarnation of Vishnu to destroy the evil works of Kali. Egypt waited for Horus, who would destroy the serpent Typhoon. The Arabs in their tents continued to invoke a savior. In the northern part of Europe the Scandinavians directed their vows to Thor, the most powerful of the gods, so that he would slay the dragon. The distant peoples of America thought of Puru, who would send his own son from heaven, while the Mexicans prayed for and awaited a universal religious transformation, in which a mysterious sacrifice would take the place of human sacrifices. Even the Druids in their dark, impenetrable forests built an altar to Isis, the maiden from whom they expected a savior-son. The Greeks, led by Plato, looked for the fullness of truth and light. In Rome, while the Sibyls diffused the idea of a savior, Cicero spoke of a law "eternal and unchangeable," and the poet Virgil sang prophetically of a Son who would be the true emperor of the world.

Isaiah, in the fullness of his prophetic role, foresees the realization of such great hope and sings of Jerusalem as the capital of the universal kingdom of the Messiah: "Nations shall come to your light, and kings to the brightness of your rising" (First Reading). The tribes of northern Arabia, those of Midian and Ephah, and those of southern Arabia—Kedar and Nebaioth—the peoples of Tarshish as well as those of other regions, all robed in splendid garments, walk symbolically toward Jerusalem, the epicenter of all the nations of the world (First Reading).

The Messiah was born for all the peoples admitted to the same inheritance, "members of the same body, and partakers of the promise in Christ Jesus through the gospel" (cf. Second Reading). We might say that before the Incarnation, mankind was orientated to one people, the Jews; this people was, in turn, orientated to one tribe, that of Juda; the tribe to one family, that of David, and this family finally converged in the Messiah. With the Incarnation, history, now qualitatively transformed, again begins to grow: Jesus founds a family (His own and that formed by the apostles and disciples); He forms a family in order to dwell among a people, and through this people He wishes to conquer all mankind spiritually. If we wish to represent this concept graphically, we can make the Greek letter Chi (X), the symbol of Christ and of His universal kingdom.

The coming of the Magi is both a confirmation and a summation of this consoling truth. Tradition tells us there were three, representing the three continents known in the world of that era. Melchior was a Persian king, Balthasar an Indian, and Gaspar an Arabian; through them many different peoples were represented at the court of the King of heaven and earth. But who were these Magi? The word *magus* in the singular can be interpreted as *soothsayer, diviner;* in the plural it means *learned, wise.* These wise men (whatever their number—three, five, or twelve) were certainly versed in the sacred sciences of India, Chaldea, and Egypt. Possibly they had heard about and meditated on the prophecies of Daniel, that leader among wise men, about the coming of the Messiah (Daniel 1:20); they must have known the prophecy of Balaam, a soothsayer in Mesopotamia:

> I see him, but not now.
>   I behold him, but not nigh:
> A star shall come forth out of Jacob,
>   and a scepter shall rise out of Israel;
> It shall crush the forehead of Moab,
>   by Jacob shall dominion be exercised
>
>   (Numbers 24:17-19).

Led by a providential light, the star, they came at last to adore God-made-man, these representatives of all mankind.

The meaning of Epiphany is wonderfully pointed out by the Holy Father. Paul VI says: "The Epiphany is the day when we celebrate the manifestation of Christ, light of humanity! It is the day of the opening to faith which establishes relations of communion and salvation with Jesus Christ the Savior, for all peoples, for each individual! It is the day which guides men toward their center, their leader, their Messiah.... It is the day of truth, the day of unity!... It is the day which attracts vocations; each one his own but all tending towards Christ our brother and Lord! Each one of us should feel called and urged to go out along the paths of life, along the roads of the world both near and far, to announce the great and good news...the Gospel. This is the day par excellence for the meeting with the pagan and secular world; it is the first missionary day!" (Angelus address of Paul VI, January 6, 1972)

PASTORAL REFLECTIONS

1. One lesson is this: *God can reveal Himself in the most natural event.* From the point of view of science, it seems probable that the star that appeared to the Magi was nothing but the meeting of the planets Jupiter and Saturn in the constellation of the fish. That is what John Kepler, the celebrated astronomer, thought. In 1603, at Prague, he observed the unusual brightness of such a phenomenon, which according to calculations also took place at the time of the birth of the Messiah.

2. Another lesson we can learn from the conduct of the Magi is that *correspondence with faith* is difficult. The friends and relatives of the Magi surely advised them not to undertake so long a journey, without a definite destination, through the desert, filled as it was with pitfalls and all kinds of risks. Perhaps some of them thought the Magi, who were looked upon as wise men, were mentally somewhat unbalanced. Nevertheless the latter, though they had no definite proof, set out on their way toward the Messiah, equal to the sacrifice asked of them, fortified only by an interior certainty. The test of their faith reached its height when they found themselves face to face with the humility of the Messiah. Accustomed to pomp and luxury, as Orientals were, they found themselves in front of a helpless Baby, between two simple creatures, Mary and Joseph. Notwithstanding all this, however, the Magi, as the Gospel tells us, believed and adored their Redeemer, thus becoming the first representatives of all future converts from paganism.

3. But the most beautiful lesson of today's liturgy seems to be the *interior conversion* of the Magi themselves: "...they departed to their own country by another way" (Third Reading). In biblical terminology *route* may also refer to moral conduct. Contact with the Messiah had transformed the very souls of the Magi: they had been wise in human science and in astronomy, but now they received the light of faith and heavenly wisdom.

They came as visitors and returned as missionaries; they had been sad and perplexed, but now they were happy and joyful. Abandoning Herod forever, they were resolved to preserve in their hearts all the perfume of divine friendship given them by Jesus. Contact with God is not a constraining, formless thing; it is an ethical encounter which produces in him who accepts it a total conversion of heart, an uplifting transformation of soul in order to make him worthy of belonging to the very family of God.

FIRST SUNDAY OF LENT:

The Covenant Between God and Man

> Readings: Genesis 9:8-15
> 1 Peter 3:18-22
> Mark 1:12-15

The covenant between God and man is the point of departure and of arrival for all the religious thinking of the Old and the New Testament. God had a program of holiness, an ideal of ineffable communion for creation: time and space were to be the meeting point between His intervening mercy and man's interior aspirations. The covenant of love established in Paradise from the very beginning was, alas, broken because of the refusal of Adam and Eve as the official representatives of all mankind. But God, whose benevolent plans are never thwarted, with infinite patience picked up the fragments of that shattered friendship and began to rebuild it for the good and glory of the very man by whom He had been betrayed.

After the first failure and the catastrophe of the flood, the Lord said to Noah: "Behold, I establish my covenant with you and your descendants after you.... I establish my covenant with you, that never again shall all flesh be cut off by the waters of a flood,... I set my bow in the cloud, and it shall be a sign of the covenant between me and the earth.... I will remember my covenant which is between me and you and every living creature..." (First Reading). This is the promise of a cosmic alliance, a universal covenant: the rainbow, made of water and light, touching the sky at its vertex and sustained at its ends by the earth, whose center is man, is both a symbol and a divine guarantee.

It will be useful to recall the intermediate stages between this luminous beginning of the covenant with Noah and its culmination as seen in New Testament writings; these form, as it were, periods of hope for the People of God. Having shown His plan of goodness, God continues to unfold His dialogue through Abraham by confirming the pact of the covenant; He chooses the founder of a family to establish friendship with a multitude, and Abraham, by obeying the call of God, becomes the "father of believers," even as Adam had been constituted the father of the living (cf. Genesis 12:3). On Mt. Sinai God goes on to lay down the terms of the covenant with the whole people: the Jews become God's people; the worship of the Most High becomes the national religion of the Israelites. But as the pact with Abraham pointed to and moved toward a nation, so at the foot of Sinai it reached out to an even vaster covenant: God was looking to all of mankind.

The prophets, in reminding the Jews of the greatest religious happening in their history, the covenant of Mt. Sinai, developed a theology of the covenant, stressing its moral obligation and its affective aspect. The covenant, they said, is a free gift of God, who loves His people as a bridegroom loves his bride. God is the shepherd, the vinedresser of Israel; Israel is His flock, His chosen vineyard. Israel, the prophets insist, must be faithful to the covenant, for infidelity brings suffering, exile, punishment. Yet the prophecy consoles the Jewish people, declaring that whatever may happen, the covenant marches on toward its wondrous fulfillment in the life and work of the Messiah to come.

With the death of Christ this covenant of friendship between God and His people is sealed once and for all for the whole of mankind: this is the dominant theme of the four accounts of the Last Supper given by the Synoptics and St. Paul. Finally on the day of Pentecost the Church, moved by the Holy Spirit, sets out on its journey in every direction of the world in order to propose to men the prospect of becoming the holy People of God. This history of the covenant, which at the same time allows us to understand God's love for His creatures, will have its ultimate fulfillment when time is no more. St. Paul reminds us that notwithstanding and contrary to all appearances, our history moves on irreversibly to the merciful design of salvation realized forever by Christ. St. John in turn bids us rejoice in a preview, as it were, of the final setting of human-divine friendship in the supernatural vision of a "new heaven and a new earth" in eternity (cf. Revelation).

In the course of its history Israel unceasingly recalled the prophetic event of the covenant: the commemoration was a time uniting grand liturgical celebrations with a renewal of the promise of fidelity. Such a celebration took place at Mt. Ebal and Mt. Garizim under the leadership of Joshua (Joshua 8:30), in Jerusalem under Josiah (2 Kings 23:23) and again under Ezra and Nehemiah (Nehemiah 8). Lent is a propitious time for confirming or renewing the covenant with God. On the day of baptism the Christian, freed from the state of mere creaturehood, enters the mystic ark of the covenant with God, in intimate friendship with Jesus Christ (Second Reading).

PASTORAL REFLECTIONS

In the sight of God and of Christ there are three classes of persons, just as there were on Palm Sunday when Jesus entered Jerusalem triumphantly as a king: in His presence there are enemies, indifferent people, and intimate friends. The purpose of the covenant between God and man is to establish a deep and intimate friendship between the creature and the Creator through Jesus Christ. In order to be effectively united with Christ in true friendship, the following most necessary conditions must be fulfilled:

1. *Union with His word.* The friend of Christ places his confidence in the Gospel (Third Reading); he has the interior certainty that Jesus is above all truth, and this often against tangible evidence. The friend of the Lord makes the Word his yardstick for every intention and every exterior action; indeed, it is by faith that Christ lives in our hearts (cf. Ephesians 3:17).

Union of will. "The meeting of God's loving and saving will with the obedient and happy will of our human heart is perfection, holiness" (Paul VI, June 14, 1972).

2. *Union of heart and of affections.* The Lord stands at the door of our heart and knocks; the friend opens the door and the friendship of hospitality, that friendship which surpasses all human knowledge, is established between the two (cf. Revelation 3:20). If encounter with human beings is a grace, this encounter with Jesus is grace par excellence. Through Jesus this friendship then ripens into intimacy with the Trinity:

If a man loves me,
he will keep my word,
and my Father will love him,
and we will come to him
and make our home with him (John 14:23).

3. *Union of intention, of sacrifice.* The friend of Jesus promptly unites himself with the salvific action of Jesus. For this reason he accepts penance, the suffering that is a prolongation of the passion, that mysterious means of redemption for others (cf. Third Reading).

In this way the friend of Christ acquires the interior and exterior splendor of our Lord, becoming a believer, a follower, a collaborator (cf. John 14:21). In this way the covenant becomes substantial peace and blessing; we experience that "all the ways of the Lord are indeed grace and truth for those who observe his covenant" (Responsorial Psalm).

SECOND SUNDAY OF LENT:

The Value of Christ's Sacrifice

Readings: Genesis 22:1-2, 9, 10-13, 15-18
Romans 8:31-34
Mark 9:2-10

The entire Old Testament moves toward the New as the leaves and flowers of a tree culminate in fruit. Today's liturgy gives us a clear, typical picture of this movement. Abraham, the husband of Sarah, longed to have a son. God promised him countless descendants; twenty years later Isaac was born. The contrast between fulfillment and promise grew sharper when God commanded the old patriarch to sacrifice that only son. The Lord said to him: " 'Take your son, your only son Isaac, whom you love, and go to the land of Moriah, and offer him up as a holocaust on a height that I will point out to you....' When they came to the place of which God had told him, Abraham...reached out and took the knife to slaughter his son. But the Lord's messenger called him from heaven. 'Abraham, Abraham.... Do not lay your hand on the lad...for now I know that you fear God...' " (First Reading). There is no doubt that the request was most painful to Abraham: he had to choose between love for his son and the will of God. We need not be surprised at this heavenly command if we remember the period in which Abraham lived, when men had such a profound sense of the absolute dominion of God that even the sacrifice of human beings did not seem incredible to them. We must also consider that Abraham was doubtless given a special grace to fulfill this painful mission, inasmuch as God always grants the necessary strength to carry out His commands. Our entire psychological reaction of irritation will vanish if we keep in mind that this was an execution in intention, not a bloody one, already carried out. All this was to be a lesson that we might understand the true historical sacrifice of the Son by the Father for love of us.

It is St. Paul who recalls for us the typology of this Old Testament episode, which he explains in the immolation of Christ: My brothers, he writes to the Romans, "He who did not spare his own Son but gave him up for us all, will he not also give us all things with him? Who shall bring any charge against God's elect? It is God who justifies; who is to condemn? Is it Christ Jesus, who died, yes, who was raised from the dead, who is at the right hand of God, who indeed intercedes for us?" (Second Reading) The Apostle of the Gentiles, while playing down the other motives of Christ's death, underlines the aspect of mercy. Christ became a victim not only to satisfy divine justice, as non-Catholics prefer to think, but rather to show forth His goodness. It is characteristic of the lover to give himself, and when love is infinite, the gift is total. So far as the Father is concerned, being infinite love, He wished to reveal to us His own love in the Incarnation, that gift of the Father (John 3:16) and the witness of the Son through the passion: "Greater love has no man than this, that a man lay down his life for his friends" (John 15:13).

The sacrifice of Christ, prefigured by that of Abraham, also differs sharply from this one and from all ancient sacrifices in its universality. "Christ died for all," St. Paul tells us. Had the Redeemer been offered by someone, His sacrifice could have been applied for the benefit of this or that individual, but by "offering himself freely to his passion" He was able to extend the fruits of that same sacrifice to all men of all ages. It may be noted, finally, that in virtue of this offering to the Father for love of His brothers, Christ was able to enter into His glory, constituting Himself the mediator of grace and mercy to all who, directly or indirectly, accept His covenant of love. In this way history became qualitatively changed through the sacrifice of Him who was born, died, and was glorified in order that divine mercy might be poured out in the hearts of men.

PASTORAL REFLECTIONS

1. In these days there are some people who mistakenly try to devaluate *the salvific power of the cross of Christ,* as if our salvation depended principally on some personal, social dynamism. But this ineffable sacrifice alone "cancelled the bond which stood against us with its legal demands; this he set aside nailing it to the cross" (Colossians 2:14). Vatican Council II, while opening itself up to the era of the whole man with loving optimism (cf. Constitution on the Church in the Modern World, 1) does not hesitate to make the cross of Christ the focal point of religion. It would be wise for us not to forget this teaching lest we fall into a neo-Pelagianism and "the cross of Christ be emptied of its power" (1 Corinthians 1:17).

2. But the true follower of the Redeemer not only fixes his eyes on the cross of Jesus as the fountainhead of all blessings, he not only cherishes in his heart sentiments of gratitude to Christ for His sacrifice, but he is even *ready to carry the cross* in order to be an instrument of redemption for his fellow men. The Son of God suffered not that men might not suffer but that their sufferings would be like His—redemptive, elevating. Every one of us certainly has something hard to accept in his own life. In the face of this reality each person is confronted with two alternatives: either to become a perpetual malcontent, a pessimist, at odds with everything, or, after having done what is possible for his own peace, to unite to the sacrifice of the Redeemer the sufferings that enter into his own program of life. Given the ordinary lack of spirituality, we seem to succumb to certain sufferings that appear insurmountable, undeserved. But then God Himself comes to our aid, giving us some kind of Tabor, just as He did for the three beloved apostles, Peter, James, and John (cf. Third Reading).

3. Here we would do well to recall an incident in the life of Professor Alfred Blalock of the University of Baltimore, the pioneer in heart surgery. Every spring the

little girl on whom he had performed the first heart operation used to travel about four hundred miles to bring "good Papa Alfred" a bouquet of flowers. "Papa Alfred" used to acknowledge that *token of appreciation and gratitude;* it was enough to repay him for all he had done for the child. Must not man do at least as much for God?

THIRD SUNDAY OF LENT:

The Cross and Man

> Readings: Exodus 20:1-17
> 1 Corinthians 1:22-25
> John 2:13-25

The whole life of Christ moves toward the cross. For this reason the evangelists devote special care to the account of the Savior's journey to Jerusalem, the holy city, where He would consummate His sacrifice. St. Luke's narrative centers around the journey of Jesus to the place of His crucifixion (9:51—19:28). St. John, too, after his account of the wedding at Cana, immediately presents Christ in Jerusalem, where for the first time He foretells His death and resurrection (Third Reading).

The great preacher and theologian of the cross, however, is St. Paul. After being thrown from his horse on the road to Damascus, he was converted by Christ crucified and risen (Galatians 1:16). From that moment on, the cross on which the Lord died became for him the one sign of the power and wisdom of God in opposition to the petty shrewdness employed by men regarding salvation. He writes to the Christians of Corinth, "Jews demand 'signs' and Greeks seek 'wisdom'; but we preach Christ crucified, a stumbling block to the Jews and folly to Gentiles, but to those who are called,....Christ the power of God and the wisdom of God. For the foolishness of God is wiser than men, and the weakness of God is stronger than men" (Second Reading). It is characteristic of the genius and the saint to be creative in finding new ways to carry out their undertakings. Jesus Christ contradicts all criteria of action by choosing the cross as the instrument of salvation for men and glory to the Father.

Through the cross salvation comes to the creature in its abundance, and that in every sphere of his being and acting. We may be permitted to underline our dignity as the first conquest of the cross: if a God dies in such humiliation in order to save His creature, that is an unquestionable sign of the latter's dignity. What adds weight to this conclusion is the inspired word which declares that Christ suffered for the sake of man's dignity (Hebrews 2:9). In this way the cross becomes the silent vindication and constant defense of the value of man against all private and public acts of violence and tyranny, which would make man a guinea pig, a mere tool (cf. Constitution on the Church in the Modern World, 18).

Then there is the profound rapport between the Crucified Himself and our interior life. He loves us, not in an abstract, Platonic way, but in a real way, touching all the negative aspects of our life. By means of His cross He has indeed established intimacy with every creature, achieving solidarity with the mystery of our unhappiness through suffering and abandonment. The author of the letter to the Hebrews continues in the same vein: God became man that He might reveal His mercy, and He brought this work of love to perfection by submitting to the trial of suffering in order that He might more effectively help us (cf. Hebrews 2:17-18).

In this connection it would be well to recall part of the memorable discourse Paul VI delivered at the conclusion of the Way of the Cross on Good Friday, 1972. He said: "The crucified speaks to you, man who is suffering, to you, the man worn out by fatigue, by the worries and sufferings of your life. He speaks to you, who are sick, to you, who are poor, to you, who are on the fringe of society. He speaks to you, the man who is weeping, to you, the man who perhaps mocks in order not to get himself involved, to you, the man on the verge of desperation.

"Who is it who speaks to you and who calls you? It is the man of sorrows, the man who knows suffering (cf. Isaiah 53:3). Even if no one else is, Christ is your colleague in suffering.... Christ is with you, He suffers with you.

"...Has not Christ become identical with you no matter what your misfortune...?" (March 30, 1972)

The fundamental reason for the cross is the remission of sins. Even if we are weak, God does not reject us, but He always remains with us to deliver us from our sins. He was crucified between two thieves, probably two guerrillas condemned by Roman authority, as if to establish and proclaim in a palpable way what His mission was: to die for sinners. God makes it His business to forgive all sins always, provided we remain close to His cross.

PASTORAL REFLECTIONS

1. Everyone loves because he knows or thinks he will receive a return of love. We can reply to divine love in two ways, one theoretical, the other practical. We must, first and foremost, give the place of honor to the cross. It is good to insist on the fact that our religion is a looking on Him who was pierced (cf. John 19:37). St. Felix of Cantalice went to the home of a celebrated Roman lawyer. Finding him in the library immersed in reading, the saint said to him: "It would be a misfortune for you if all these writings were to make you forget the book of books—the crucifix." Those who are truly faithful follow "the cross-bearing Christ" (Constitution on the Church, 41).

2. One night in 1741 an old man was shuffling along a dark street in London. It was George Frederick Handel, who for forty years had composed immortal music for the English court and for all of Europe. Kings and queens had honored him. But now jealousy and rivalry

had succeeded in having him and his works banned from the English court, and he was reduced to utter poverty.

Half-paralyzed, discouraged, he was dragging himself along the street when he saw the facade of a church. He entered, and overwhelmed with bitterness, cried out: "My God, my God, why have you forsaken me?" In despair he returned to his poor dwelling, where he found a large package on his table. He tore it open and found a book entitled *Sacred Oratorio,* together with a letter from the author, Charles Jennings, a poet of sorts. Handel was furious, but he read the letter, in which Jennings begged him to begin work on the oratorio immediately, adding, "The Lord wills it."

As he leafed through the text unwillingly, Handel came across the passage: "He was spurned and avoided by men.... He looked for sympathy, but there was none; for comforters, but he found none" (cf. Isaiah 53:3; Psalms 69:21). Reflecting on this glorious example and led by the grace of Jesus crucified, George Frederick Handel set to work anew and for years he continued to compose lovely harmonies expressing love of God and of his neighbor.

3. It is indispensable that we show our love for Christ by *obeying his commandments,* as he himself enjoined on us (cf. John 14:15). The first reading recounts for us the ten commandments as a witness to our love for God through complete solidarity with our neighbor.

FOURTH SUNDAY OF LENT:

The Love of God

Readings: 2 Chronicles 36:14-16, 19-23
Ephesians 2:4-10
John 3:14-21

The ancients had only one idea about God—His absolute greatness. They thought of God as the supreme

Lord of the universe, to whom everything had to be referred. With Plotinus, Greek philosophy reached the point of sensing that God is love, but this divine essence was still thought of as being wholly static, like water in an Alpine lake that has no outlet. Christianity, on the contrary, rests on the lively confidence that "God is love" (1 John 4:8): the center of giving within himself (the Trinity) and of diffusion outside himself (creation, revelation, incarnation, redemption, communion with man). The good news is precisely this love-gift of God (the agape) as opposed to love of pleasure (eros) and love of friendship (philanthropy), types of human love.

In the Second Reading St. Paul enlarges upon the free gift of divine love, shown to us in Christ. Writing to the Christians of Ephesus, inhabitants of a splendid city, who might delude themselves into thinking they were something in the history of salvation, he tells them in a clear-cut manner: "But God, who is rich in mercy, out of the great love with which he loved us even when we were dead through our trespasses...for by grace you have been saved through faith; and this is not your own doing, it is the gift of God—not because of works, lest any man should boast. For we are his workmanship, created in Christ Jesus for good works, which God prepared beforehand, that we should walk in them." The relationship between God and man is not one of commutative justice, where there is giving and receiving; nor of generosity, where much is given and little received; it is a relationship of free love on the part of God, who gives Himself to us without our being able to give Him anything in exchange. In this sense we may say that God is not "just" toward us, but only "good."

If mankind is insistently called to respond to such love, this collaboration is not on the level of being, causal, but only on the level of action, of merit, that is, for the fructification of the gift received. But what must we do? St. John, like St. Paul, repeats that the classic means of corresponding with love is to believe in the saving power of Christ. "God so loved the world that he gave his only Son, that whoever believes in him should not perish but have eternal life" (Third Reading). The Lord expects us to believe in Him, in Him alone. There is a difference between understanding and believing: the former is primarily an act of the intellect and is concerned with an idea; the latter is primarily an act of the will in order to adhere to a person. In the concrete, to believe means to accept the person of Christ with all that this implies and all that it can imply; it is a sharing in the very life of the Savior, choosing it as the model of our own actions. To believe is to pledge oneself to live "according to the new man," the mystic continuation of Jesus in time. To believe is to have the interior certainty that all history revolves around the death, resurrection, and glory of the Son of God. Finally, to believe is to have the intimate, undeviating conviction that in virtue of the merits of the Redeemer we too shall be wholly glorified in eternity. This response, given in faith, is not a kind of pacifism, but a personal agreement with Jesus, proclaiming His word, professing His life, and witnessing to His glory.

Small wonder, then, if this dialogue between the gratuitous love of God and our attachment to Him often results in a kind of tension like a painful gestation. Were not the Hebrew people, though the object of God's love, also a people in distress? The First Reading gives enough indications of such a state. The Jews were punished when they showed themselves unworthy of God by breaking His covenant of love. So it is: to separate oneself from God is to ruin one's life. Secondly, precisely because God loved His people He did not allow them to perish, but by awakening in them a deep yearning for His friendship, He drew them back to Himself. Similarly, our moments of defeat and misfortune are the ones that can bring us back to God more completely. Francis Thompson describes God as "The Hound of Heaven," who pursues man passionately, not to enslave him, but to restore him when he has worn himself out, or has been injured along the path of material things in the belief that they will give him complete happiness. God's method is this: to show His power in human weakness (cf. 2 Corinthians 12:9).

If God permits His friends to be tested, it is also because there can be no genuine love without sacrifice: to learn to love means to begin to suffer. To be loved by God, to be favored by Christ, involves a risk: it is equivalent to taking one's stand with open eyes for that which is eternal, spiritual, and struggling against all that is contingent, finite. Finally, the Lord, wise teacher that He is, does not hesitate to discipline those whom He loves (cf. Hebrews 12:6) in order to help them attain genuine maturity in His love, the essential purpose of life. Does not a mother discipline her little son so that he may attain a high ideal? Here we have the law of the grain of wheat which by dying produces much fruit (cf. John 12:24). Even trials are the fabric of goodness: "All is grace."

Instead of complaining we ought rather be grateful to God for His love toward us and cry out to Him: "Let my tongue cleave to the roof of my mouth if I do not remember you" (Psalm 137:6).

PASTORAL REFLECTIONS

1. *I am loved by God.* Revising the formula of Descartes, "I think, therefore I am," the theologian Hans Urs von Balthasar synthesized Catholic theology in the statement: "I am thought of and loved by God, therefore I am." A popular American song has it: "You are nobody as long as nobody loves you." Therefore, when I discover that God loves me with a love of donation, then life becomes sweet, I feel enveloped in tenderness and shelter, as when a bride is led by the hand to her bridegroom, or when a child rests securely and comfortably

in his mother's arms. To believe in God's love for me is to possess life most truly; it makes me want to dance for joy.

2. *The characteristics* of this divine love for us are mainly four: *gratuity, creativity, preference, communion.* The love of God for us is based not so much on our merits as on the exclusive benevolence of the Lord. Almost always we have some motivation for our human loves: often it is distributive justice, a giving for a receiving. But divine charity is poured out upon us without any reason of merit on our part: God loves us because it is His nature to love. In the second place, it is to be noted that in loving us God confers upon us dignity and worth: "Because you are precious in my eyes, and honored... I love you" (Isaiah 43:4). The highest dignity of the human creature is to be loved by the Creator. Such divine charity is, furthermore, preferential, even exclusive. In the eyes of the Lord, each one of us is as if he were the only one in history. God singles us out to love each one individually, with His whole love, as if there were no one else in the world. The love of God, finally, creates union and confirms it. God loves us in earnest, and it is He who always makes the first step to eliminate divisions, misunderstandings and separations between us and His Heart. It is always God who through a continuous and merciful strategy of love seeks to re-stabilize and enrich the relationship of fidelity contracted between ourselves and Him on the day of our baptism, a relationship we so easily break through our sin or weaken through our lack of correspondence.

3. *The messenger and fashioner of this whole poem of charity is Christ crucified.* The cross is the sign of the victory of this immeasurable divine love for us. For each one of us Jesus has an exclusive love, a single love, for He has given Himself "for me." His love is completely disinterested, healing, for He gave His life for us sinners. His charity is prevenient, unsurpassable, liberating, freely bestowed. Every kind of person is loved by

Him: the sinner, the unbeliever, the weak, the unhappy; we are all enveloped continually by this immense and unfathomable love. Because of this, our life reflowers continually in a hope that is never disappointed, it breaks out in a victorious hymn of paschal joy (cf. Paul VI, March 24, 1978).

FIFTH SUNDAY OF LENT:

Sin and Satan

Readings: Jeremiah 31:31-34
Hebrews 5:7-9
John 12:20-33

The passion of our Lord is a radical call for us to meditate on the existence and the action of Satan in our lives. There are three falls of Satan. First, because of his pride he fell from heaven to earth together with the other angels (cf. Luke 10:18). Here he ruled like a lord until the coming of the Messiah; he had direct power even to incarnate himself in individuals (it is well known that at the time of Christ there were many people possessed by the devil). With the Savior's death, Satan suffered his second great defeat: he was relegated to his own realms of darkness: "Now shall the ruler of this world be cast out" (Third Reading). At the end of time, with the second coming of Christ, the devil will finally be completely vanquished and condemned to hell forever (cf. Revelation 20:7-10). At present, however, even though he is held in check by Christ, the evil one does not cease to spread abroad his destructive violence, his noxious campaign for the moral fall of mankind. This is a truth constantly preached by the Church, also in the documents of Vatican II (cf. Constitution on the Church, 16; Constitution on the Church in the Modern World, 13, 37). She keeps on recalling it even though few people think about it.

The existence of the devil leads us to another consideration: sin. It is not difficult to be convinced of this terrible possibility and reality. Did not Christ die to overcome Satan and to destroy sin? But even prescinding from the unquestionable victory of the Son of God, is there anyone of us who is not aware of the snares of evil, like an underground siege? "Man is ill in the very depths of his being," Paul VI recently declared. We find ourselves so weak, especially in our will: often we sincerely promise to be good, but we continue to choose error rather than truth, what is useful rather than what is honorable, vice rather than virtue: "I see what is good but follow what is evil." Man, it is said, is a microcosm, a world in miniature: undoubtedly he has within his soul starry heavens, snow-capped peaks of high ideals, living waters of good resolutions; but he also has insidious woods, treacherous swamps, deserts, evil-smelling waters. No one is absolutely pure. "Let him who is without sin among you be the first to throw a stone at her" (John 8:7). "If we say we have no sin, we deceive ourselves" (1 John 1:8).

For our consolation, however, be it said that the real sinner is not the one who falls, but the one who loves his sin. There is a difference between a fault of weakness and a deliberate sin: the former is the result of an innate weakness; the latter is due to perversity of will. A person may be walking the way of virtue and perfection, and yet he may happen to stumble and fall: that is a weakness common to all of us. If, on the contrary, a person deliberately decides to enter upon the road to evil and if he arranges everything with this in mind, he is truly "the sinner." It is precisely this deliberate sinning which is diametrically opposed to God and can lead to perdition: from attraction to evil we pass on to consent, from consent to a fall, to repeated falls, to habit, and from this last to despair, and from despair to possible eternal damnation. Vatican II has not hesitated to confirm the existence of hell and the possibility of falling into it (cf. Constitution on the Church, 48).

But for every sin there is a remedy: the goodness of God. "I will forgive their iniquity, and I will remember their sin no more" (First Reading). What is Christianity? It is the encounter of the heart of God with our misery. By means of His passion Christ has merited complete pardon. There is no question here of legal pardon, apparent pardon, like a sick man trying to hide his infirmity by wearing a precious cloak of gold; it is a matter of authentic re-creation of our being, a real transformation from the state of a sinner to that of a "new being," ontologically remade, elevated. In the presence of this wonder St. Augustine declared that the justification of a soul is a greater work than creation itself.

The manner in which pardon is granted is likewise munificent. According to psychologists, there is no satisfaction in a gift unless it is accompanied by some external sign. Well, then, the sacrament of penance—that free and felicitous sacramental miracle—takes into account this human need. By entrusting the bestowal of this inexhaustible pardon to the priests of the Church, Jesus also wished to give us a sensible and reassuring sign of the pardon granted. The very limitations of the confessor, his own moral weakness ought to help him dispense divine pardon more abundantly to those who, like him, are weak by nature or might be discouraged by the weight of their sin. Precisely to make this same mercy flow more generously and easily in the drama of sin in man's life, the Church has promulgated norms regulating general sacramental absolution.

This season of Lent is a suitable time for calling upon God and saying to Him: "A clean heart create for me, O God" (Responsorial Psalm). Whatever our moral state may be, we should not be afraid: Christ is our powerful and most compassionate advocate (cf. 1 John 3:1), and the sacrament of penance is such an easy means of attaining the joy of refreshing pardon, a means in complete keeping with our nature. Jesus went out to meet His suffering and death for this very purpose, "to be the source of salvation" (cf. Second Reading).

PASTORAL REFLECTIONS

1. "The sinner is at the very heart of Christendom," says Charles Péguy. Who can appreciate the light better than one who has known the darkness? Or enjoy the heights better than one who has suffered the depths? Or relish the joy of being re-accepted better than the prodigal returning to a merciful Father? The first Easter message of Christ sent the apostles to the ends of the world with the commission to forgive sins in His name; it was like a *spontaneous release of His divine mercy, pardon and peace.*

2. In his famous and important encyclical, *The Mystical Body*, Pope Pius XII enumerates for us the *benefits of frequent reception of the sacrament of reconciliation.* He tells us: "By it, genuine self-knowledge is increased, Christian humility grows, bad habits are corrected, spiritual neglect and tepidity is purified, the will is strengthened, salutary self-control is attained, and grace is increased in virtue of the sacrament itself." We will do well to profit by these benefits.

3. In his Angelus Message for the fourth Sunday of Lent, the Holy Father urged the faithful to *prepare for the approaching feast of Easter* by the reception of the sacrament of penance. "Brothers! Easter is drawing nigh!" he reminded them. "We must prepare for it...to make it our Passover.... It is a question of preparing to celebrate, each in his own conscience...the miracle of liberation from sin, the miracle of recovering our lost life, that is, rising again with the Risen Christ. This sacramental participation...calls for an interior act of humility, confidence and courage,....but if it is carried out sincerely, it is the most significant, the finest and the most strengthening act of the year..." (Pope Paul VI, March 20, 1977).

PASSION SUNDAY (PALM SUNDAY):

The Man of Sorrows

Readings: Isaiah 50:4-7
Philippians 2:6-11
Mark 14:1—15:47

The liturgy of Palm Sunday presents the passion of our Lord and invites us to meditate on its elements: Christ's humiliation, obedience, and desire to be sacrificed. St. Paul writes to the Philippians, citizens of Asia Minor: "Though he [Jesus Christ] was in the form of God, he did not count equality with God a thing to be grasped, but emptied himself, taking the form of a servant,...he humbled himself and became obedient unto death, even death on a cross! Therefore God has highly exalted him and bestowed on him the name which is above every other name..." (Second Reading). We are accustomed to thinking about the humiliation of the Son of God at the moment of the crucifixion, and that is understandable. But according to Pauline thought, the most profound humiliation of the Word took place in the Incarnation, when the Son made the leap from the infinite to the finite, from the eternal to the contingent, from the state of perfect glory to that of humanity, subject to all its limitations except sin. Through this self-emptying, which we might call ontological, Jesus wished to reach the very depths of humiliation in keeping with the human nature He had assumed. He submitted to bodily humiliation, offering His back to those who struck Him, His cheeks to those who plucked His beard, His face to those who buffeted and spit upon Him (cf. First Reading). After the scourging, Pontius Pilate will present Him to the crowd as "the man of sorrows." His humiliation of soul was also unspeakable. He was abandoned by His apostles, betrayed by His friends, vilified by the mob, and laughed at by His enemies. The crucifixion itself, reserved by Roman law for slaves and for criminals of subject peoples, taking place outside the city walls lest the sacred confines of the holy city be defiled, could not but be a cause of humiliation and sadness for the most holy soul of Jesus.

Another element completes the interior offering of Jesus: obedience. His entire life was a generous and total *yes* to the will of the Father for the benefit of His fellowmen. In obedience He became incarnate (cf. Hebrews 10:5); His food was to do the will of Him who had sent Him into the world (cf. John 4:34); He does nothing except what pleases the Father (cf. John 8:29). His passion was undoubtedly the moment of His supreme obedience. He could have freed Himself from His enemies and overcome them with His infinite power; He could have refused to drink the bitter chalice of suffering. Instead, He chose to do the will of the Father, and when He had finished the task that had been entrusted to Him, He surrendered Himself into the hands of the Father (cf. Luke 23:46): "It is finished" (John 19:30).

Humiliation and obedience had their generous fulfillment in the free sacrifice desired by Christ. He predicted His passion three times (cf. Matthew 16:20; 17:22; 20:17). He overcame the opposition of the apostles, who wanted to prevent His going to meet the cross, as, for example, when He called Peter a "satan" because the latter did not want to hear anything about this subject (cf. Mark 8:33). In a word, the Lord steadfastly longed for the hour of His sacrifice in order to accomplish the salvation of mankind (cf. Luke 22:15).

But why all this? Adam and Eve brought sin into the world through their pride and its fruit, disobedience. Christ wanted to remedy the situation by humility and obedience.

Jesus was obedient because He was humble, and He wished to manifest His obedience through humility. But because He wished to give Himself totally to the very end, His humility unfolded itself in humiliation, and His obedience in sacrifice. Moreover, He moved steadfastly toward His self-immolation in order that men might have in Him, their Redeemer, the perfect model of love for the Father and practical love for His fellowmen. He, the Lord, absolute Perfection, eternal Truth, loved the world not in so many words but above all by sacrificing Himself for us for the glory of the Father. The Virgin Mary too, the new Eve, called by God to collaborate directly in the salvation of the world, promptly surrendered herself to the twin virtues of humility and obedience: "Behold, I am the handmaid of the Lord; let it be done to me according to your word" (Luke 1:38).

PASTORAL REFLECTIONS

After having examined these doctrinal aspects in a pastoral vein, we may be permitted a few reflections:

1. Despite our cleverness in avoiding humiliations, we are not seldom *forced to encounter them.* These may come from the egoism of our neighbor, from unexpected circumstances, from ourselves, especially in the evening of life. What to do? The follower of Christ knows how to accept this "martyrdom of the heart," in order to return love to Him who first loved us, confident that—as in the case of Christ, so also in his—the moment of humiliation providentially coincides with that of an unseen glorification before God.

2. We were estranged from divine friendship through the disobedience of our first parents; now it is up to us to find our way back in *humble obedience* to all that divine Providence has ordained for us. One soul used to pray: "Lord, give me the courage to change what I can change, and to accept all that I cannot change."

3. In a terse phrase, the evangelist simply says: "They crucified him." Our Lord died at three o'clock in the afternoon; at that very moment the paschal lamb was being offered in the temple of Jerusalem to com-

memorate the freeing of the Jewish people from the slavery of Egypt. The blood of the victim was sprinkled on the altar, and the people were invited to partake of the sacrificial flesh. For us too the true Pasch is not simply an historical or emotional commemoration; it is *an entering into the sacrifice of Christ* through the sacraments in order that we may receive life from the supreme fact of our salvation.

EASTER SUNDAY:

The Victory Over Death

Readings: Acts 10:34, 37-43
Colossians 3:1-4
John 20:1-9

The whole liturgy is a feast of joy, a pure, irresistible joy that diffuses itself like the waves of the ocean, and desires to invade the whole universe. The Church does not cease to repeat, as if to sound the very depths of her exultant enthusiasm, "Alleluia, alleluia, Christ is truly risen, alleluia!"

The first reason for this paschal joy is the certainty that Jesus is truly God. He had worked miracles to tell us that He was God, but He promised, He prepared the way and awaited the time of His resurrection to convince and ratify definitively His identity as the Son of God. On several occasions Jesus had said that He would lay down His life and on the third day would take it up again (cf. Matthew 27:63-71; Luke 24:6-7; John 2:19).* In His human weakness He could be crucified, but in His divine power He rose again to life. That empty tomb shall remain, for all time, a constant challenge to those who

---

*Christ insisted on the "third day," for according to the belief of that time, the soul left the body after the third day. Compare the account of the death of Lazarus, whose body was in decomposition because it was already the fourth day after his death (cf. John 11:39).

deny His divinity. With His resurrection He has displayed His power to confirm that He is indeed the Lord (cf. Romans 1:3; 2 Corinthians 13:14).

Our paschal exultation comes, in the second place, from the fact that in the resurrection of Christ our history has found its center, its explanation: the resurrection is like the "hinge" of time, as the empty tomb is the "hinge" of space. In His rising, Jesus directly takes the reins of the life of man and inserts Himself into human history as supreme Master, as a dynamic force in rendering positive all the events of our times. The third evangelist presents for us the resurrection and ascension of the Messiah as the prophetic moment in which the power of Christ is projected into history: from now on, Jesus will not cease to be mystically present with us on our way through the world, just as after His resurrection He followed the two disciples going to Emmaus (Luke 24:13ff.).

But the Savior remains among us not to prevail over us but to provide, not to dominate us but to sublimate us. He is risen for us. As God He could not die; if He has died and is risen again it is only in order that we may be vivified in Him, victorious through Him (1 Corinthians 15:21-22). It must be noted too that Christ did not die for humanity in the abstract, but for each individual person; thus too His resurrection is not simply a generic fact of history, but an event which concerns and touches, at least potentially, every single person. It is St. Paul who offers us this consoling application: "Jesus, who was put to death for our trespasses and raised for our justification" (Romans 4:25), for every creature, "each in his own order" (1 Corinthians 15:23).

But our joy is augmented and continues to spread out, like concentric circles ever increasing in size, at the thought that this victory of Christ pervades every dimension of our existence. The uplifting and vivifying power of the resurrection effects first of all our rebirth to a new, celestial life. As we light our own little candles from the Paschal candle, so from the glorious risen body of Christ there emanates grace and holiness. "O night, terror of demons! Paschal night, awaited for a year! O nuptial night of the Church, which gives birth to the newly baptized and despoils the sleeping demon! Night in which the Heir introduces the heirs into eternity!" (Asterius of Amasea, c. 400) It is quite revealing that Easter coincides with spring, when everything is awakening to a new life, to rebirth, to supernatural life.

Another source of the paschal joy which floods the People of God is found in the verity that sorrow and suffering has been transformed. Doubtlessly, that Good Friday had been for the apostles, for the disciples, for all those people who loved Jesus, the destruction of their hopes; the cross seemed to have inexorably broken down every ideal of life, every dream of victory. But Jesus rises, He appears! After all, then, the sorrow, the humiliation, the defeat had a meaning! But there is more: In His rising, the Lord definitively overcame death. "Death and life have contended in that combat stupendous...Christ from death is arisen, the Victor King, ever reigning!" Holy Church gratefully sings in her liturgy. If through one man death came into the world, through another Man the resurrection has come to us (cf. 1 Corinthians 15:21). Christ is the "firstborn from the dead," and He has begun the procession of the redeemed.

To be less incomplete in mentioning the joyous notes emanating from the Christian Pasch, we cannot fail to add that because of Christ's resurrection, our own body, too, will be glorified after death. Again it is St. Paul who assures us of this truth: "If the Spirit of him who raised Jesus from the dead dwells in you, he who raised Christ Jesus from the dead will give life to your mortal bodies also through his Spirit who dwells in you" (Romans 8:11). Our Savior, the Lord Jesus Christ, "will give a new form to this lowly body of ours and remake it according to the pattern of His glorified body" (Philippians 3:21). Thus while here on earth we bear the image of Adam, in heaven we shall resemble the second Adam, the Lord Jesus (cf. 1 Corinthians 15:49).

PASTORAL REFLECTIONS.

1. *Christ yesterday, today, and forever* (cf. Hebrews 13:8). Not only has Christ split our history in two —the time before Himself and the time after—but He also continues to remain the eternal Lord of time and of souls. Napoleon Bonaparte made a pointed observation: "Where are Caesar Augustus, Pompey, Alexander the Great, King Cyrus of Persia? Only their names are written in the books, to the indifference of many scholars, but Jesus Christ is everywhere present and His sign of failure—the crucifix—is displayed in all parts of the world. It is Jesus who continues to attract thousands, millions of souls who feel the vivifying presence of this patron and savior of humanity, entrusting themselves to Him who is physically invisible but spiritually fascinating, electrifying."

2. *Christ is our true Savior.* In instances in which Jesus deals directly with individuals (Nicodemus, the Samaritan woman, and others) or with groups (as when He gave the discourse on the Eucharist at Capernaum) He seems to follow a pattern: first He searches into the souls of His hearers, He sounds out the most profound needs, the most acute yearnings; secondly, He offers His very self to satisfy in the individual the thirst for the infinite and to elevate him to a supernatural dignity. This is precisely what Christ is to each of us. Pope Paul VI said this in addressing a large audience of young people: "We wish to tell you that the radical solution to your problems does not lie in a set of 'things' but in 'Someone.' Someone in whom all the values you are secretly seeking are united.... If you wish to be and to remain always young, follow Christ! He alone is the Savior of the world. He alone is the true hope of mankind..." (Paul VI, February 25, 1978).

3. *Christ is our assured hope for life after death.* Outside the context of resurrection, history can appear

to be nothing but a vain series of events, each in itself and all as a whole meaningless: birth, growth, old age, death, and then nothing, a horrible nothing. The resurrection has broken this closed circle and has inserted into it a hope, an expectancy, the assurance of a new condition, a life transfigured and made eternal by love! The Christian is joyously aware of this, and at Holy Mass every Sunday, the weekly "little Easter," the whole Christian community cries out with confidence and interior certainty, like an innocent child, "Dying, you destroyed our death; rising, you restored our life; Lord Jesus, come in glory!"

SECOND SUNDAY OF EASTER:

The Blessedness of Those Who Believe

Readings: Acts 4:32-35
1 John 5:1-6
John 20:19-31

To the eight beatitudes proclaimed by Jesus in Galilee, at the beginning of His ministry, the Risen Lord added a ninth. Appearing to His apostles in the cenacle, He said to the unbelieving Thomas: "Have you believed because you have seen me? Blessed are those who have not seen and yet have believed" (John 20:29).

Faith is a blessing first of all because it completes our knowledge. We have the light of the sun for the body, the light of knowledge for the mind, the light of faith for the soul. Without faith, man's knowledge is greatly limited indeed. But with the help of faith, it can invade the very regions of the divine, even to the throne of the Most Holy Trinity. When faith comes to the aid of our natural knowledge it makes us able to distinguish truth from falsehood, the essential from the secondary, the permanent values from the transitory and illusory. It is precisely this luminous opening of the horizon to the whole world, to human and divine history, which gives us a sense of interior contentment and blessedness.

Furthermore, faith is a blessing because it gives us the sensation, rather the certainty, that despite all the contradictions of life God still has a merciful design for us, a design which leads to eternal happiness. It is only faith that gives meaning to our sufferings. If we consider all the trials and sorrows which must be encountered, more or less, as man makes his way through life from the cradle to the grave, what consolation or comfort is to be found except that which comes from faith? The one who has no faith naturally ends in despair, but the person whose life is anchored in faith can remain serene and joyful. "I am seventy years old and I have never been happy," said the unbelieving Goethe, though he had at his command all the pleasures life could offer. "I am seventy years old and I have never been unhappy," was the statement of St. Leonard of Port Maurice, who spent a long life in penance, while St. Francis of Assisi admitted, "I am looking forward to such joy that to me every pain is a delight."

Faith is a blessing because it gives strength to act. The world belongs to those who believe. It is faith that forever fashions man. The energy to live, the enthusiasm to act are somewhat dangerous when man does not know the driving force of his whole existence. Inertia is always the sister of enigma, of doubt, of fear. The steps of the one who does not know where to go are slow, tired and uncertain; but for the person who has the gift of faith the goal is fixed, everything is clear, worthy to be experienced and mastered, and treading the pathways of time becomes graceful, like the sequence of Gregorian music. As the rays of the sun illumine every peak in a range of mountains, so the light of faith shining on the panorama of life makes it interesting, transfigures it, inviting the believers to wholehearted activity to be worthy of their status as creatures, as sons of God. The book of the Acts of the Apostles breathes an air of fervor and social kindness on the part of the first Christians because they were "a community of believers" (First Reading).

Faith is beatitude because by it a Christian possesses Jesus Himself. In biblical language, to know, to believe, means to come into intimate union with the person in whom one believes. Hence, to believe in Christ means to possess and be possessed by the very Word of God Himself. St. Aurelius Augustine explains: "He who believes in Christ penetrates into Him; penetrating into Him, he possesses Him; and possessing Him, he shares His life." St. Peter himself told us so long ago: "Without having seen him you love him; though you do not now see him you believe in him and rejoice with unutterable and exalted joy" (1 Peter 1:8). There is no doubt that our greatest joy is to belong intimately to Christ, and our greatest nobility is to be able to sign ourselves as "a friend of Jesus."

One final reason for the blessing accruing to us from faith: it is a pledge of our eternal life. The ascent to the divine is a work of faith. The Gospels give abundant testimony of this: "He who believes and is baptized will be saved" (Mark 16:16); "...that whoever believes in him should not perish but have eternal life" (John 3:16); "This is eternal life, that they know you, the only true God, and Jesus Christ whom you have sent" (John 17:3). Most insistent upon this rapport of faith and salvation is St. Luke: on four different occasions he uses the expression, "Your faith has saved you" (7:50; 8:49; 17:19; 18:42). For St. Luke, Christ has the great mission of saving mankind through faith. The very thought that through faith life can have a positive conclusion gives joy and enthusiasm. But another truth that we often encounter in the Gospel is this, that our faith can mean salvation also for others. The paralytic of Capernaum had no faith himself, but he was saved by the faith of those who brought him to the feet of Jesus (cf. Matthew 9:2-6). Lazarus was raised from the dead because of the faith of the two sisters, Mary and Martha (John 11:1-44).

PASTORAL REFLECTIONS

1. In the world there is any amount of noise, and certainly there is no lack of entertainment, but there is no joy. In the depths of many souls there is a sediment of annoyance, of aversion, of discontent caused by a sense of futility. Even those people who do not accept the world as it is and would like to change it are often a prey to sadness. Joy is a rare pearl, more so now than ever before. If we wish to possess once again this blessedness, we must *clothe ourselves anew with light,* live to the full our Christian faith. Sometimes there are succinct ideas which reflect, as in a concave mirror, the whole vision of the world. Such is the idea of our history as given to us by faith. Philosophy is the research of the reason of things, of beings; faith in God is the answer. Philosophy examines human truths and builds upon them; faith offers the meaning of existence. Philosophy places question marks about God; faith is God interrogating man in order to teach him the wonders of supernatural realities and to guide him toward the fullness of life. To lose faith is to lose the meaning of existence and the ultimate reason for action. With faith, everything acquires significance. For this reason, faith is that which "overcomes the world" (Second Reading).

2. *To be a Christian one must have faith.* The only true *Weltanschauung* of the Christian is that of faith, which far from being contrary to science and human thinking is a stimulus, comfort and richness to them. St. Paul, employing a phrase from the prophet Habakkuk (2:4) states that "the just man shall live by faith" (Romans 1:17). Faith is in truth the "foundation that sustains the religious edifice" (Paul VI, October 12, 1977).

3. *The characteristics of faith:* In the "Porta di Santa Marta," the exterior door on the left side of St. Peter's Basilica, wrought by the artist Scorzelli in 1971, we can read some lines of the hymn of faith composed by Pope Paul VI: "O Lord, I believe! I desire to believe in You.

O Lord, grant that my faith be pure. O Lord, grant that my faith be free. O Lord, grant that my faith be joyous. O Lord, grant that my faith be lively. O Lord, grant that my faith be humble. Amen."

THIRD SUNDAY OF EASTER:

The Value of Suffering

Readings: Acts 3:13-15, 17-19
1 John 2:1-5
Luke 24:35-48

During Lent we have had occasion to meditate upon suffering and the cross of Christ. The biblical readings of this third Sunday of Easter offer us an occasion to reflect upon the mysterious fruitfulness of suffering in our lives.

The ancient Greeks accepted suffering as something which could not be avoided. Pain, they thought was caused by the envy of the gods. The Persians attributed it to the influence of a wicked god. The peoples of India, thought that it came from the body, from matter, and for this reason they sought to annihilate it in nirvana, or in the psychological extinction of every desire. The philosophers think far too much about it and arrive at nothing; the romanticists make of it an esthetical distraction; the pragmatists would like to suppress every form of pain, while the hedonists busy themselves trying to avoid every kind of suffering. Others become so bitter over suffering that they use it as a reason to rebel against God. Christ did not eliminate pain and sorrow, but He transfigured it into a positive reality. In the Christian concept it is something like "the bitter seed of an apricot which was cast by the wayside: it fell and was forgotten about. Twenty years later, in that same place, a beautiful apricot tree was in full bloom" (René Bazin).

In the first place, suffering ennobles us. The person is born through an act of love, he grows in suffering.

There are no wounds without a battle, but neither is there victory without a battle. One who does not know how to suffer runs the risk of never growing up in spirit. An old proverb suggests this prayer: "Lord, now and then let me meet an enemy, so that I may ever be in fighting trim." In activity we become masters of things, but in suffering we become masters of ourselves. Tears are not lamentations; they brighten our eyes so that we can see ourselves better. A person who is able to suffer begins to understand, one who understands has the possibility of loving, and only one who loves is worthy of life. The great men of the past have almost always been the ones formed and chiseled in the school of suffering. The saints became authentic personalities for the very reason that they were able to accept pain as the purifying and strengthening factor of their genuine moral values and standards.

But according to the promises of the Gospel, suffering is most often the way to eternal salvation. The death and resurrection of Jesus are not in reality two moments that follow upon one another like "the one first and then the other," but they form the very center of the cosmic itinerary and the spiritual dynamism of history. As it was written, Christ suffered and rose again from the dead on the third day (Third Reading), so that mankind, purified from its sins and practicing penance, could be converted, that is, could be turned to God (First Reading), entering into the friendship of God. Even when the Lord said that He was "the way" to go to the Father, He referred particularly to His death and resurrection as the point of passover for all those who would be His followers: it is through Him, therefore, that we pass from sorrow to love, from death to life, from sadness to joy. This magnificent spirituality was the theme of the early catechesis of the apostles. St. Peter confirms this: "But rejoice insofar as you share Christ's sufferings, that you may also rejoice" (1 Peter 4:13); and Saint Paul, the theologian of tribulations, never ceases repeating that authentic Christian life is to be immersed in the death of Christ in order to participate in His resurrection (Philippians 3:21; Ephesians 2:6; Colossians 2:12; Romans 8:17). We are not born to die, but in Christ Jesus we suffer and die only to be born anew. Our cross united with the cross of Jesus is the dynamic principle of our resurrection itself (cf. also Mark 10:28).

According to the categories of Christian asceticism, suffering can be further a means of salvation for our neighbor. As there is such a thing as solidarity in the physical field, in the intellectual and the social field, so also and even in a greater degree does it exist in the supernatural realm. As Christ made Himself "an expiation for our sins, and not for ours only but also for the sins of the whole world" (Second Reading), so also the Christian has the sublime possibility of collaborating in the salvation of the world by means of suffering.

It is quite clear that Christ as our Head suffered all that He could suffer to merit salvation for us, and He wills to continue to suffer in His Mystical Body to apply the same salvation to all mankind (cf. Colossians 1:24). We instruct and teach others through our words, but we save them through our sufferings.

Sorrow is, finally, "the test of the supreme love of God" (Charles de Foucauld). It is in suffering that our faith becomes religious fidelity. One who does not know how to suffer for the beloved does not love; who suffers but a little for the person beloved, loves but a little; who suffers much, loves much. He who desires to suffer immensely for the person beloved, he loves truly, without measure. "A calm and quiet life that leads to God, this is good; a life of pain lived in patience and in union with Christ is of greater value; but to find one's happiness in a life of pain and suffering, this surpasses everything: it is the perfection of love" (Master Eckart).

PASTORAL REFLECTIONS

1. *Much of our suffering comes from ourselves.* In this study on suffering, let us not forget that more than a few of our troubles are caused by ourselves, occasioned

by the bad use we make of our liberty. A biblical example: The people of Israel insist upon having a king, such as all the other Oriental peoples had. The aged prophet Samuel warns them of all the social and economic troubles such a choice would bring upon them; he tells them their only King must be God. Other kings would rather oppress them, making them pay heavy taxes, carrying away their Israelite sons and daughters as slaves; they would requisition the people's cattle and vineyards and other properties. But the people continue to demand a king as their head, and Saul is elected. Though God had made known through the mouth of Samuel that He did not want His people to have a king, He made a pact with Saul, let him be anointed, and granted him all the rights of kingship over the people of Israel. Nevertheless the Israelites had to pay for their erroneous choice, for the prophecies of Samuel were all verified (cf. 1 Samuel 8ff.). God permitted that His people suffer even greater trials because of the erroneous use they made of their liberty. So it is also for us.

2. *But the Lord knows how to draw good from evil.* God's way is not that of punishment but of forewarning, not of beating down but of saving and recovering. Often it is through the very pain we suffer that the Lord recalls us to Himself. The little child in the midst of his toys might easily forget his mother, but let her once go out of the room and disappear from his sight. He sets up a cry until her return. When she is once more near him he clings to her, his toys are forgotten and he has found greater sweetness in being with his mamma. The Lord who loves us more than even our mother can love, permits the failure of our little earthly ideals and the destruction of what we thought were very important projects, so that after an excusable reaction of sadness, perhaps even of anger, we can sense the need and the happy lot of turning to Him, our sovereign Lord.

3. Undoubtedly, *sorrow* is a constant source of sadness and pessimism, but if it is seen thus with mystical vision and *lived in union with Christ,* it can become a

"fortunate misfortune," a rocky cliff of gold. A plant uprooted and transferred to another place may have a new lease on life, and the same holds for our sorrows when they are placed in the very heart of God. Sanctity is a mysterious plant which does not grow, flower and fructify if it is not watered with tears and blood. On Calvary there were three crosses: one that redeemed, that of Jesus; one that was redeemed, that of the good thief; and the third that remained indifferent in the face of salvation. May the crosses in our life be like the first two: redeeming and redeemed.

FOURTH SUNDAY OF EASTER:

The Mission of the Good Shepherd

Readings: Acts 4:8-12
1 John 3:1-2
John 10:11-18

Already among the Sumerians, the Babylonians, and the Assyrians, the word "shepherd" was used to describe a sovereign who took attentive care of his subjects, sustained the weak, gathered the dispersed. The Egyptians thought of their divinity as a shepherd protecting the people like a flock of sheep. The Greece of Homer's time also speaks of shepherd kings whose duty it was to govern and feed the people entrusted to their care. But the idea of shepherd is dear, above all, to the Hebrews, perhaps because they were, at least at one time, a nation of shepherds; perhaps also because many of their national heroes, such as Moses and David, were shepherds. The principal reason is, though, that the prophets had sung of the future Messiah as a good shepherd (cf. Ezekiel 34:12-16). Judaic liturgy, in fact, prescribed the reading of this thirty-fourth chapter of Ezekiel during the feast of the dedication of the Temple. In this text the prophet in the name of God censures the false shepherds of the people of God and foretells the future Good Shepherd.

Christ Jesus was well aware of this historical and biblical background, and on the feast of the dedication of the Temple He took up this ancient liturgical text the people had just heard and presented Himself to them as the Good Shepherd. In a most appealing discourse He outlines the qualities of a true shepherd. This is the theme of the Third Reading.

First of all, the shepherd leads the sheep. He is not led by the flock, but he is the one who guides, who chooses the direction and the destination. Certainly the sheep do not know which roads to take, which paths to follow, the conditions of the different ways; but they are sure that in following their shepherd they will have abundant pasture, rich in every way. The same can be said for the Christian: just like any other person he does not know how his life will unfold, but in his heart he holds a great trust: he is sure that at the end of the road there will be the great surprise of an eternal communion with God.

During the journey, it is the duty of the good shepherd to protect his flock from all dangers. The hireling—says Jesus—abandons his sheep and runs away in face of danger, but the good shepherd remains there to protect the sheep entrusted to him. Man is a being threatened from all sides: he is threatened by the egoism of his neighbor, by uncertainty, by sorrow, by time itself which absorbs every existence. Christ frees us from all these dangers. In following Him as the good shepherd, we see the others no longer as our aggressors but as sheep of the same flock, members of the same company; our uncertainties and fears of the unknown are overcome too in the sense that however obscure the pathway, it has a certain and infallible goal: eternal life. Because of this positive and wonderful goal, the very rush of time and even death itself are overcome and conquered forever.

Another task of the shepherd is to revivify the sheep that are critically wounded along the way. Christ does not limit Himself to simply encouraging and urging along those who fall by the wayside, but like a divine pelican, He nourishes with His own blood and with the power of His redemption every wounded, sinful man. And even if we continue to hurt ourselves, to inflict mortal wounds upon ourselves, He the fount of infinite love will not cease pardoning us, caring for us, continually offering us redemption to the very last moment of our lives, in order to number us among the flock of His elect.

In this marvelous office of mercy Christ has an intimate rapport with each individual person. We usually think of the flock as an anonymous thing, a uniformity in which all individuality disappears. In the flock of the people of God, however, each one is regarded, each one is loved as if he were the only one. If a mother gives herself wholly to one of her children she cannot at the same time give herself wholly to another. Jesus, who has perfect knowledge and infinite love, can be totally and simultaneously available to each and all. He Himself has confirmed this: "I know the voice of each one of my sheep, and each one knows me." Làszlo Mécs, a Hungarian poet, sings of this consoling truth in these words: "I knew only that there was Someone who loved me. Someone who is greater than every silence, greater than every love and joy, greater than the world and greater than heaven. I knew it. He loves me. This is everything!" How beautifully we can combine these lyric thoughts with the Psalm of the Good Shepherd: "The Lord is my shepherd, I shall not want!" (Psalm 23)

The third liturgical reading continues to enumerate the prerogatives of Christ as the Good Shepherd, stressing lastly the victory which will be His. There is a noteworthy parallelism between Jesus as Shepherd and Jesus as Head, who is "to unite all things in him, things in heaven and things on earth" (Ephesians 1:10). Not only was the Savior the visible shepherd of Israel, but He also continues to be the invisible and invincible guide of the Church, which for this reason is called His house, His bride, His body. He is God-with-us—Emmanuel—for He "dwelt among us" (John 1:14) in order that the world and its history, despite alternating vicissitudes, will advance toward spiritual perfection until the great day when He will call together the whole flock, separating the sheep from the goats at the Last Judgment (Matthew 25:32ff.).

PASTORAL REFLECTIONS

1. *The figure of the Good Shepherd* was the earliest and the most touching representation of Christ in *the first centuries of Christianity.* Lovely paintings on this subject, dating from the end of the second century, are to be found in the catacombs of St. Callistus, Priscilla and Domitilla in Rome. Throughout the ages the Church has stressed this mission of Christ as the Good Shepherd (Constitution on the Church, 6, 18, 27, 28; Decree on the Ministry and Life of Priests, 11, 18, *et al).* It is good for us all, for our sanctification, to belong to the mystical flock of Him who is in the midst of men to serve them.

2. *To believe in Jesus Christ.* The apostle St. John wrote his Gospel to convince men that Jesus is the Son of God. One who truly believes this will entrust himself to Jesus, dedicate himself to His love alone. It is most necessary for us as Christians to surrender ourselves to Christ, to follow Him fondly, trustingly. Jesus is the Messiah, the Christ, the King sent by God; He is Son of God and son of man; He is the Omnipotent, the Savior, the Good Shepherd. "Though He appeared a long time ago," said our Holy Father, "He is near us in a perennial presence, and with the inviting fondness of a brother He is our teacher, our guide and our savior" (Paul VI, December 25, 1976).

3. But *our following of Him will grow in perfection if we love the Savior as a friend.* It is proper for the human heart to find in one particular friend an ideal of perfection which is attractive and inspirational in the excellence of its moral beauty. The Christian religion, our faith, presents Christ to us as the perfect ideal, as a friend who is all beauty and interior splendor. "The Word of God," affirms St. Augustine, "is beautiful as the

perfect image of His Father; He is beautiful in the womb of the Virgin Mary, where He assumed perfect humanity without losing divinity. He is beautiful in the miracles He performs, in the words He speaks, in the life He leads. Christ is always beautiful, as well when He sacrifices His life as when He conquers death. He is beautiful when He is sacrificed upon the cross, when He descends into the tomb, and when He rises again. His beauty continues to shine upon our souls!"

FIFTH SUNDAY OF EASTER:

Authentic Apostolate

Readings: Acts 9:26-31
1 John 3:18-24
John 15:1-8

The first condition of Christian apostolate is to remain in the love of Christ. Jesus told His apostles: "As the branch cannot bear fruit by itself, unless it abides in the vine, neither can you, unless you abide in me. I am the vine, you are the branches. He who abides in me, and I in him, he it is that bears much fruit..." (Third Reading). St. John insistently speaks of "remaining in Jesus." Eleven times he mentions it in the fifteenth chapter of his Gospel, and at least sixteen times in his letters. There is no doubt that if we want to produce fruits of sanctity and of apostolate it is indispensable that we remain united to Christ. As the heart sends blood to every part of the body, so does our Savior nourish and make fruitful the whole of His Mystical Body.

The way to become true apostles, therefore, is to be "touched and transformed" by love and by divine grace. The shepherds and the magi became propagators of the message of salvation after they had experienced contact with the Savior (Luke 2:20; Matthew 2:1-12). The apostles became truly apostolic only after the descent of the Holy Spirit on the day of Pentecost (cf. Acts 2). When St. Paul was visited by the Lord on the way to Damascus, at that very moment there was born in him the driving urge to action (Acts 22:10). "The love of Christ impels me," he stated.

The Holy Spirit is Fire and Light. For this reason, the two principal directions of the apostolate are those of charity toward the neighbor and the spread of truth. In reference to the first point, it is well worth repeating that between the love of God within us and our love of the neighbor there is an inseparable relationship, a necessary link. St. John reminds us of this: "his commandment is this: that we are to love one another... those who keep his commandments remain in him and he in them" (Second Reading). Without this vital insertion of self into Christ, it will be difficult to make a generous gift of self to the other. There may be ulterior reasons for generosity: emotional reflexes, occasional insights into human solidarity, but it will not be easy to practice true self-giving in charity for the simple reason that no one can give what he does not possess, and no one can continue to give of himself without receiving. But the gift of the Spirit is also the power of light: for this reason, whoever is immersed in the love of God tends to make the Gospel message vibrant, diffusing the truth with constancy, courage and fidelity.

In the first reading we read that St. Paul had been "preaching boldly in the name of the Lord." The example of this intrepid and forthright apostle forces us to a bit of reflection which might even seem like a reproof. Today in the world people are afraid of being messengers of truth, bearers of light. Some speakers on religion prefer to pour out their verbal tirades on less interesting aspects of the sacred, and try to diffuse unwholesome ideas, oftentimes artfully falsified for economic or editorial purposes. And the very experts in religion, the Catholics, the children of light and of love, usually stand by in silence, and even if they do speak, their reaction is timid, weak, as if they were suffering an inferiority complex or social fear, or as if they were obliged to accept such things without retort.

When the Germans were victorious over the French in 1870, a French officer Gougenat des Mousseaux went to find Bernadette, the seer of Lourdes. She was in a convent in Nevers. The officer asked her if she were not afraid of the Germans, who even then were advancing toward Nevers. She replied, "Ah, no. I have no fear at all." "Are you sure?" the officer insisted. "Very sure," she repeated. "I am afraid of only one thing in this world —the bad Christians!"

The authentic apostolate has two fundamental laws, mentioned in the book of Wisdom in chapter 8: to act "strongly and sweetly," which is the manner of God. Strongly in regard to the defense of the doctrine, sweetly in the manner of presentation. There must be clear delineation between truth and falsehood, between good and bad, between God and the demon, but at the same time the apostle must be patient and lovingly approachable with his listener. St. John the Baptist spoke frankly to his audience, without reserve and reticence; strong in the Spirit, St. Stephen the deacon fearlessly denounced his adversaries for their sin. St. Peter, too, proclaimed the truth aloud to the crowds, saying that it was impossible to keep silence about it for this was the will of God and of the Risen One. St. Paul knew very well that speaking the whole truth would probably incur imprisonment and even martyrdom; nevertheless, he preached with freedom, with decision, with no fear whatsoever. Fear is a bad companion for any action, and "he who is afraid of men will hardly be able to do any good for them," as St. Ignatius of Loyola pointed out. It goes without saying that in addition to being firm and clear in spreading the truth, the apostle must also be respectful, gentle, very human. This holds very especially for our own day. Our "Good Pope John," that artist of dialogue, stated almost as an echo of St. Augustine: "You must be inflexible with error, but indulgent with the erring." The two values of objective judgment and subjective comprehension render the apostolate valid and efficacious.

It is needless to belabor the point that in this courageous work of the apostolate sufferings and contradictions will be encountered. The Divine Master predicted it: "I send you out as lambs in the midst of wolves" (Luke 10:3); "If they persecuted me, they will persecute you" (John 15:20). But the battle must not discourage. To fight for the right is good, for it is to love. If men oppose and misinterpret those who are dedicated to doing good, this is only one more reason to trust in God alone. Such confidence in Him will give security and tranquillity of heart, for the divine approbation is the wellspring of interior peace (cf. Second Reading).

George Washington had hardly assumed command of the American troops when he was informed that in one town his soldiers had suffered a defeat. The general did not lose his composure but asked if the men had fought. The answer was a definite "Yes!" "Then," he concluded, "our states are safe."

PASTORAL REFLECTIONS

1. *Liturgy and apostolate.* "Religious celebrations tend to continue, in thought, in outlook, in action, that is, in conduct, and precisely in the newness of the good and in the firmness of love. They are not like candles which are extinguished at the end of a feast, but are lights that remain lit somehow in conscience to enlighten the path of time in front of us. In other words, moments of spiritual intensity survive, especially in the guiding resolutions that the religious feast has inspired in us.... Christian mentality tends to convert the momentary and transient contacts of inner light into the faithfulness of promises..." (Paul VI, January 2, 1977).

2. *The testimony of the apostolate.* In the first centuries, the Christians professed their love for Christ by going cheerfully toward their martyrdom. When in the fourth century the prospects of martyrdom receded, many Christians sought to substitute it with voluntary

martyrdom, retiring into the deserts of Thebaide to practice renunciation, vigilance, fasting and obedience. Our martyrdom today is apostolic action (cf. Constitution on the Church; Decree on the Lay Apostolate).

3. It remains to us yet *to make our own the prayer* of a great soldier of Christ, St. Ignatius of Loyola: Eternal Word, Only-Begotten Son of God, I beseech You, teach me true generosity, to serve You as You deserve, to give without counting the cost, to combat regardless of wounds, to work without seeking repose, to sacrifice myself without expecting any other reward than the knowledge of having fulfilled Your holy will. Amen.

SIXTH SUNDAY OF EASTER:

Christians: Witnesses of Goodness

Readings: Acts 10:25-26,34-35,44-48
1 John 4:7-10
John 15:9-17

In antiquity the supreme motive for action was force; in the oriental Greek culture it was wisdom; in the Roman empire, law held sway; in our western world it is now technology and the positive sciences. But in the Christian religion, that which is decisive is charity, goodness. It is not so much a love of pleasure or of esteem, but the love which is self-giving, an effusion of goodness, a love like that of the heavenly Father who loved the world so much that He sent His only Son to the world that we might have life through Him (Second Reading).

As an actual response to the love of God for men, we are all invited to love one another with a very special love, a supernatural love given to us by Christ. It is the apostle St. John who points out to us the unique relationship between the love of God and the love of our brethren: "Love one another even as I have loved you" (John 13:34); "As the Father has loved me, so have I loved you...love one another as I have loved you"

(John 15:9-12). He makes of it an explicit command: "This I command you, to love one another" (John 15:17). Fraternal love is, therefore, the badge of the followers of Christ; the true disciple of the Master is distinguished from others because he has learned this one thing: Love your neighbor with the heart of God.

If we should seek for motives for being spreaders of kindness, we must begin with the basic fact of our creaturely solidarity. No man is an island, and each one has need of the others; each one is bound to the others in his life, his development, his activity. There is a fable which brings out a point of interdependence: The tiger has need of the forest to save him from being caught, and the forest has need of the tiger to avoid being cut down. Charity is a law of communal perfection, benevolence is an encouragement in life, and being in harmony with others is an expression of true nobility.

In the second place, we must preserve a loving unity with our neighbor because, living in the grace of God, we are for that very reason the children of God. Now, what is the pride of the son? To resemble his father. Well, then, in reflecting on the program for Christian living as St. Matthew develops it so clearly in chapters five, six and seven of his Gospel, we notice that the invitation to be perfect as the Father in heaven is perfect (Matthew 5:48) is addressed to the followers of Christ with specific reference to charity. Then if we consider that our neighbor is, at least potentially, a child of God, it follows clearly that we cannot say that we love the Father without at the same time including in our love His sons. The Apostle of love tells us the same in his well known text: "If anyone says, 'I love God' and hates his brother, he is a liar" (1 John 4:20). Furthermore, in Christianity Jesus is the Head and the Christians are the members of a single organism: the Mystical Body. It is our very belonging to this People of God that obligates us as Christians to look upon others as ourselves. "He who says he loves God and does not love his neighbor," comments St. Augustine on this point, "is like a person who embraces someone while stamping on his feet." Another of his metaphors is that a person without charity is like a flame that has gone out.

Finally, we may not forget that the divine judgment pronounced upon us will be made on the measure of our love. Even the ancient non-Christian religions, for example Buddhism, threaten with hellfire those who treat their equals unjustly. But it is only Christianity which points to the day of judgment as the time of reckoning for the charity we have practiced or not toward our fellowmen. If as disciples of the Master we have been given His mandate to love one another, it is logical that we shall one day be examined and judged according to it. At the close of our life we shall be judged according to our love, and each one will receive according to that which he has given. Eternal life will be the prize of our kindness. God came to us by becoming Man; we arise to God through humanity. It is again the fourth evangelist who calls our attention to this fact: We know "that we have passed out of death into life, because we love the brethren" (1 John 3:14).

The supreme difficulty, however, is to put into practice this wonderful program of Christian charity. The Gospel offers us a solution, a classical means: to remain in Christ and persevere in His love (cf. Third Reading). Enriched and advanced in divine love, we shall not find it so very difficult to radiate this love to those around us, for "the fruit of the Spirit is love, joy, peace, patience, kindness, goodness, faithfulness..." (Galatians 5:22). And Pope Paul VI expresses it like this: "It is the love of God in us which becomes comprehension, help, dedication, generosity" (Paul VI, May 8, 1964). Remaining in the love of Christ, we can in this way continue in time the Incarnation and its ineffable story of goodness and kindness. In this way God will love men not only with His own heart but also with the hearts of men. Another thought from St. Augustine: "He who has charity conceives the Word; he who practices charity gives birth to the Word."

PASTORAL REFLECTIONS

1. *Our resolution* can be but one: to do what the Lord has commanded, *to love our brothers.* To be loving and kind is an adventure more wonderful and more arduous than going around the world in a sailboat, or shooting through space in a spacecraft. It is loving kindness which remains forever, for God is love, or rather, God with us is love. Where there is love, there is God.

2. *The Week of Charity.* The real misfortune of the world is that of not loving. Let us, therefore, make of the days of our week a journey of love, like this:

Sunday, the Lord's Day: At all times, see in your neighbor the likeness of Jesus. The defects of your brother belong to his humanity, but the reality is divine: every person is a creature of God.

Monday: Treat your neighbor as you would treat Jesus. He, the Lord, desires this for the good of all.

Tuesday: Be more ready to give than to receive, in imitation of Christ whose whole life was a gift of mercy for the life and salvation of men.

Wednesday: In your dealings with your neighbor transform all into charity, gentleness, genuine collaboration. Be understanding, loyal, optimistic.

Thursday: Remember that the measure you use for others will be the measure God uses for you. Judge not and you will not be judged.

Friday: Do not draw unfavorable conclusions, do not complain, do not criticize. Your charity must be limpid and clear, like the pupil of an eye which cannot suffer even a tiny grain of sand upon it.

Saturday: Welcome your neighbor with every mark of benevolence. Your charity must fit this description: Kindness toward all, always and at any cost.

3. *A Prayer:*

Make us worthy, O Lord, to serve our brethren in the whole world, especially those who live and die in poverty, hunger, abandonment. Give them today, Lord, their daily bread, material bread and moral bread, through our hands. Give them peace and joy through our love, our comprehension, our solidarity.

Lord, make us channels of Your peace.
Let us seek rather to console than to be consoled,
to understand rather than to be understood,
to love rather than to be loved.
For it is in forgetting ourselves that we find ourselves,
it is in pardoning that we are pardoned,
it is in dying to ourselves that we are awakened to eternal life. Amen.

ASCENSION:

The Ascension and Heaven

> Readings: Acts 1:1-11
> Ephesians 1:17-23
> Mark 16:15-20

After having given His own His final instructions on the kingdom of heaven, Jesus led them to Mount Olivet where "he was lifted up, and a cloud took him out of their sight. And while they were gazing into heaven as he went, behold two men stood by them dressed in white. 'Men of Galilee,' they said, 'why do you stand looking into heaven? This Jesus, who was taken up from you into heaven, will come in the same way you saw him go into heaven'" (First Reading).

In these words, St. Luke places the story of the ascension of Jesus between the two comings of the Lord. For him, "sacred history" begins with this event and concludes with the second coming of Christ, the Parousia. Likewise the third reading, taken from St. Mark, reports the fact of the ascension with particular reference to the miracles which the apostles worked in the name of and through the power of Him who ascended into heaven.

Here a question comes to our minds: Is there really a heaven, a paradise? The whole of the New Testament bears witness to this reality. If we but open the Gospels and leaf through them, we become aware that heaven is the central and insistent promise: the entire Sacred Book is a warm invitation to our eternal destinies. Jesus always made a distinction between earthly life and heavenly life, with the former at the service of the latter. Furthermore, does not the Incarnation itself stand as a providential guarantee and hope of heaven? St. Augustine tells us that God became man so that man might become God. Christ is the point in which human nature encounters the divine nature in closest communion, making it possible that where God is, there man can also be. Proceeding from this principal we can deduce that "the ascension of Jesus is a triumph not purely personal for Him alone, but collectively; when the Lord arose and ascended into heaven, not only have we been confirmed in our right to possess paradise, but we have also effectively entered there with Him, for the members of the (Mystical) Body must be there where the Head is" (St. Leo the Great). This is also the desire and plan of Jesus who has asked the Father for our perfect union with Him in a full and eternal joy (cf. John 17:21; 16:22).

Reason cannot but affirm the tenets of revelation. Among the many arguments which can be adduced to prove the existence of this heavenly city, the psychological approach can serve us well. Here on earth we are all seekers of happiness, complete happiness, but no one ever finds it. It is useless to waste words repeating that perfect felicity does not exist in the streets of time. On the contrary, how sad are our days! Even should we with great effort immerse ourselves into a state of trance, tasting every elixir of long life, consulting every recipe of psychoanalysis, still we could never, never annihilate the distance between our desires and the desired satisfaction, nor would we cancel our condition of pilgrims and exiles. The root of every spiritual tension is fundamentally metaphysical: it is eternity which creates our anguish, our restlessness. If then there were no paradise, God would have condemned us to a continual imbalance, to a continual search for a situation we could never realize. We would then have to conclude that God created us merely for His own whim and fancy. Rejecting this fantastic hypothesis, we are obliged to draw the inherent conclusion that the heavenly Father has arranged in His Providence to still our insatiable thirst for perfect happiness up there in the bright city of the spirit. Eternal beatitude is the goal of the pilgrimage of the People of God (cf. Constitution on the Church, 9, 21, 25). The Church herself will arrive at her fulfillment only in the glory of heaven (cf. On the Church, 2, 9, 48); she will have her true beauty, her true splendor, only as the Church of eternity, the Church of the Apocalypse (cf. Paul VI, June 7, 1972). And it is precisely in heaven where each and every Christian, guided and almost transported by the Church, will be able to participate in the banquet of an endless, unbounded joy, united with all the blessed of the heavenly Jerusalem (cf. On the Church, 50, 51). God will understand us, will love us totally. In paradise the sad and nostalgic dirge of every human heart will become a wedding song of perfect love.

PASTORAL REFLECTIONS

1. As we travel toward our Fatherland, *let us not be overly concerned about the acquisition of things.* Certainly we must use with joy and gratitude the things which God in His wisdom and Providence offers us, but we must not abuse these terrestrial realities, nor idolize the things which are intended to be a help to us, not a hindrance, on the way. God has created and given us everything so that here on earth we may live a new life of grace and in heaven, an undying life of glory.

2. *To make the journey well,* to assure ourselves a secure voyage over the sea of life, so often dangerous and deceptive, toward the eternal shore, *we must use a ship that cannot flounder.* Many centuries ago St. Augustine already described this metaphor to us: "During this voyage the waves and the tempest make the sea very rough. But at least we are inside the ship. Outside, death would be inevitable. Anyone trying to swim in the

midst of these wild billows, however strong his arms might be, is sooner or later to be overcome by the mighty ocean and swallowed up within it. To cross this ocean one must be within the ship.... This ship is the Church" (Sermon 75, 24; P.L. 38, 4756).

3. *Let us be constant in doing good.* The recompense is promised not to the one who begins, but to the one who perseveres. The Christian will not be asked how he began but how he finished. Paul began badly but ended well. Judas began well but ended badly. Many start off, but not all arrive at the goal. Our good deeds are done in vain if we stop doing them before we come to the end of life. Perseverance to the end makes our whole life worthwhile. Our efforts are pleasing to God if we keep trying and never give up until the task is done.

The thought of our heavenly Fatherland, luminous goal of our pilgrimage, makes us ardent and constant in the work of our salvation. It equips us with strength and wings for the final crossing, to arrive at our felicity in God. St. Paul wrote to the Christians of the little city of Ephesus: "The Father of glory...give you a spirit of wisdom and of revelation in the knowledge of him, having the eyes of your hearts enlightened that you may know the great hope to which he has called you, what are the riches of his glorious inheritance in the saints, and what is the immeasurable greatness of his power in us who believe" (Second Reading).

SEVENTH SUNDAY OF EASTER:

Faith, the Fountain of Holiness

Readings: Acts 1:15-17, 20-26
1 John 4:11-16
John 17:11-19

Several times already we have meditated together on the gift of faith as necessary for our existence, as a criterion of Christian authenticity, and as a fountain of blessedness. On this Sunday, following the guidance of the third reading, we shall round out this theme by considering faith as the practical means of our sanctification.

It is generally agreed that our existence depends upon light. The plant absorbs light, this light, stored in the vegetal world, enters in turn into the animals as they consume plant life. There it is transformed into protein, an essential energy-building substance. This protein is subsequently modified and adapted to the organism of man, for whom flesh meat is a most important nutrient. It can further be stated that our whole life, all our actions, our technical inventions and applications, depend upon light in its various and mysterious powers. Much the same could be said, but in the interior and supernatural level, about faith which is "the divine life, the newness, the energy; it is the rebirth and salvation" of man's spirit, as Pope Paul VI stated. It is through the light of faith that we pass from being simple creatures of God to being His very children, sharers of His own divine life. It is known that the verbs "to know" and "to believe," in a biblical sense, signify a vital communion, an intimacy between the one known and the one who knows. St. John expressly says that "whoever believes in the Christ is born of God." In the thought of the fourth evangelist, faith and divine life are correlative terms. The third reading of today also highlights this most encouraging and consoling thought: "Father, I have given them your word; and the world has hated them because they are not of the world.... I do not pray that you should take them out of the world, but that you should guard them from the evil one.... Sanctify them in the truth; your word is truth" (John 17:14-17).

But how does this spiritual growth, this sanctification come about?

Because we are men, the Word of God enriches us in the first place in our intellect and our will. Surrendering ourselves to eternal truth, we are in a position to grasp and solve the problem of life with all its intricacies, like a professor who can work out a problem on the blackboard if he knows the facts and the procedure. Our limited human knowledge can become true wisdom and good sense only if it is enlightened and sustained by the light of eternal Truth. This is the message of the Scriptures, from the sapiential books to the letters of St. Paul, who points out our social folly in transgressing the divine message (cf. Romans 1 to see how forcefully he states it). St. James, too, lovingly invites his readers to accept the truth of Christ in order to be effectively wise (James 1:5-6). Through faith, the will is very powerfully strengthened; the Bible is like a mighty treasury of sublime revelations which disclose the infinite, eternal realms of God. Well now, if youth is hope and hope is a presage of the future, it is not difficult to conclude that the man of faith, having a prevision of this panorama of inexhaustible goals and conquests, will for that very reason live in a state of perennial youth of spirit.

But the positive effects of truth are those of a supernatural and ascetical order. Once we have received the word of God, it becomes in our soul a standard for comparison: the Word of the Lord is like a mirror which reveals that which we are and that which we should be. Very often we disdain the eternal Word simply because it accuses us of our moral wretchedness. He who fears the light can be accused of fearing to see himself as he really is. The divine Word is, in fact, "sharper than any two-edged sword, piercing to the division of soul and spirit" (Hebrews 4:12-13). Should it happen that this divine Word finds us in a morally erroneous position, this "power of God leading everyone who believes in it to salvation" will cleanse and heal us, as the Lord Himself has promised and as St. Peter taught (cf. Acts 15:3). It is for this reason that the masters of the spiritual life tell us that it is easier for a person to communicate daily and remain in mortal sin than for one to meditate on the Word of God and yet remain in mortal sin. A second spiritual effect is an invitation to a complete severance from the mentality of the world. Those who have been instructed by the Word of God see further than simple human prudence; they evaluate things and events and look at history from God's point of view, with an eye to eternity.

It is also necessary for the apostle of the kingdom of Christ to be imbued with eternal truth. The dynamic essence of the apostolic vocation is to be separated from the common way of thinking, in order to be "priests of truth."

But the most beautiful effect, ascetically speaking, that the Word of God can produce in our souls is our assimilation to Christ. There are three modes of knowledge: the chronicle of things and events as they are presented in the newspapers; professional knowledge such as that which takes place between superiors and subjects, between managers and workers in a factory; but the true knowledge is that vital relationship, that which exists between two persons who love each other, as for example between a betrothed pair or between husband and wife. Captivated by a Truth-Person which is Christ, we find ourselves transported as it were from a zone of purely terrestrial vision to an ineffable intimacy with the Savior: "I live by faith in the Son of God, who loved me and gave himself for me.... I know whom I have believed" (Galatians 2:20; 2 Timothy 1:12). This is the lucid testimony of St. Paul. Christian faith is not an abstract theory, it is the very Person of Christ who enters into our heart. Faith is to choose to love and be loved by Jesus our model, the reason for our vocation, the ideal and the reward of our life. Sanctity is living in Christ, being possessed by His love. "By this we know we abide in him and he in us, because he has given us his own Spirit.... So we know and believe the love God has for us" (Second Reading). It is no wonder then that the gift of faith is considered by the Church as a pledge of life eternal. Faith and life eternal: these are the alpha and the omega of the salvation which comes to us through Jesus Christ, author and finisher of our sanctity.

PASTORAL REFLECTIONS

1. Faith, however, comes through hearing (cf. Romans 10:17). *Jesus Christ has given us the example in accepting the inspired words.* He, the eternal Word, did not disdain to veil Himself with the human words of Sacred Scripture.

a) Throughout His life Jesus was our exemplar by doing all that had been written about Him. His actions from birth to death had as normative criterion the fulfillment of the Scriptures (cf. Hebrews 10:5; Micah 5:1; Matthew 2:6; Hosea 2:1; Matthew 2:15; John 19:30).

b) For the Son of God, the Bible was a book of prayer, from His first official act as an Israelite in the Temple of Jerusalem when He was twelve (Deuteronomy 16:16; Luke 2:41-50), to the hymns He recited before His passion (Psalms 112-117; cf. Mark 14:26). Furthermore, on the cross He prayed invocations drawn from the Psalms: "My God, my God, why have you forsaken me?" (Psalm 22:2); "Father, into your hands I commit my spirit" (Psalm 31:6; cf. Luke 23:46).

c) The inspired word of the Old Testament was for Jesus the basis and continual reference in His preaching, for example when He presented Himself as the Messiah (Isaiah 61:1-2; Zephaniah 2:3; Luke 4:21); when He spoke of the living water, symbol of grace, on the occasion of the feast of the Tabernacles (cf. Zechariah 14:16-19; John 7:37-38); again, when on the feast of the Dedication of the Temple, referring to chapter 34 of Ezekiel He presented Himself to the world as the Good Shepherd (Ezekiel 34; John 10).

d) It can be said, further, that all the preaching of Jesus was in harmony and rhythm with the Sacred Scriptures, from His first dialogue with Satan in the desert (cf. Deuteronomy 6:16; 8:2-3; 34:1-4; in comparison with chapter 4 of Mark), to the farewell discourse with His apostles (cf. Leviticus 9:22; Luke 24:50-51).

2. *Every believer can be inspired by the Word of God.* A very consistent patristic theme, which was given much importance in antiquity and tends to be reaffirmed in these our own times, conceives inspiration as the action of God not only upon the prophet but also upon the person who receives the message of the prophet, the reader or listener. St. Gregory the Great says that the writer and the reader both find themselves under the touch of the Holy Spirit. This is so because the Bible is not just any book, a theory; but it is Someone, God, the Holy Spirit, who continues to work in souls and to speak to our hearts. "It is this Spirit," comments St. Augustine, "which never ceases to inspire the preacher, the listener, and the liturgical assembly." This is the true mystique of the exegesis of Holy Scripture, its effectiveness in the strengthening of faith and sanctification of souls.

3. Here then is a conclusion we must draw: Rather than searching through the Bible for expressions which support our way of thinking and living, or our manner of interpreting the Christian life, let us rather be completely docile to the Word, let us permit ourselves to be pervaded by it so that it can reveal to us who we really are and be effective in us as a pattern of all goodness and all sanctity. There are some who seem to shield themselves from being touched by the Word of God, like those who open an umbrella in the rain so they do not get wet. Others, instead, react like the rock which receives the rain water but lets it run off. Quite different from these two types, the faithful Christian receives, accepts and absorbs into himself the words of the Bible, like a dry desert which absorbs the rain water, so that he produces, as Jesus said, abundant fruits of joy and holiness (cf. John 14:12; 15:11; 17:3).

PENTECOST:

The Descent of the Holy Spirit

> Readings: Acts 2:1-11
> 1 Corinthians 12:3-7, 12-13
> John 20:19-23

Pentecost, the most solemn feast for the Jews, was the annual commemoration of the covenant God had contracted with the people on Mount Sinai. Fifty days after the Israelites had left Egypt (the word pentecost actually means the fiftieth day), at daybreak God came down to the top of Mount Sinai, in the form of fire, accompanied by thunder and lightning and the loud blast of trumpets (Exodus 19:16-18). When the Hebrews accepted the law of the Lord they became the "People of God." Fifty days after the resurrection of the glorious body of Christ from the tomb, about nine o'clock in the morning, the Holy Spirit descended with the accompaniment of the same natural phenomena: fire, sound, wind and storm. "When the day of Pentecost had come, they (the disciples) were all together in one place. And suddenly a sound came from heaven like the rush of a mighty wind, and it filled all the house where they were sitting. And there appeared to them, tongues as of fire, distributed and resting on each one of them. And they were all filled with the Holy Spirit and began to speak in other tongues as the Spirit gave them utterance.... Each one heard them speaking in his own language...the mighty works of God" (First Reading).

Pope Paul commented on this singular event: "The fact is that the Church was born at that moment. Her body, composed of men of this world, received its supernatural animation which penetrated it entirely, infusing new unity into that assembly that was called the Church, and at once conferring various and distinct functions on this or that member of the ecclesial assembly, as on a special organ for the benefit of the whole organism. The Church was born, from that first seminal hour, hierarchical and communitarian, constitutionally one, organized and united (cf. 1 Corinthians 12:4ff.)" (Pope Paul VI, May 17, 1972). Through the work of the Holy Spirit, God was incarnate in Christ; through the same Holy Spirit, Christ vivifies the Church. Thus the Church can continue the same mission as Christ and repeat His salvific acts. The same Holy Spirit, no longer bound to the historic person of Jesus, no longer conditioned by the Hebrew nation and a specific epoch, can work in a universal dimension without being subjected to and blocked by human caprice or the historical vicissitudes of men. It is this same Spirit who chooses His missionaries, continues to consecrate them so that His message will arrive to all mankind (cf. Acts 2:17), yes, even to the ends of the earth (Acts 1:8).

The pentecostal Church will change the history of man because, fortified by the Holy Spirit, she alone will be able to eliminate sin and transform humanity from within, to form the true family of God. "Receive the Holy Spirit," said Jesus; "If you forgive the sins of any, they are forgiven; if you retain the sins of any, they are retained" (Third Reading). The first duty of the Church is not so much to offer new social ideas, but rather to purify humanity through the Holy Spirit. "The Church prays! Her first task, her first duty, her first purpose is prayer" (Paul VI, April 12, 1978).

But the principal scope of the Holy Spirit is that of making us live in mystical communion between ourselves and God, between ourselves and our neighbor. Sin divides, the Spirit unites; sin creates opposition, the Holy Spirit instead realizes a wonderful dynamic union even while respecting the ontological differences of each member. Human towers of Babel are built up by sin, but through the Holy Spirit we have cenacles of peace and communion. St. Paul illustrates this positive aspect of the Holy Spirit in the well known comparison: "For just as the body is one and has many members, and all the members of the body, though many, are one body, so it is with Christ. For by one Spirit we were all baptized into one body.... All were made to drink of one Spirit.... There are varieties of gifts but the same Spirit" (1 Corinthians 12:12-13; 4).

This indeed is true communion.

Communism is a purely exterior juxtaposition; the life of an institute may be a moral concordance. The true Church, however, is a functional, organic unity through the presence of the Holy Spirit. One thing placed upon another gives the idea of space; one thing after another suggests the idea of time. One thing within another is unity; and one person in vital communication with another is Church. But this can be had only through the presence and the power of the Holy Spirit who unites (Ephesians 4:3), who consecrates our persons (2 Corinthians 1:22), who is our life, our activity, our most sublime transformation in Christ Jesus (Galatians 5:25; Romans 8:9, 13; Ephesians 4:30). In brief, through the Holy Spirit our whole existence becomes a divine adventure.

PASTORAL REFLECTIONS
culled from an address of Pope Paul VI:

1. *"The work of the Holy Spirit is the determining factor of the Christian religion.* It is transforming for that privileged part of humanity which enters into the range of its influence; it is decisive for our salvation.... We have not yet perhaps studied properly the theology of the Holy Spirit and the realities that derive from His action on the human soul. These are, in the first place, grace, and then His gifts (cf. Isaiah 11:2) and His fruits (Galatians 5:22), as well as the ways through which the

Holy Spirit is normally conferred on us, prayer (cf. Luke 11:13) and especially the sacraments, the vehicles of grace, that is of the action of the Holy Spirit in us." It is necessary, then, to meditate upon this "divine Unknown" and enjoy His powerful forces for sanctification.

2. "There is one rule: an ordinary requirement is called for from anyone who wishes to pick up the supernatural waves of the Holy Spirit; *it is inner life.* The appointment for the meeting with the ineffable Guest is fixed inside the soul. Sweet Guest of the soul, the admirable liturgical hymn of Pentecost says. Man is made the 'temple' of the Holy Spirit, St. Paul repeats to us. However much modern man, and often also the Christian, also the consecrated, tend to become secularized, they cannot, they must not ever forget this fundamental rule of life, if the latter is to remain Christian and animated by the Holy Spirit...Pentecost has had its novena of meditation and prayer. Inner silence is necessary to listen to the Word of God, to experience His presence, to hear God's call.... We must give inner life its place in the program of our busy existence: a primary place, a silent place, a pure place. We must find ourselves again in order to be fit to have the life-bringing and sanctifying Spirit in us. If not, how can we listen to His testimony? (cf. John 15:26; Romans 8:7)."

3. "Another question is the old one, but very much in fashion today, which contrasts *the religion of authority with the religion of the spirit.* The latter is preferred by adversaries of the institutional, hierarchical Church, who claim the freedom of a democratic Church, living in the spirit expressed by the religious sense of the community. We still know in some way how this criticism expresses itself. We think that the question, if raised within the Catholic Church, is an attack on the very existence of the Church and leads to extinguishing the real flame of Pentecost.... It disregards the thought of Christ and of the whole of Tradition..." (Paul VI, May 17, 1972).

TRINITY SUNDAY:

The Church, Gift of the Trinity

>Readings: Deuteronomy 4:32-34, 39-40
>Romans 8:14-17
>Matthew 28:16-20

The liturgy of today, particularly in the third reading, asks us to meditate upon the dynamic center, the wellspring of our spiritual life: the most Holy Trinity. Revelation makes known to us the Father, the Son and the Holy Spirit. The Gospel of St. Matthew tells us: "Go therefore and make disciples of all nations, baptizing them in the name of the Father and of the Son and of the Holy Spirit, teaching them to observe all that I have commanded you; and lo, I am with you always, to the close of the age" (Matthew 28:19-20).

The activity of the Triune God is manifest not only within the divine nature, but also outside this trinitarian intimacy, imprinting the divine seal and image upon its works. The very world in which we live is, in reality, a world filled with the Trinity; the divine stamp appears most evident in man, in whom St. Augustine already envisaged trinitarian traces in the three human characteristics of intelligence, will, and sentiment. And is not the family a trinitarian sign through the presence of the father, the mother, and the child who unites in love the two parents? Even our divinized life reminds us of the trinitarian datum because the authentic man is composed of body, soul, and spirit; it is this which makes us images of God. In addition to these particular aspects we cannot omit mentioning that our whole spiritual and mystical life is stamped with the image of the most Holy Trinity. The Second Vatican Council continually reminds us that we are saved by the Father, by means of the Son, through the power of grace and love of the Holy

Spirit. It is no wonder, then, that the most Holy Trinity has particular and constant vital connections with the Church, "the universal sacrament of salvation" (Constitution on the Church, 48). For this reason, Church and Trinity are correlative, integral terms. We cannot understand the history of the Church apart from the Trinity.

In the first centuries of Christianity the worshiping community had a profound sense of the activity and the liturgical primacy of the most Holy Trinity. The historical beginnings of the Church commenced and moved outward in the name and the power of the Blessed Trinity. Every Eucharistic gathering, ever social initiative, every Christian document was sealed with the sign of the Trinity as its beginning and its end. Actually we are still reminded to do the very same, but perhaps we do not sense, as did the early Christians, the importance and the urgency of referring our whole interior and spiritual attitude to the honor and glory of the Holy Trinity. Nevertheless, this mysterious and ineffable life of the Trinity will continue to flow copiously throughout history by means of the Church, even to the end of time.

Man can assume one of the three attitudes in relation to the gift of the Church and her spiritual riches: he may refuse it, he may passively accept it, or he may receive it gratefully and let it yield abundant fruit in his life. We must admit it: there are those who fight against the Church; there are those who accept the Church as an historical fact, as something that cannot be disregarded; but there are also those who understand and love the Church, and they receive this gift not to set it aside but to collaborate with it and make it fruitful.

In order that the Church may truly produce supernatural fruits in us, it is necessary that we be attached to her not in the critical spirit of a schoolboy but with the fond attachment of a son, who will speak about her with love and loyalty whenever he has the opportunity.

It is not just, neither is it a mark of historical intelligence to settle on the structures of the Church as objects of criticism. It is necessary instead to study the richness which she perennially bestows. Christ grew and changed physiologically in His human nature, remaining nevertheless the Son of God. Similarly the Church may put off many things she has assimilated through different times and circumstances, but for the believing Christian, she remains the dynamic and salvific presence of Christ. For one who knows her well, she joyously remains "the old fountain of the village which continues to give men the limpid and pure water of grace and holiness."

But we must respond in an operative and responsible manner to the dynamism of the Holy Trinity in the Church. On the day of our Baptism we were assumed into the divine intimacy, in communion with the whole Trinity. It was the triumph of our spiritual nobility: we received—St. Paul enthusiastically reminds us in the second reading—the divine Spirit through which we can truly call God our Father. We must do everything in our power to make this divine life bear fruit in us. This divine life was a total gift. If one has the natural talent for music but never uses it, the gift vanishes. If a student is admitted to a college, a university, but never attends the classes or follows the lessons, he squanders money and learns nothing. Similarly, this "seed of eternal life" planted graciously and freely by God in our hearts requires our cooperation. What is the Christian life? It is a constant occasion to collaborate with the grace of God.

PASTORAL REFLECTIONS

1. *The Mystery of the most Holy Trinity is a mystery of life.* Every creative act, every act of love pours forth from it. Our God is not a god of the dead, not an idea, a supreme individual far away from the world of men and quite detached from them. He is the very perfection of life and donation in the ineffable communica-

tion of the Three Persons, always living and life-giving. The whole story of salvation, initiated with creation, actuated in the redemption and perfected through the invisible presence of the Holy Spirit, constitutes the significance and the magnificent epic poem of the trinitarian mystery. With creation the Father begins the dialog with man; with redemption the Son fixes in time, for always, a bond of friendship between divinity and humanity; and through the Holy Spirit the same God transforms man and transports the whole of humanity towards "the new heavens and the new earth" of eternal beatitude. The people offer their sufferings, their sorrows, their actions, their prayers, that all these gifts may complement the sacrifice of the Lord.

2. *The history of salvation is being carried out* historically, in time, *by means of the Church* whose soul is the Holy Spirit. Consequently we must fear and avoid but one thing: to cut ourselves off from the Church. If a member of our body—a hand, a foot, a finger—be severed from the body, it will dry out and die, it will decompose, while the body inhabited by the soul remains alive and intact. Thus also the Christian is alive, is Catholic, as long as he is united to the Church. Now if he would want to separate himself entirely from the Church, he would lose the breath of the Spirit and the vivifying strength of grace. We can know that we are still living mystically united to the Church if we are animated by a desire to preserve charity, to love truth, to promote unity and to arrive at eternity. These attitudes are a sign and guarantee that we are living under the influence of the Holy Spirit (cf. St. Augustine, Sermon 267).

3. Only *if we bear good fruits* can our image as a creature of God become also a likeness of God Himself, because a true divine likeness implies the presence of sanctity in us. And only by participating in divine life can we legitimately be worthy of the great mystery of salvation, which has its mysterious, unfathomable origin in the most Holy Trinity, Father, Son, and Holy Spirit.

CORPUS CHRISTI:

The Eucharist in the Church

Readings: Exodus 24:3-8
Hebrews 9:11-15
Mark 14:12-16, 22-26

In life, in all life, there is osmosis, interaction. In minerals there is no exchange, therefore they have no life. But in plant life, in animal life, in man there is vital exchange with the ambience within the kingdom: there is life. More specifically, the union of bodies gives life to the child; the union of minds can produce culture; it gives birth to new ideas. In a similar way, communion of God with man is the source of man's supernatural life. The Lord called this divine communion the Eucharist, supper—that is the most common time for exchange. Generally three things are done at this meal: first there is dialogue, then there is exchange of gifts, thirdly there is the sharing of the food. The liturgy for the feast of Corpus Christi invites us to reflect on this threefold division, though the love of Christ remains one and indivisible.

First of all there is the listening to the Word of God. The three readings which the festive liturgy places before us for our consideration is like the first moment of encounter. In the Eucharistic celebration the People of God are first of all invited to hear the words of truth: "Moses wrote all the words of the Lord.... Then he took the book of the covenant, and read it in the hearing of the people; and they said, 'All that the Lord has spoken we will do' " (First Reading). After having listened to the message of salvation on the part of God, the Christian people respond to this word by reciting the Creed, a proclamation of their adherence to and acceptance of all that God has revealed. "The obedience of faith is to be given to God who reveals, an obedience by which man commits his whole self freely to God, offering the full submission of intellect and will...and freely assenting to the truth revealed by Him" (Constitution on Divine Revelation, 5).

The second moment of this intimacy between God and man, through Christ, is the exchange of gifts. Once for all times Jesus consummated His sacrifice on Calvary, but He incessantly presents it to the Father for the life of all the generations throughout time: "Brothers, Christ entered once for all into the Holy Place, taking not the blood of goats and calves but his own blood, thus securing an eternal redemption.... Therefore he is the mediator of a new covenant...those who are called may receive the promised eternal inheritance" (Second Reading). The essential theme of history is not so much politics, conquests, technology; it is rather the Lamb that was slain, "worthy...to receive power and wealth and wisdom and might and honor and glory and blessing" (Revelation 5:12). Studies of the organic functioning of the human body show that it is a story of blood: every 29 seconds about 3 liters of blood pass through the heart; in seventy years, about 250 million liters have passed through, enough to fill 12,500 railway tanks. This little story of our corporeal self is like a symbol of the true story of humanity, that of the blood and the purifying sacrifice of Christ, which is continually being poured out upon the social fabric of mankind. Every day there are about 350,000 Holy Masses celebrated, more than 14,500 every hour. In each one is lifted up the chalice containing the blood of Christ, in merciful remission of the sins of all men. Upon this gesture of infinite donation follows the response of the creature: at the offertory some of the faithful bring to the altar bread, wine and other things for the sacrifice, as tokens of interior donation. The people offer their sufferings, their sorrows, their actions, their prayers, that all these gifts may complement the sacrifice of the Lord.

When we are invited to a meal, after we have exchanged words and gifts, we take our places at the table to partake of the same food. The sharing of a meal is a response to a psychological urge for a common element which unites us, binds us in an effective friendship. What man tries to do, God accomplishes fully in giving us His very self as food for our souls. "And as they were eating, he took bread, and blessed, and broke it, and gave it to them, and said, 'Take; this is my body'" (Third Reading). In Holy Communion, the most profound union is effected between God and man. In the Incarnation, God entered into relationship with all mankind in general, but in the sacrament of the Eucharist, every person who receives Him becomes the universe of God, a tabernacle of divinity; through this sacrament our weakness is united to the power of the Lord, our misery to absolute value, our existential insignificance to magnificence, time to eternity, earth to heaven, the finite to infinite. The Lord Himself said, "He who eats my flesh and drinks my blood abides in me, and I in him" (John 6:56). The tangible response of the creature is given not directly to God, for God has no need of us, but to the brethren loved for the love of God and in His love. Christian love for the neighbor, in this way, is the outpouring of the love of God diffused in our hearts. The desire for social solidarity is the effect of our living communion with God Himself through Christ.

PASTORAL REFLECTIONS

1. *The Eucharist is "center and summit" of the Church.* As the humanity of Christ is the great sacrament of the love of the Holy Trinity, and the Church is the great sacrament of the love of Christ, similarly the Eucharist is the heart of the Church and of the liturgy. The Conciliar decree on the Ministry and Life of Priests tells us in paragraph 5: "The other sacraments, as well as every ministry of the Church and every work of the apostolate, are linked with the Holy Eucharist and are directed toward it. For the most blessed Eucharist contains the Church's entire spiritual wealth, that is, Christ Himself, our Passover and living bread. Through His

very flesh, made vital and vitalizing by the Holy Spirit, He offers life to men. They are thereby invited and led to offer themselves, their labors, and all created things together with Him. Hence the Eucharist shows itself to be the source and the apex of the whole work of preaching the Gospel. Those under instruction are introduced by stages into a sharing in the Eucharist. The faithful, already marked with the sacred seal of Baptism and Confirmation, are through the reception of the Eucharist fully joined to the Body of Christ."

2. *And it is this belonging to the same Body which effectively makes us brothers.* "The real and sacramental body of the Lord nourishes the spiritual and social body which we are.... The Eucharist becomes in us the great source of brotherly love, of social charity... establishing thus a correspondence between the two communions, one with the living, personal Christ in heaven, the other with Christ present in men, who have become our brothers by identical love.... The lesson of love, which gushes forth from the Eucharist, must therefore find us all pupils ready to forgive, to do good, to serve our neighbor, to the full extent of our possibilities. This is not utopia, it is not hyperbole.... After the Eucharist, this will be the distinguishing feature of the true disciples: the art of loving one another (John 13:35; 15:12). This is the root of human society, not based on selfishness, hatred, vendetta, violence, but on love" (Paul VI, June 1, 1972).

In another place the Holy Father says: "The love received from Christ in the Eucharist is communion with Him and for this very reason it is transformed and manifested in our communion with our brothers, actual or possible, such as all men are for us. Nourished by the real and sacramental body of Christ, we become more and more the Mystical Body of Christ.... Let us repeat with St. Augustine: 'O Sacrament of piety! O Sign of unity! O Bond of charity! He who wishes to live has the wherewithal!' And so may it be for us!" (Paul VI, June 12, 1977).

3. *A final synthesis:* The Trinity is nothing other than the reciprocal donation of God from within His mysterious Being, one in nature and three in persons. The feast of Corpus Christi—the Body of Christ—is like a trinitarian dynamism within the heart of time. Jesus said, "I am the way, and the truth, and the life" (John 14:6). He is our constant way to the Father because He purifies us with His sacrifice; He is our truth through His very word; He is our life because He gives Himself to us as food for our souls. Through the Eucharist-Word we move toward God; through the Eucharist-Sacrifice we can be united to God and live in Him; through the Eucharist-Sacrament we are assimilated into the very divinity itself: "In him we live and move and have our being" (Acts 17:28). In the Incarnation, God became like unto us; in His Word He became our friend; in His Sacrifice He became our Redeemer; in Communion He becomes our food; and all this so that in heaven He may be our reward.

BAPTISM OF THE LORD:

The Savior and the Holy Spirit

> Readings: Isaiah 42:1-4, 6-7
> Acts 10:34-38
> Mark 1:7-11

The Holy Spirit entered the lives of patriarchs like Isaac and Joseph, warriors like Gideon and Jephthah, kings and leaders like Moses, Saul, and David. He consecrated and strengthened all the prophets. The privileged object of the action of the Holy Spirit was the Virgin Mary in three decisive moments: her Immaculate Conception, the Annunciation, and the day of Pentecost.

Now since the Messiah was the point of reference of all this preparation for salvation, and likewise its effective consummation, as a human being he could not but be at the center of the Holy Spirit's action. The prophet Isaiah sees Him consecrated by the Spirit through the Father from the moment the plan of salvation was conceived:

> Behold my servant, whom I uphold,
>   my chosen, in whom my soul delights;
> I have put my spirit upon him....
>
> I am the Lord, I have called you in righteousness,
>   I have taken you by the hand and kept you;
> I have given you
>   as a covenant to the people,
>   a light to the nations (First Reading).

The baptism of Jesus in the Jordan is like the public investiture of the redemptive mission of the Messiah. We might say that the eternal consecration of the Son in the Holy Spirit on the part of the Father and its manifestation on the day of His baptism are, in a certain measure, like the conception and birth of the same Messiah. So the second evangelist narrates: "In those days Jesus...was baptized by John in the Jordan. And when he came up out of the water, he saw the heavens opened and the Spirit descending upon him like a dove, and a voice came from heaven, 'You are my beloved Son; with you I am well pleased' " (Third Reading). The Father and the Spirit solemnly reveal to the world the Son as the long-awaited Messiah for the redemption of men. Precisely at this moment in Christ's life the history of the supernatural age, the new creation of the children of God, begins. Just as at creation the Spirit of God in the form of a bird "swept over the waters," like a fructifying life-force (cf. Genesis 1:2), and as after the deluge the dove carried a plucked-off olive leaf as a sign for all humanity now delivered from evil (cf. Genesis 8:11), so in a clear and unmistakable way the Messiah received the Holy Spirit in order to be consecrated the true and only Savior: "God anointed Jesus of Nazareth with the Holy Spirit and with power. He went about doing good and healing all who were oppressed by the devil, for God was with him" (Second Reading).

If we wished to linger over the relationship between Christ and the Holy Spirit, we would have no difficulty in showing that all of prehistory and the life and action of the Messiah were sealed by His vital and efficacious union with the Spirit, who dwelt in Him permanently in the fullest measure not only as a Person of the Trinity but as an abiding and decisive force of action and of victory. The Messiah is, in fact, described by the prophets before His birth by the action of the Holy Spirit; He was conceived as man solely through the work of the Holy Spirit. At the beginning of His public life, inaugurated by His baptism in the Jordan, the Holy Spirit leads Him into the desert, where He fasts and prays as did Moses and Eliah. Through the Holy Spirit He overcomes the temptation of the devil to found a kingdom of riches, honor and power, and in the power of the same Spirit He returns to Galilee, where He begins His preaching.

All the miracles He performs bear the seal of the Spirit, in virtue of which He drives out devils, heals the sick, frees those enslaved by sin, raises the dead. His prayer too is made in the Holy Spirit, through whom He exults and is glad. On Tabor Christ is transfigured by the power of the Spirit, and His resurrection is the fruit of the Spirit of God. After His resurrection, on Easter evening, the Redeemer gives His apostles His Spirit as a sacramental grace, and on Pentecost the Spirit comes down upon the Virgin, the apostles, and the disciples as a wellspring of charismatic, apostolic action to complete the mission of the Messiah.

PASTORAL REFLECTIONS

1. In the Bible the word *spirit* has a variety of meanings. In particular, it signifies the *wind* with its double, irresistible power of overthrowing houses and felling cedars and of making life germinate by carrying seeds or by transporting rain clouds. Aside from figures of speech, whoever *possesses the Holy Spirit* feels within himself the power to *destroy evil and sin*, and is urged to be born anew, to grow, and to develop within himself the divine life of grace. The word *spirit* also means *breath*, vital breathing. Respiration is just as normal and important as a healthful external atmosphere. If a person wishes to be spiritual, he must inhale deep breaths of fresh air from God's country; he must converse with the Spirit and thus reach maturity.

2. But the word *spirit* when joined to the qualifying word *holy*, means the power of God, which *enters into, transforms, and consecrates* a person for a program of good; it is like the complement of inhaling—exhaling the things that come from within. The Messiah was consecrated by the Spirit for the salvation of the world.

Every Christian, too, made a temple of the Spirit on the day of Baptism and vivifed by the same Spirit in confirmation, precisely because he has been spiritualized, is destined for the apostolate, has a mission of goodness, has, as Paul VI puts it, "an inspiration for doing good."

3. In his poem "The Golden Sunset" Edgar Allen Poe (+ 1849) imagines earth, sea, and sky as being permeated with rays of light and with spirits. This could well be a beautiful and appropriate image of *the action of the Spirit of God on the tangible events of history.* The seven gifts are gifts of the Holy Spirit that envelop our life and vocation as children of God, and that give them direction and a positive momentum towards the good.

SECOND SUNDAY IN ORDINARY TIME:

The Search for and the Possession of God

Readings: 1 Samuel 3:3-10, 19
1 Corinthians 6:13-15, 17-20
John 1:35-42

The providential action of God enters history not in an unexpected happening or by what might be called shock treatment, but silently, as blood courses through the veins, as light beautifies objects in our home. Samuel was sleeping in the temple of the Lord. The Lord called: "Samuel, Samuel!" "Here I am," he replied, and ran to Eli. "I did not call," Eli said. "Lie down again." This happened three times. Then Eli understood that the Lord was calling the youth. So he said to Samuel, "Go, lie down; and if he calls you, you shall say, 'Speak, Lord, for your servant hears.' " God called Samuel again, and the boy received the disclosure of God regarding the salvation of Israel (cf. First Reading).

The lessons revealed by Samuel, whom St. Peter considered the first of the prophets of the Old Testament, are many. There is no need to wait for God to reveal Himself directly in a visible manner. Frequently He merely whispers to us. His invitation comes to us through the Incarnation by way of poor human language, even though what is said is wholly divine. God speaks to us in this way because He does not wish to violate the spontaneity of our love and of our response. Sometimes we can be so ignorant that we do not regard as divine His voice, which comes to us, as it were, in three languages: that of natural creation and conscience, that of Church history and our own experience, and the supernatural language of revelation and personal inspiration.

Samuel is not satisfied until he comes in contact with the person to whom the voice belongs. An idea, a concept, a word, particularly when it is abstract and passing, cannot be the final measure of our choices until it is anchored in the concrete, in a person. This is true especially for religious experience: our reason, listening to or trying to speak about God, does everything in order to come into contact with divinity. Samuel does not stop his search because he does not know who is speaking; the going may be slow, but it must continue; it is not necessary to understand everything all at once. What is important is that we continue to look for contact with God in every voice, in every event. The search may last all our life, but this in itself means to be worthy of the infinite benevolence of God, for to seek the Lord is to possess Him already. The first encounter between God and man is in the sphere of faith, in adherence to the word of God. Revelation, like a ray of light, touches man, and if he opens his soul to it through faith, communion between creature and Creator already exists.

The Gospel gives us a picture of the person who wishes to hear and follow Jesus Christ. "The next day John...looked at Jesus as he walked, and said, 'Behold, the Lamb of God!' The two disciples heard him say this, and they followed Jesus. Jesus turned and saw them following, and said to them, 'What do you seek?' And they said to him, 'Rabbi (which means teacher), where are you staying?' He said to them, 'Come and see.' They came and saw where he was staying; and they stayed with him that day, for it was about the tenth hour" (Third Reading). John recalled that "four in the afternoon" about seventy years later. It was one of the highest spiritual moments he had ever had. Andrew was with John; then Peter joined them, then all the rest. And so the band of Christ's followers begins the procession of the People of God. This Gospel story vividly underlines the primacy of practice over theory. Christian life is a vital communion with Christ beyond all knowledge; the former may sometimes even be a preparation for the latter. The Magi "came" (action) and "saw" (knowledge). Jesus said to the first two disciples: "Come and see."

Without insisting too much on this decisive point of Christian action, let us notice that if Christianity is a fact, a mystical encounter between Christ and us, it is logical to think that to live our Christianity more easily, we must first be ready to be loved by Him and then to live on in His love (cf. John 15:9). This union will then be a light, an intuition for grasping the meaning of the ideas that prepared us for encounter with Christ. Such was the case with the disciples at Emmaus, the apostles after Pentecost, and St. Paul after his conversion. Relying on this priority, the Curé of Ars used to suggest to the Parisian intelligentsia who made religious objections that they go to the sacraments first of all; afterwards, he said, would come discussion, and often there was no request for it. St. Augustine summed it up when he said: "I believe that I may understand." This is equivalent to saying, "I entrust myself to God; I observe His law in order that I may understand it." Even from psychology we know that in the end one believes truly what one does. Jesus put it thus: "For every one who does evil hates the light.... But he who does what is true comes to the light..." (John 3:20-21). If these ideas are correct, it is certainly ridiculous to search for the faith while living in sin.

PASTORAL REFLECTIONS

1. If the United States is a great nation, one of the reasons is that the American character is practical rather than discursive. Americans are not afraid to begin something even if it is difficult. There is a proverb that says, "If you think something can't be done, do it right away, for you might wake up in the morning to find that someone else has already done it." In the book of the Hindus, the Brahama, we read: "A man becomes good by good deeds, and bad by bad deeds." In a word, our actions shape our psychological and intellectual dispositions. *The expert* is the man who has stopped philosophizing and *has begun to act.*

2. In order to be enthusiastic in doing good, we evidently need a teacher, one who invites us, who urges us on to great things. To us too Jesus says: "Come and see." The greatest thing we can do in life is *to experience deeply the friendship of Jesus,* even if we can do it only once. In our earthly condition we are given a marvelous opportunity: we can fall in love with Christ. The love of Jesus never deludes us; it does not grow weary; it does not fall away. On the contrary, it can create in our souls unsuspected harmonies swelling to such a degree that we cannot but sing for very joy. Two thousand years ago some fishermen with rough manners and calloused hands had this experience; women dragged to the depths of evil, like the Samaritan woman and the Magdalene, felt this love and remained fervent unto death, unto martyrdom. The following of Christ is indeed the most beautiful adventure of love.

3. Naturally, in order that the way may be easy, there is one condition among many, of which St. Paul

reminds us today (Second Reading): purity of heart. All that we have is a gift of God and must be used for His glory. *Everything is a source of joy if it is used properly.* If we were to use the Liberty Bell in Philadelphia to make some hammers for a blacksmith, all Americans would be insulted. If we used the flag, the symbol of a country, to clean sidewalks....

Voluntary impurity, pursued and systematic, not only impairs the dignity of the body, but is an affront against God, who has given us this power to be used fruitfully for our own life and for His glory. Impurity is a denial of ourselves; it obscures in us the resplendent image of God, the Creator and Perfecter of our very life. Therefore it is well to pray with the Psalmist, "Behold, I come to do your will, O Lord" (Responsorial Psalm).

THIRD SUNDAY IN ORDINARY TIME:

The True Followers of Christ

Readings: Jonah 3:1-5, 10
1 Corinthians 7:29-31
Mark 1:14-20

In times past, especially in Greece, disciples listened to their teacher, but learned by imitating his actions: knowledge was experience; culture, a matter of seeing. In Israel too the rabbi or teacher had the duty not only of imparting concepts and ideas, but also of completing the formation of his own followers by the example of his personal behavior. It is known that at the time of the Messiah the discrepancy between teaching and practice compromised the effectiveness of the teaching of the Scribes and Pharisees. John the Baptist, echoing the prophets, boldly preached the need of coupling doctrine with practice, a condition that would be fully realized in the Messiah.

From the very beginning of His public life Christ showed Himself as the teacher par excellence, unique among His kind, the one worthy of being followed because His teaching agreed with His practice, and His deeds were in complete accord with His words. But there were other differences between Christ and other teachers. In the first place, it was He who chose His disciples; the disciples were not free to choose Him. The choice was His, and His too the invitation "Follow me." His authority, far from being humiliating or crushing, was the result of His own extraordinary power, His sovereign word; it was genuine messianic urgency which demanded a prompt response. Besides, He called His followers to Himself not only to instruct them, but to communicate to them His love, His own person. There is a certain purity of wisdom in Buddha, Confucius, Socrates, and in Mohammed's Koran, and we can also become their disciples; but only in Christ does doctrine coincide with life, and teaching with the person (cf. Mark 1:1). Another difference is this: while the pupils of a Jewish teacher, once they had been instructed in the law, could leave their master to set themselves up as teachers and to guide others, the followers of Christ become His followers by sharing completely His life in every one of its aspects. To follow Christ means to keep step with Him to the very end, with all the risks of His companionship. Nay, more: the Divine Master points to the cross as the distinguishing mark of His true disciples. Life indeed is realized through death, love through suffering, and the cross is the road to the resurrection. This mystery of redemptive suffering is not understood all at once (and that is providential), but often, as in the case of Peter, we come to grasp its meaning at the end of our life. Finally, through personal imitation of the Master, the disciple becomes capable of showing forth in himself and outside himself the salvific riches of the Savior: thus imitation is transformed into witness. St. Paul, that great imitator of Christ, could declare to the Corinthians: "Be imitators of me as I am of Christ" (1 Corinthians 11:4-6).

Today's liturgy points out and develops several ascetical characteristics of the followers of the Messiah. "Follow me," the Lord said to Andrew, Simon, James, and John, and they "followed him" (cf. Third Reading). The first disciples left everything, even their father. Jesus seems to demand complete detachment, the renunciation of riches, of security, even of love for our dear ones, and this wholly and irrevocably. He likewise declared: "No servant can serve two masters" (Luke 16:13). To love is to choose. To choose one thing, one person is in itself to sacrifice so many other things; it is to renounce the other person: here we have the alternative dynamics of love. But what about the providence of earthly realities? The Christian does not have a Manichean attitude toward things: he uses them without abusing them, he serves them without making idols of them, he takes pleasure in what can be good along the way, but he does not burden himself with things that are a drawback. The follower of Christ is the man who makes use of things in order to serve God, not the man who wants to use God in order to gain possession of things.

St. Paul explains this attitude of interior detachment without contempt, of controlling earthly things without rejecting them: "I mean, brethren, the appointed time has grown very short; from now on, let those who have wives live as though they had none,...those who rejoice as though they were not rejoicing, those who buy as though they had no goods, and those who deal with the world as though they had no dealings with it. For the form of this world is passing away" (Second Reading). This stand will hardly be attractive to novices in the spiritual life, but it is the requirement and the dialectic of the following of Christ. Indeed, the ideal Christian is the man who, as it were, plunges into the kingdom of God, accepting its program, the Gospel. "The reign of God is at hand! Reform your lives and believe in the Gospel" (Third Reading).

PASTORAL REFLECTIONS

1. In the biblical sense, to believe means to receive and to accept with one's whole being (intellect, will, and heart) the truth that has been proclaimed. The follower of Christ is one who *lives according to the Gospel,* acts according to the Gospel, fights, suffers, and hopes for the Gospel in order to be a member of the kingdom of God. The disciple of Jesus is always spiritually tuned in to pick up the mysterious message constantly proclaimed by the Gospel, "the mouth of Christ." Here is the real penance of the Christian: this constant beginning again according to the word of Christ, this uninterrupted turning (metanoia) of his thoughts to those of the Master.

2. Granted that *this ideal of evangelical perfection is not easy* when the light is switched off. In the sphere of human love it is easy to get married but difficult to remain faithful to complete conjugal love; so it can likewise happen that those who accept the Lord's call with joy, at times find their obligation burdensome and difficult. The call is the Savior's gift, but the response is ours—and we, alas, are so weak, so changeable.

3. *But we must not lose courage* if we sometimes fall by the way, if we must acknowledge some infidelity, some sin. In the first reading the prophet Jonah tells us how the people of Nineveh did penance and received complete pardon from God. It is a consolation to remember that God is always ready to forgive offenses. "But you, our God, are kind and true, patient, and ruling all things in mercy" (Wisdom 15:1). Since God is Love, He would cease to be God if He ceased to love and therefore to pardon: it is His task to save what was lost, to recover what was abandoned, to heal what was injured, to receive into His embrace those who have deliberately withdrawn from Him, those who have betrayed Him. Certainly we must cooperate, at least by praying again and again: "Your ways, O Lord, make known to me" (Responsorial Psalm).

FOURTH SUNDAY IN ORDINARY TIME:

The Prophet

Readings: Deuteronomy 18:15-20
1 Corinthians 7:32-35
Mark 1:21-28

A prophet is one who speaks for God, in His name, and at His command. He is a servant of the Word of God, a minister of divine messages. In God there is neither past nor future; but when the prophet delivers his message to us, it often seems to be present but it may also be fulfilled in the future. It would be well to know, too, that from the eighth century B.C. onward, when writing came into common use, the prophet did not limit himself to announcing the will of God, but he put it down in writing as an aid and as a supplement to his prophetic apostolate. The prophet-writers are divided into major (Isaiah, Jeremiah, Ezekiel, Daniel) and minor (there are twelve) according to the length or brevity of their writings.

But what was the doctrine which the prophets disseminated under the inspiration of God? For His Chosen People God had an ideal of divine union, of sanctity; for this reason He intervened whenever the Jewish people strayed from the path of justice and virtue. By His threat and permission of chastisement, God wished to draw His people to Himself again according to a covenant of ineffable love, such as that between father and son. In addition to this aspect of actual Providence, God inspired certain persons to speak in His name in order to prepare men for the coming of the Messiah. To this end there is a kind of curious logic in the prophecies of the Old Testament: they foretell the interventions of God, and these, in turn, refer to the Redeemer as the one true Prophet; thus the word of the prophet is functionally that of the Messiah. The central theme of the first reading is precisely this interdependence and subordination of prophecy to Christ, the prophet par excellence. "Moses spoke to the people, saying: 'A prophet like me from among you...him you shall heed.' And the Lord said to Moses, 'I will raise up for them a prophet like you,...and I will put my words in his mouth, and he shall speak to them all that I command him. Whoever will not give heed to my words which he shall speak in my name, I myself will require it of him' " (Deuteronomy 18:15-20).

From the beginning of His public life, Christ was fully conscious that He was the sole Voice of God, toward which the other prophetic voices pointed. At the beginning of his Gospel, St. Mark tells us: "...they went into Capernaum, and immediately on the sabbath he entered the synagogue and taught. And they were astonished at his teaching, for he taught...with authority.... They... were amazed. They questioned among themselves: 'What is this? A new teaching...with authority!' ...At once his fame spread everywhere throughout all the surrounding region of Galilee" (Third Reading).

If we had to point out the qualities that constitute the superiority of Christ the Prophet in comparison with the other inspired ministers of the divine Word, we would be inclined to say something like this: Jesus is the true prophet, for He speaks not only in the name of God but as the Son of God, equal to the Father, having the same authority as the Father. Christ is a prophet not only now and then and at intervals, but always and in the fullest measure. Every word of His is a message, every action of His is a lesson not only for a people, but for all mankind. He does indeed base His own statements on the earlier prophets as if to declare definitely that He knew that everything the Father had revealed through the prophets was being fulfilled in His own person. Furthermore, Christ speaks with a very definite purpose: to found the kingdom of God on earth; His words deal primarily with the forgiveness of sins and the overthrow of the devil, as today's Gospel tells us.

We must not forget that His prophetic authority, after all, derived from the very human way in which He spoke. Jesus knew Hebrew, the language of the Bible; He knew Aramaic, the language of the people; probably He was not unacquainted with Greek, the principal language of the Orient; and possibly He knew Latin, the language of the Roman conqueror. Whatever be the case, it is certain that His word was at once persuasive and forceful, mild and revolutionary, captivating and refined. Whoever heard Him had the impression of having been blind heretofore; listening to Him, a person felt as if He were immersed in the sea of eternity. In the music of Christ's words, the world, life, and human beings took on a new light, an unsuspected dimension. He was indeed the most captivating of speakers.

PASTORAL REFLECTIONS

1. What had been foretold by the prophets was verified in Jesus to the last detail. What the Savior Himself foretold was fulfilled in the course of a generation: for instance, the martyrdom of some of the apostles, and the destruction of Jerusalem by the Roman general Titus. Now *this law of prophecy become history* ought to make us confident and eager to accept the Gospel message, on the basis of which we shall be judged.

2. A second reflection: Prophecy still continues in the Church, mainly through the hierarchy, but also as a gift of the entire People of God (cf. Constitution on the Church, 12). But anyone called to exercise the prophetic office in the name of Christ may never forget something very important: in the first place, *the prophet must be in communion with the Church.* The charisms granted to the faithful, as St. Paul points out (1 Corinthians 14:26-33, 40), are subject to discipline, to the charism of pastoral authority in charity. "...Religious and canonical obedience, which is required of us in the ecclesial economy, is not only in harmony with the real freedom of the children of God, but is its foundation and guarantee...and is at the basis of our being as men,

Christians, Catholics, chosen to follow Christ" (Paul VI, February 2, 1972). A person may prophesy, drive out demons, even work miracles, but if he does not do the will of the Father, if he does not remain in the Church, he will not be recognized by Christ, much less loved by Him (cf. Matthew 7:21-24).

3. Furthermore, the prophet must ever keep in mind that his work will be effective only if it is spoken by a child of God in sanctifying grace and if his preaching aims at overcoming the sins of the world, if it recognizes and possesses in an authentic way the biblical "power of God." It will likewise be profitable if the discourse itself is short, profound, unified, simple in delivery. These, it seems to us, are *the essential qualities of the prophet of the new covenant.* To act in this way it is evidently necessary to be ever in harmony with eternal Truth: "Oh, that today you would hear his voice: 'Harden not your hearts...' " (Responsorial Psalm).

FIFTH SUNDAY IN ORDINARY TIME:

The Apostolate of Truth

Readings: Job 7:1-4, 6-7
1 Corinthians 9:16-19, 20-23
Mark 1:29-39

The liturgy of last Sunday underlined the continuity of prophecy in the New Testament. Today's liturgy urges us to consider the missionary dimension of the Church in relationship to the spread of the Gospel. In this way the plan of God is fulfilled: the prophets of the Old Covenant spoke in order to keep alive the hope of the Messiah, foreseeing some aspect of truth; Christ came, and "by giving Himself brought us every form of newness" in a definitive manner (St. Irenaeus); the Savior then founded the Church so that the salvific message might be spread over the whole world.

The first chapter of Church history opens with the dynamic vision of the Church on the march for the spread of eternal Truth: "Go into all the world and preach the gospel to the whole creation. He who believes...will be saved; but he who does not believe... will be condemned" (Mark 16:15-16). Mindful of this supreme command and fortified by the power of the Spirit, the apostles present and proclaim themselves the depositaries and messengers of the Gospel. For the sake of spreading it, they even renounce serving the poor at table, for they are of the opinion that the greatest charity is that of truth, and they are convinced that from truth every other act of charity derives its impetus and development. Hence the action of all these fervent apostles aimed at evangelization in order to make the world yield to the truth of Christ.

The liveliest and most powerful model of the apostle is St. Paul. He opens himself to the pagan world with a trumpet blast of victory, with a program of fiery zeal, and with a vitality that bursts forth: "For if I preach the gospel, that gives me no ground for boasting. For necessity is laid upon me. Woe to me if I do not preach the gospel! For if I do this of my own will, I have a reward; but if not of my own will, I am entrusted with a commission. What then is my reward? Just this: that in my preaching I may make the gospel free of charge.... I do it all for the sake of the gospel, that I may share in its blessings" (Second Reading).

The purpose of the Church is the spread of the Gospel; her reason for existence is to safeguard and hand on the Word she received from her Founder. What is the Pope but the one who must feed the lambs and the sheep? (cf. John 21:16-17). He is the "word of God with us." And the bishops and priests—are they not the custodians and authentic teachers of Christian doctrine? (cf. Constitution on the Church, 25) A minister of God may remain a minister even if he does not celebrate the Eucharistic mystery, but if he gives up preaching he denies his own consecrated vocation. The Church is so closely bound up with the ministry of the word that she has entered into treaties and concordats with secular powers in order to safeguard the liberty to preach as her first need and inalienable right. Even if she is bound in chains or reduced to slavery, as Paul was, she can still continue to be the Church precisely because she can still diffuse the word of the Lord, at least secretly.

The layman, too, as a son of the Church, has the mission to receive and spread the Gospel. Like the apostles and together with them, from the very beginnings of Christianity, the disciples of Christ—men like Stephen, Philip, Barnabas, and Silas—are filled with zeal for preaching. In the last chapter of his letter to the Romans, St. Paul draws up a list of these apostolic lay missionaries: Aquila and Prisca, Andronicus and Julia, married couples; Rufus, Urbanus, Apelles, Apaenetus, Caius Vibius Firmius, and Caius Vibius Ampliatus, gloriously buried in the catacombs of St. Priscilla; a Mary and other women with Greek names are also mentioned: Tryphoena (the delicate one), Tryphona (the sumptuous one), and Persis (the Persian woman). These lay apostles had taken to heart the words of Christ, "You are the salt of the earth.... You are the light of the world" (Matthew 5:13-14). And through their apostolate "a large company was added to the Lord" (Acts 11:24). Nor may we overlook the fact that in this regard Vatican II has insisted anew on the duty of the apostolate of the laity, who must witness to the truth (cf. Constitution on the Church, 35), so that the Gospel may penetrate deeply into their mentality, their customs, and their social activity (cf. Decree on Missionary Activity, 21).

PASTORAL REFLECTIONS

1. What is history? It could be defined as *"the game of truth."* Affirmations and denials give rise to tensions, to friction between individuals and between classes; *yes* and *no* plow the deep furrows of unity or discord. "The world lacks God, lacks faith, lacks what can come to it

from God.... When you walk in the darkness, you don't know where you are going.... Man today is in the world without knowing where he comes from, where he is going, and why he lives. The reason of life evades him. Modern man is very clever, but he does not know why he works. The sense of life evades him.... You need a light. And this light is faith, our religion, it is Christ's Word.... When in a dark room, at night, a light is lit, the eyes see things. Things acquire a place, a form, a meaning. Well, what gives a meaning to our life is the central light of faith.... From truth comes charity, love, liking for the world, for things, for others. There comes the impulse to the apostolate" (Paul VI, March 19, 1972).

2. Christians must be convinced that it is impossible for them to be true disciples of Christ *if Christ Himself does not exercise His function as master* along the whole gamut of their existence, if they lose contact with His word. Our life as believers began when we acknowledged and accepted Jesus Christ, but our faith-life will develop only if it is deeply rooted in the living, life-giving soil of the Word of God, from which it receives its vital nourishment through the full blossoming of the spirit. God Himself has deposited this divine word in the Church; only the Church, according to the will of her Founder, is the guarantee, interpreter, and support of our religious convictions. The follower of Christ may not let himself act according to changing styles that pass away, but must remain firmly attached to the Truth that remains (cf. Paul VI, April 19, 1972).

3. *The faithful Christian is by his very makeup an apostle* of and in the truth, conscious of the fact that the salvation of mankind is a truly royal action, most pleasing to God. Interiorly, the life of Jesus is holiness for us; exteriorly, it is apostolate. Christ wants to continue to love through our hearts, to give with our hands, to look kindly through our eyes, to enlighten through our voice, which joyously disseminates His word, the only word that is Truth!

SIXTH SUNDAY IN ORDINARY TIME:

Sin and the Sacrament of Penance

Readings: Leviticus 13:1-2, 44-46
1 Corinthians 10:31—11:1
Mark 1:40-45

For the ancient Hebrews the worst disease that could afflict a human being was leprosy. Inexorably the body of the leper disintegrated until it was reduced to a mere skeleton. Furthermore, deprived of all family and social contact, the leper wandered about alone, like one rejected, and this not only as a sanitary precaution, but also that he might not pollute the sanctity of the Chosen People. Finally, from a religious point of view, the person afflicted with leprosy—according to the then reigning mentality—was considered the world's greatest sinner, one who, as a punishment, carried in his very flesh the clear signs of divine reprobation.

Jesus upset completely this socio-religious standard of the Old Testament. Like a Savior, He stooped down to the leper, symbol of fallen humanity and of the sinner, and brought him back to full life on the threefold level of bodily health, social fitness, and reinstatement into divine friendship.

Biblical exegetes are wont to see in this miracle of the cure of the leper a type of the sacrament of penance, above all in its effects. By means of this sacrament Christ continues to stoop down to all who have erred, to outcasts, to those emarginated from life, and today—if one may say so—to drug addicts and those alienated by sin.

The first and most sublime effect of penance is that of restoring anew the interior life of the sinner. It is common Catholic doctrine that the sacrament of penance is an authentic supernatural re-creation of our soul, as if we were receiving a second baptism. Indeed, it constitutes one of those marvels which St. Augustine does not hesitate to declare greater than creation itself. As a consequence of this mystic transformation from a state of sin to a new life of grace, it follows that the one pardoned becomes the joy of the Trinity. And it was Christ who, by accepting death as an outcast, outside the Holy City, brought together these two deep abysses: that of the moral degradation of the sinner and that of the infinite perfection of the Father. Nay more: Christ, by healing us and placing us once more in vital union with the Eternal, also makes us fit workers of the earthly city.

By the grace of God, received or increased by means of this sacrament, we can have sufficient strength to avoid evil and to advance in virtue: something that is of undoubted advantage to society as such. In this connection it is well to mention again that when God saves He effects in us a salvation that is in all respects complete.

Continuing the parallelism with the Gospel narrative, it will not be out of place to explain why the sacrament of penance demands the confession of our sins to God's minister. There should be no difficulty in this regard if we recall that, according to the principles of psychology, our nature needs to see, to hear, to experience through visible signs the pardon granted to us by Him who loves us. God wants to make us feel His pardon in a manner wholly human, both sensibly and emotionally, through the voice and the heart of the priest. The objection of the moral weakness of the confessor does not hold, since just as God became man to show forth His mercy in a high degree, so He intends to make use of finite creatures, sometimes even of sinners, to pour forth more abundantly and more surely His own ineffable love of redemption; indeed it is the consciousness of our own moral weakness that urges us to be generous in God's name toward our brothers.

If we are imbued with this theological view regarding the sacrament of Penance, we shall spontaneously resolve to approach it often voluntarily. We are told that St. Charles Borromeo used to go to confession every day in order to be holier and to purify in himself the ecclesial community, for it remains true that "the soul that uplifts itself, uplifts the world." Don Bosco ends his biography of St. Dominic Savio by declaring that this youth was able to reach sanctity because he had used the sacrament of Penance well and frequently.

PASTORAL REFLETIONS

1. *The first victim of sin is the sinner himself* inasmuch as he becomes insincere with himself, deceitful toward others, cut off from God. St. Teresa of Avila calls the devil "that poor fellow who cannot love." Granted, all of us can be wounded by the vicissitudes of life; all of us can make mistakes, but the hypocrite dissimulates them, the vicious man repeats them voluntarily, and the sinner truly desires them. To fall into the mud is certainly bad, but to want to sink in the mire is disastrous; it is the ruination of one's own life.

2. But the sinner is also a disgrace to his fellowmen. From the very first pages of the Bible sin is branded for its *negative effect upon society.* Such is Cain's sin of religious jealousy, the sin of lust at the time of the deluge and the sin of pride manifested in the building of the Tower of Babel (cf. Genesis 4:1-16; 6:11-13; 11:1-9). Hence we must agree with the philosopher Charles Baudolaire who says that the fullness of civilization is the elimination of sin. Vatican II also declares that only if man is freed from sin can the human family become more truly human and more united (cf. Constitution on the Church in the Modern World, 40).

3. But how free ourselves from sin? Man can cut off an ear, gouge out an eye, but he cannot heal himself of himself. So too in the sphere of morality: all of us can be sinners, but *only Christ can save us:* He is our Savior (cf. Luke 5:32; Constitution on Revelation, 4). Christ Himself, recalling the prophecies of the Book of Numbers, said that just as Moses lifted up the serpent in the desert so that everyone who looked at it would be cured of his

wounds (cf. Numbers 21:8-9), so by the death of Christ on the cross He would overcome every sin and every curse.[1] "We will," says Pope Paul VI, "be humble and sincere: we will recognize the complex and urgent accumulation of our many deficiencies, of our unsatisfied needs, of our chronic infirmities,...and we will find a solution and comfort and a remedy for this unfortunate situation in Christ's Redemption" (Paul VI, April 7, 1976).

SEVENTH SUNDAY IN ORDINARY TIME:

The Divine Mercy

Readings: Isaiah 43:18-19, 21-22, 24-25
2 Corinthians 1:18-22
Mark 2:1-12

Taking up again and developing the theme of last Sunday, we recall that though we continue to offend Him by sin, God reveals toward us the tenderness of a Father and Redeemer.

This consoling truth was clearly proclaimed even in the Old Testament. The inspired book of Exodus declares that God is "a merciful and gracious God, slow to anger and rich in kindness and fidelity, continuing his kindness for a thousand generations" (34:6-7). The Psalmist says,

 As a father pities his children,
  so the Lord pities those who fear him,
 For he knows our frame;
  he remembers that we are dust (Ps. 103:13-14).

The heart of God, the prophets sing, is moved with compassion for our misery; He surrounds His people with abiding affection and love even as a mother cradles her

---

[1]. It is well-known that in Asia, Egypt, and Palestine the serpent also had a healing power. In Greece, Aesculapius himself, the god of medicine, was represented by an entwined serpent.

own child close to her heart and as the water of the sea envelops the reef.

By His deeds, His words, and above all by His sacrifice, Jesus conclusively fulfilled this good news of divine goodness. He revealed the merciful countenance of the Father, entrusting to us, for our hope and comfort, the unforgettable parable of the lost sheep, of the lost coin, and of the prodigal son. Christ came to earth not to give evidence of wonder-working power or to seek renown but, like a physician, to save those who were lost through sin. If He healed not a few persons, He did it to manifest His love poured out in every direction; if He accepted crucifixion between two sinners, it was that in them He might have two witnesses to hand down to all generations His mission as the Lamb immolated for the forgiveness of sins; if His own death took place outside the holy city of Jerusalem, it was that He might be able to redeem all homeless exiles, all those abandoned, outcasts, outlaws—today we could well add: drug victims, emarginated persons, alienated people—those who at one and the same time are victims of sin and themselves sinners. In a word, He awaits all, and He says to each sinner: "Come, I will wipe out your sins; as for myself, I will not remember your faults." God is love; if He stopped loving, He would cease to be God.

Through the centuries the theme of divine mercy has been illuminated by Christian writers. In the first place, St. John the evangelist reminds us that if sin is great, the heart of God is still greater. "Our sins," Saint Cyril of Jerusalem remarks, "if placed one on top of the other, will never tower above the forbearance of God, just as our injuries will never surpass the skill of the physician." St. Lucy Filippini, foundress of the Pious Religious Teachers (Maestre Pie), explains: "When men give themselves, they impoverish themselves; but God enriches Himself in pardoning, for only in this way does His love become mercy." And St. Therese of the Child Jesus adds this lovely thought: "I will reveal one of my most intimate secrets to you. Yes, for a long time I have believed that our Lord is more tender than a mother. A mother is always ready to pardon the faults of her little one; that is just what God does for us. And my nature is such that fear makes me draw back, whereas with love I not only move forward in Jesus, but I fly. For this reason," the little saint of Lisieux concludes, "my way is to be happy always, always to smile, whether I fall or gain a victory!"

Let us then always remember this, especially at the moment of death. We are told—and with this I shall finish—that when Bossuet, the great French preacher and apologist of the seventeenth century, the chaplain of the court of Louis XIV, lay at the point of death, his friends reminded him of the many good services he had rendered to the Church and society; but he murmured, "This is not the time for talking or balancing accounts, but rather the time for believing and entrusting oneself wholly to the mercy of God!" So be it. The badge and program of Christians is precisely what the apostle of love, St. John, taught: they are the ones who despite all the apparant contradictions of life and of history, believe in the love of God.

PASTORAL REFLECTIONS

1. By taking away sin, *Jesus heals and changes man* from within. Just as night makes us think about love, and death reminds us of life, so the experience of our sins, pardoned by Christ, can change our life into a more vigorous and joyful one. Man is like a two-faced being, capable of evil and of good; a creature that can be sucked up by the frustrating experience of sin and likewise be drawn by the inviting prospect of virtue. But the love and pardon of Christ can impress itself on him so as to make him truly the most beautiful image of Christ (cf. Paul VI, September 12, 1976).

2. As the sinner is a negative element in society, so the man who has been sanctified, restored by grace, is for that very reason *a benefactor of that same civil society*. Before his cure, the paralytic of the Gospel

(Third Reading) was a burden for his fellowmen, a passive element; but after he had been cured by the Redeemer, he became free in thought, bold in expression, diligent in action, and generous in self-giving. It is precisely our sins that make us a dead weight in history, even though we may make a great deal of noise and attract not a little attention; whereas if we are truly holy, purified by the mercy of God and lifted up by His infinite love, we can efficaciously and joyfully contribute to the advent of a society built according to the measure of sons of God.

3. *According to the Gallup Poll of September, 1976, the religious sense* is more widespread in the United States than in Europe. This opinion poll revealed that for 56% of the American people faith is "very important," while only 27% of the Europeans gave the same response; 94% of the American people declared that they believe in "God or in a supreme being," whereas in Europe the percentage is only 78%; 68% of the people in the United States believe in a life beyond, whereas a single country of Europe has a proportion of 48% who believe in an afterlife. It would be wonderful if the United States continued to be preeminent in this sphere also—as a country beloved by God and the Redeemer.

EIGHTH SUNDAY IN ORDINARY TIME:

The Mystical Marriage

Readings: Hosea 2:16-17, 21-22
2 Corinthians 3:1-6
Mark 2:18-22

On this eighth Sunday, before entering the season of Lent, the Liturgy of the Word wishes to sharpen the wonderful picture of the covenant between God and humanity by presenting to us our Lord as the Spouse who seeks every occasion and means of union with our souls. The prophet Hosea writes:

The Lord says:

"Therefore, behold, I will allure her,
and bring her into the wilderness,
and speak tenderly to her....
And I will betroth you to me forever;
I will betroth you to me in righteousness
and in justice, in steadfast love, and in mercy."

The Lord, then, calls us to Himself with the desire and tenderness of a young bridegroom, and this not because He needs us, but rather because we have a fundamental need of Him (First Reading).

Not only Hosea, but practically all the prophets, sang of God as the Spouse who seeks to bind us to His love by giving us joy. Above all, Jeremiah, the spiritual heir of Hosea, takes up the symbolism of marriage and extols the "age-old" love of God for His people (Jeremiah 31:3). As a consequence of a severe interior trial, the prophet-psychologist came to understand that life is never disastrous, because in every situation, mysteriously and constantly, the goodness of God reveals itself. Enlarging on this theme, the prophet Isaiah in turn defines God as "a jealous Lover," who wants to win over His creature despite the latter's sin and infidelity (cf. Isaiah 54:4-8; 61:10; 62:4ff.).

The theme of marriage between God and humanity was so deeply and habitually felt by the Jewish people, that God Himself inspired the writing of a book, *The Song of Songs*, on this theme. According to the generally preferred dating, it was composed about 300 B.C.

But what are the motives and the consequences of this nuptial union between God and His creature? Several ideas have already been mentioned. Let us develop them still further. "Sociality, which is spoken about so much today, certainly remains, but the individuality of a particular person is drowned in the multitude of people.... How often it can happen to each of you, and perhaps several times a day, that you are in the midst of the human crowd, living in the same skyscraper, having a place in the world of human work,... and yet you feel lonely and isolated. You are surrounded, it is true, by a zone of collectivity: common language, the same nationality, profession and organization...but you feel yourself a stranger, interiorly different and almost alien among the others" (Paul VI, September 15, 1976).

But if the love of God for us is constant, even jealous, persistent to the point of overtaking and possessing us, it remains joyously true that in life there is at least someone who is seeking us, who truly wishes us well. Precisely this is the good news of Christianity: it is not man who seeks God—as is the case in other religions—but God who eagerly seeks His creature.

Usually when a lover notices gross defects in his partner, he withdraws from her. Not so God. For while man seeks love in order to be fulfilled and enriched, God for His part wishes to draw us to Himself in order to enrich us and to give Himself to us. The greater our weakness, says St. Paul, the more glorious is the power of divine mercy (cf. 2 Corinthians 12:9). How significant history is on this point! Just at the time of the prophet Hosea, the Assyrians oppressed and conquered the Northern Kingdom, Israel; discord, murder, and fraud to gain possession of the kingdom were rampant within. Yet at this very moment God was pictured by Hosea as a lover seeking His people. The son of Beeri—that was the name of the prophet's father—made abundantly clear to his fellow-citizens the certainty that God, far from repudiating His covenant with man, called him more intimately to Himself and wanted to embrace him with a sweet and enduring love such as that between husband and wife (cf. Hosea 2:20ff.).

On the level of personal history too the prophet teaches us the same lesson. He had married an evil woman who bore him three sons. Discovering her infidelity, he at first drove her away, but later, at the command of God, he had to take her back and definitely reinstate her in his love as her husband. Indeed, it was this sorrowful experience in his own married life that led him to describe in an inspired manner the intercourse between the generous, inexhaustible love of the Lord and the persistent infidelity of His Chosen People. The good news of Christianity, then, contains the assurance that God loves us with a love that pardons—that is, that after having bestowed His beneficent love upon us as His dear children, He pours out upon us His pardoning love when we have been unfaithful.

This inexhaustible love of God is certainly not always recognized in its possessive intensity. By definition God is "He who loves," or better still, "He who returns." His love has, as it were, a twofold movement: He seems to withdraw, but only that He may return to us more desirous of Him. He—and this too in the manner of married couples—seems to create in us the impression of having lost Him, but only in order to give us the joy of having Him appear unexpectedly and even more in love with us. In a word, the path on which God encounters His creature here below is like a trail that winds through the desert. To be specific, between the initial encounter of our first joyful meeting with God and the culminating point of our nuptial union with Him, we may have to undergo trials, as happened to the Jewish people on the journey to the promised land, as happens too between married people; we may have to undergo separations, pains, misunderstandings, contradictions, delusions; but all this will serve—in the method of the divine teacher—to purify our love for God and to make us ever more worthy of His friendship. And when we make this discovery—no matter whether it be early or late—we shall experience anew the delight of belonging to the Bridegroom, just as we did at the time of our first religious fervor, just as at the time of our departure for the Lord's country; then our life will seem to regain its song of perennial youth.

PASTORAL REFLECTIONS

1. Through the Incarnation *God has placed His tabernacle among us forever.* The tabernacle of the Jews was transported through the desert from one stopping place to another of their journey. And now, not only will the love of God always be with us, but it will follow us in every trial, in every situation.

2. This love of God for us will be above all *a pardoning love.* Unfortunately, along the path of our earthly existence, we too may fall, we may be unfaithful to God, repudiate Him, in a sense be sorry that we have given Him our word, until we arrive at the point of regretting having set out on this adventure of love. But we must not be discouraged: God is a Spouse who, even though He has been betrayed and rejected, continues to court us like the most enamored lover.

3. By a mysterious and spontaneous impulse, the person who is inflamed with love tends to *express and to diffuse it* even in his most ordinary contacts with his fellowmen, and becomes an instrument of Him "who has qualified us to be ministers of a new covenant" (Second Reading—2 Corinthians 3:6). The apostolate is really nothing other than the fire of love that has been enkindled in our hearts and that strains, through an interior force, to be ignited exteriorly (cf. Luke 12:49).

NINTH SUNDAY IN ORDINARY TIME:

Keeping the Sunday Holy

Readings: Deuteronomy 5:12-15
2 Corinthians 4:6-11
Mark 2:23-28; 3:6

After Pentecost and the feast of the Most Holy Trinity, another wonderful season of heavenly blessings begins. God is certainly present in history to sanctify it and to make of all men a holy people, a holy nation. It remains for men to be aware of this sanctifying presence of God, this mystical unfolding of divine life.

Today's liturgy lays down some conditions necessary to put ourselves in accord with this universal plan of salvation: the Sunday rest and the sanctification of the day.

The Sunday rest is the theme of the first reading taken from the book of Deuteronomy. The Lord said: "Six days you shall labor, and do your work, but the seventh day is a sabbath to the Lord your God; in it you shall not do any work...remember that you were a servant in the land of Egypt, and the Lord your God brought you out thence with a mighty hand and an outstretched arm; therefore the Lord your God commanded you to keep the sabbath day."

To learn to rest is a sign of interior liberty, a quality of the sons of God. A conscious laying aside of work is, above all, a sign of the supremacy of the spirit over matter: man ought to show himself superior to any economic advantage. It is necessary to stop work every now and then to avoid the illusion that we are quite indispensable; after all, the world will carry on without us, without our work. Let us be busy but not preoccupied. The world existed before we came on the scene and will carry on to better itself even when we are gone.

It is necessary periodically to call a halt to our activities to prevent ourselves from living in only one dimension: that of the body, matter, thus running the risk of letting our spiritual values become atrophied and psychologically one-sided and abnormal: "Man shall not live by bread alone" (Matthew 4:4). A temporary respite from our work is necessary for our very work itself. Some disciples of St. John the Evangelist were surprised to see their venerable master lose time in little pastimes. The saint had them bring him a bow and arrows, and told them to fix the bow taut, all in readiness for shooting the arrow. Then he asked, "Can this bow last long if it is so highly strung?" "No," they replied. Then the old man concluded, "Our souls too would become flaccid under constant strain." Besides, it is useful to remember that too much tension can make us nervous, easily harsh. It happens not rarely that because of the accumulation of toxins in our system, occasioned by overfatigue, we become irritable and unkind and less courteous with our neighbor, thus breaking the great precept of charity.

It may be that on Sundays we desist from physical labor but fill them instead with taxing and costly programs and meetings, demanding even greater mental stress than the usual daily round. These are not a rest, they are rather a more tiring sort of work. We must learn to use our free time profitably and plan our weekends to rest our minds and bodies.

But Sunday is above all the day of the spirit, the day of worship. It is the one day of the week when we take time to reflect on our fundamental aim in life: to feel near to God, encounter Him and enjoy His presence, and to insert ourselves into the Christian community. God floods our soul when we empty it of all earthly things, all temporal concerns. The moments of Holy Mass are eminently suited to this personal and exclusive encounter with the Father. Freedom from manual work should promote a serene activity of the soul in a threefold dimension: in prayer, in religious instruction, and in works of charity. We ought to take advantage of the opportunity to learn more about our religion on a Sunday or feastday. This can be done by reading some sound book or meditating on the Word of God offered in the liturgy. To steel ourselves against temptation and to strengthen our faith, we ought to oxygenate our soul with eternal truths and the Word of God.

Sunday is, furthermore, the time for Christian charity. The third reading, the Gospel, recalls this duty to our minds. On a sabbath day, a festive day for the Jews, Jesus cured a man with a palsied hand. It is commonly known that from the very beginning, Sunday was for the Christians a day of community, of fraternity (Acts 2:41). It must be so for us too. During the week we were busy with material concerns. Even our interpersonal meetings were often prompted by some business transaction or other. Let at least our Sunday be devoted to fraternal charity. It is related that Frederick Ozanam, after having received Holy Communion on Sunday, used to return Jesus' visit by visiting some sick person.

We have merely sketched some aspects of this "theology of Sunday." We are aware, too, of the many difficulties which interfere with our keeping the Sunday holy. What is important, however, is that we do not lose sight of the principal aim of a Sunday: a sacred atmosphere. It is only by this divine and divinizing atmosphere that such days will be highly rewarding and sublime.

PASTORAL REFLECTIONS

1. *Repose is a duty just as work is a duty.* Work and repose are two complementary terms. The rhythm of life is marked by the alternating of work and repose, of movement and quiet, of tension and relaxation, of concentration and distraction. These phases have relation and harmony just as there is relation and harmony between day and night, between giving and receiving, between the body and the mind. Repose has its place, therefore, among the important duties of man as creature of God, as a limited, finite creature who has need of replenishing himself with energy, of recharging himself with sound motivation for action.

2. *The Sunday rest must raise us up to God.* "Rest from the ordinary rhythm of work is not sheer idleness or mere exterior entertainment. It can be a propitious moment for conscience, for the formation of one's own personality, for ascent to the peaks of the soul.... It can be the hour of interior reflection, above all the hour of prayer, the hour of some 'spiritual exercises,' of interior listening..." (Paul VI, July 10, 1977).

3. *The day of rest is above all a day for good works in our own family.* During the working days of the week we often have very little time to remain with our dear

ones, to manifest to them our solidarity and benevolence. On festive days we can make up for this lack. After having participated in the liturgy of the Church, we can immerse in our "little church of the family" all our love, our comprehension, our tenderness and dedication, so that it—the family—may continue to be life, joy; that it may become more and more a reality conquering time and dominating space even to the point of becoming a little paradise.

TENTH SUNDAY IN ORDINARY TIME:

The Forces of Evil

Readings: Genesis 3:9-15
2 Corinthians 4:13—5:1
Mark 3:20-35

On her pilgrimage toward eternity the Church meets a formidable obstacle: the demon. The biblical account places him at the very beginning of human history. Adam and Eve, upon whom God had liberally bestowed gifts of supernatural life, lived in familiar intimacy with their Creator. But there was a revolt. With calculated naturalness and a psychologically perfect technique, the Evil One first tempted Eve; attacking her in the feminine weakness of curiosity: "Did God say; 'You shall not eat of any tree of the garden'?" insinuated the devil. She replied: "We may eat of the fruit of the trees of the garden; but God said, 'You shall not eat of the fruit of the tree...lest you die.' " Then the devil played on her natural pride and assured her: "You will not die. For God knows that when you eat of it your eyes will be opened and you will be like God, knowing good and evil" (Genesis 3:1-6). The devil sowed the seed of fatal doubt: perhaps God was not a benefactor after all, but rather a usurper of rights.

Adam and Eve wanted to become gods in their own right; they set themselves against God and committed the sin of disobedience. This sin brought disastrous effects upon them, but also upon their posterity. The first reading mentions some of these. Psychological division within the person: Adam and Eve hid themselves because they were "afraid"; division within the family: Adam blamed Eve and she blamed the serpent; division between man and nature, which contests his dominion over creatures; division between brother and brother: Cain kills Abel; the reign of violence and of might was unleashed. The sad consequences of this sin invade every human descendant, as a poisoned spring cannot but give out poisoned water.

Now we are calling into doubt the existence of the devil, but the Bible from Genesis to the book of Revelations is full of assertions regarding the destructive presence of Satan. Vatican II makes insistent statements on this point (Constitution on: the Liturgy, 7; the Church, nos. 6, 16, 17, 48; Missionary Activity of the Church, 3, 9; Church in the Modern World, 13, 22, 37). The saints have confirmed this truth, enriching it with proofs and testimonies without number. It would suffice to read, for example, the biographies of St. Paul of the Cross, St. Teresa, the Cure of Ars, St. Gemma Galgani. St. Gregory the Great affirms that Satan seeks to counteract the beneficent work of the guardian angel, sending a demon as companion to each one of us with the task of making use of every possible occasion to incite us to evil.

The existence of the devil is commonly accepted in art, folklore and literature of all times and of all peoples. Historical and even prehistoric documents speak of an evil force quite opposed to good. Man has always felt himself to be sinful because of a moral fault committed in his earliest history, and because of this sense of sin he has always felt the need of purifying himself through sacrifices, even human sacrifices.

We are of the opinion that the demon always makes his influence felt. He is not only the prince of this world, he is also a perpetrator of wickedness. His is a kingdom which changes tone, tactics and methods; it is he who incites temptations, he acts upon our minds and presents evil in the guise of good, as a curiosity, as a natural thing. With infernal cunning he knows how to use temperaments and inclinations for his wicked intent. At most unlikely times he invites us to sin. St. Peter describes him as "your adversary the devil [who] prowls around like a roaring lion, seeking someone to devour" (1 Peter 5:8). If nowadays he does not appear visibly incarnated as sometimes in the past, it may be because he does not need to do so anymore: he can ensnare us into sin with a little money or a bit of flesh or a bad companion. Probably Baudelaire was right when he wrote: "The most cunning trick of the devil consists in convincing us that he does not exist." And Robert Browning has this to add: "The devil is most diabolical when he is respectable."

PASTORAL REFLECTIONS

1. *Unless we overcome sin we can never have true civilization.* This consists mainly in blocking the negative influence of the power of evil. The disorder is first of all in souls, in the desire for power and prestige, in egoism, in outstripping a rival.... Democracy is not something which is decided as in a contest, or over a weekend. It is something which is constructed in the building up of man contributing to the removal of the cause of disorder within him: sin. Even the Church has its prime task not so much in combating ideas as in redeeming humanity from sin and freeing it from the devil.

2. *No matter what the sin, there is always a remedy.* The Lord said to the serpent: "I will put enmity between you and the woman, and between your seed and her seed; he shall bruise your head and you shall bruise his heel" (First Reading). It is the fruit of the Virgin, Christ, who frees us from every fault. His name is Jesus, which means not one who condemns but one who pardons, who remits the sins of the world, who conquers the evil spirit within as well as outside ourselves. To obtain this pardon from Christ we must fulfill one

condition: believe in the love of God. Though we may be obdurate sinners God asks of us but one thing: not to sin against the Holy Spirit (cf. Third Reading), that is, not to doubt the infinite love of God.

3. *Because of this trust in His love, the Christian is an optimist in hope.* All the prophets, ancient and modern, despite apparent contradictions, have placed their confidence in the positive and ultimate meaning of life: Christ has overcome and will always continue to overcome the evil in the world.

It has been written that courage is the heart of hope. It is characteristic of birds to have the courage to fly. The characteristic of the sky is to have many stars, and of the earth to yield flowers and fruits. The characteristic of one who loves is to divide his things and share with his brethren. The characteristic of a person in love is to sing and make music; and the characteristic of a Christian is to live and work in the celestial security that in the end, the good will triumph over the evil.

ELEVENTH SUNDAY IN ORDINARY TIME:

Development of the Church

Readings: Ezekiel 17:22-24
2 Corinthians 5:6-10
Mark 4:26-34

Men have founded universities to hand down their culture, schools of law to teach the application of the law; they have organized armies to have power. Jesus has founded the Church to continue His saving redemption. There is, however, a substantial difference between the human organizations and the Church: while the human organizations are always detached from their founders and can disappear with time, Christ has infused into His Church His own Spirit, His own power of life. This Church is the mystery of the God-man: God is incarnate in Christ and Christ is incarnate in the Church. The Church is, then, the continuation of Christ through the centuries. Just as the Word, though remaining the eternal splendor of the Father, grew in His human nature, so the Church, though remaining interiorly without spot or wrinkle, must grow and develop in time and history as the Mystical Body.

The first reading speaks of this irresistible growth: the prophet Ezekiel presents the metaphor of a little branch taken by God and planted in the heart of Israel, where it was to become a majestic cedar. So also the third reading, a passage from the Gospel of St. Mark, offers us this consoling truth in the delicate comparison of the seed which, when it is planted in the soil, springs up and grows into a mighty plant so large that it can shelter numerous birds of the air.

The historic development of the Church has two dimensions: it is quantitive and qualitative. No one who knows the history of the Church, even if his knowledge is only superficial, can deny or ignore the visibility of the Church among all the peoples of the earth and her universal motherhood. Impelled by divine power on the day of Pentecost she conquered the great vital centers of the world: Antioch, Alexandria of Egypt, and then Imperial Rome. While the Goths, the Franks, and the Germanic tribes fell under the might of Imperial Rome and vowed to destroy her, the Church passed into the confines of the barbarians and conquered them for Christ. Likewise in the twelfth to the fourteenth centuries, the era of the city-states, the sovereignties and republics the Church was in the fore, as also in the sixteenth century when the great discoveries of America and the Orient were in progress. It is needless to recount the miraculous expansion of the Church when even now we can state with certainty that the Church is the great universal reality, actually a cosmic reality of history. Even if she is geographically and statistically limited, her influence is felt all over the earth, like the magnet which causes invisible vibrations in all things around it.

The growth is all the more wonderful qualitatively. In the first thousand years she imposed herself in history and won all her enemies. In the second millennium she took such root in the peoples and nations and their histories that she was erroneously confused with western culture. But the second half of the twentieth century seems like the dawn of a third millennium even more resplendent and more glorious for the Spouse of Christ.

The Church of our time, of the Second Vatican Council, is so promising, active and young. Finally relieved of all nationalistic preoccupations and completely free from secular conditioning, now more than ever she is capable of assuming her role as the spiritual mother of all souls. No longer tied up with the administration of temporalities, she is completely dedicated to the defense of man and his spiritual values. With her institutional and prevalently canonical character diminished, she can present herself more and more as the messenger of the thoughts of God and manifest her role as the Bride of the Lamb, wholly devoted to the salvation of man. Parallel to the centrifugal movement of expansion in history, there has been the centripetal interior movement of ecclesial authenticity which will endure until all nations acclaim the Lord with one voice and "serve him with one accord" (Zephaniah 3:9).

PASTORAL REFLECTIONS

1. *What is meant by "catholicity of the Church"?* Pope Paul VI explains: "The scholars tell us that the first person to attribute the title 'Catholic' to the Church was St. Ignatius of Antioch, the renowned martyr of the beginning of the second century.... But the concept 'Catholic' is not by any means missing in the New Testament. It is enough to recall the final words of our Lord to the apostles, 'Go therefore and make disciples of all nations'.... The word 'Catholic' means universal and it refers directly to the 'Body' of the Church just as unity refers to the Spirit which gives it divine life... This is a marvelous mystery which makes us discover and ad-

mire the love of God for all humanity, to make brothers of all men" (Paul VI, August 3, 1977).

2. From this point it is easy to reflect that one of the principal *characteristics* of the Church is her *dynamics of movement.* Already in the Old Testament God desired the Covenant with His people to be one of "movement" in order that it could have spiritual influence on the whole of humanity. The Lord thought of His Church as a people in movement, to bring the message of salvation to all men. Certainly in her spiritual conquest the Church may identify herself with a society; but if she stops at this point, herself becoming society, she would finish by losing her mission and vocation of being mother to all people. This was wonderfully understood by St. Francis of Assisi who sent his brethren out to conquer the whole world.

3. It is for this reason that *the life of the Church is the true and only history of humanity.* Let us conclude with the words of St. John Chrysostom to a Christian of his own time: "Your hope is the Church, your salvation is the Church, and your refuge is the Church. She is higher than the sky, greater than the earth. She never grows old. She is ever young and vigorous. Holy Scripture proclaims her rock-like stability, calling her the mountain of God. Proclaims her incorruptibility calling her a queen. Calls her a daughter, because she is of the parentage of God." The Church is the paradise of time, as paradise is the Church of eternity.

TWELFTH SUNDAY IN ORDINARY TIME:

Mankind and Crisis in the Church

Readings: Job 38:1, 8-11
2 Corinthians 5:14-17
Mark 4:35-41

In the preceding chapter we lauded the progressive and irreversible development of the Church as the sign of the power of God in history. Some reader might tend to judge these words as somewhat triumphalistic, almost utopian, considering the spectacle of a Church that actually suffers, is contradicted and contested by her own children. The Church is more than aware of this sad situation (cf. The Church in the Modern World, 43). Then a question arises in our minds: How can these two diverse situations coexist? We respond by saying that the progress of the Church has to be glorious for its hope is already certitude, since the promise and the power of God is involved. Nevertheless this progress is painful and distressing because of man's free will operating in it, because God wills to respect the liberty He has bestowed upon man. Just as Christ ever remains the invincible Son of God, the supreme director of history, even though as man He had to suffer, to be misunderstood and opposed unto death, the same happens to His Bride the Church. The human soul remains untouched when a part of the body sustains a wound; the love of a mother remains unsullied even though one of her sons insults her. In like manner the Church remains always and substantially grand and spiritually majestic even when wounds or tensions appear in her body.

Let us have recourse to the teaching of Vatican Council II. It presents to us a Church all beautiful and immaculate in herself (cf. On the Church); but when it presents her in her exertions in the real context of history the same Council does not hide all the struggles and counterattacks she has had to withstand to keep abreast of these people and bring them to salvation (cf. The Church in the Modern World). The drama of the Church does not exhaust itself in the substance of her soul but in the exercise of her exterior and dynamic mission. In other words, she is all beautiful as the Bride of Christ, but she suffers in being the mother of men. We should add that particularly after this last Council she has had to suffer much in order to insert herself in the new needs of the time. We can read in the lives of Saints Ignatius of Loyola and Charles Borromeo how much they had to suffer after the Council of Trent in their efforts to implement the decrees of that Council. But hardships and trials are inherent in such a mission.

The marvel of it, however, is this, that whenever the Church seemed to flounder, to lose face, or like a little bark on the sea to be near to capsizing, she always recovered, maintained her equilibrium and presented herself more sturdy and strong than before the crisis. Using a comparison of Pope Paul VI, we can say that when the Church seemed like a tree trunk dead and dry, deprived of lifegiving sap, all of a sudden life began to throb in the tree, it put forth new shoots and leaves and produced flowers and fruits. The reason is simple: Christ is in the Church. St. Mark tells us in the third reading: Jesus asked His friends to put out to sea and they headed for the opposite shore. Quite suddenly a storm broke out and angry waves threatened to overturn the boat. The terrified apostles awakened Jesus and asked Him if He did not care whether they perished or not. Jesus woke up and calmed the sea and scolded the apostles for their lack of faith. Filled with awe the apostles asked each other: Who is this who is obeyed by even the wind and the sea? (cf. Mark 4:35-41). Likewise the first reading, taken from the book of Job, speaks of the power of God limiting the proud waters of the sea and its waves.

It is not difficult to see the intent of these readings. In the Church, the mystical ship of history, Christ keeps watch. He is ever present with her, even when He seems to sleep and apparently turns a deaf ear to those who are fearful. When the peril becomes too serious, the Lord will appear in all His power as the Son of God, as the supreme guide of the Church. He will save her, protect her from ruin, though the dangers continue to threaten. As in descending to earth the Word did not separate Himself from the Father, so in ascending into heaven He did not separate Himself from His Church. Rather, He began to be even more wholly present in His Spirit in the midst of His faithful brethren, from the very moment of

His bodily departure from them. Because of this, the Church may be attacked but she can never be conquered. History gives us a number of examples in this regard. How many kingdoms have disappeared, how many political powers have been overthrown in time! Only the Church, the vessel of the Lord, sails invincibly through the turbulent sea of history to bring us life and salvation. "Be of good cheer, I have overcome the world.... I am with you always, to the close of the age," Jesus assures us. Jesus is then the first optimist: it is "He who has promised infallibility and perpetuity to His ship the Church" (St. Pius X). Certainly she can lose some members of her crew or passengers if they cast themselves into the sea. But she as the Church remains whole and intact. With infinite mercy at her disposal she is ever ready for rescue service for those who may have gone overboard.

At times it would seem that some part of her imposing structure collapses and goes into bits; this terrifies for a while, but it is only the fear which reigned for three days after the death of Jesus, and then comes the resurrection. If some part falls or a wall crumbles, the divine Artist waits for the dust to settle and then sets about strengthening the foundations and building up anew, with the end product even more beautiful than before.

PASTORAL REFLECTIONS

1. Despite the buffets of history *the Church* will remain always beautiful, for *it is the one great and essential reality* which gives significance to *history,* to the *entire cosmos.* "The Church is God's plan for mankind; it is the kingdom of God in the world, the work of God, the building that God constructs in history, it is the People of God, it is God's covenant with man, it is the Mystical Body of Christ...Church means humanity called and gathered by the voice and by the grace of God, for Christ, in the Holy Spirit..." (Paul VI, July 27, 1977).

2. *It is her continual risk* but also her continual purpose to be always in *contact with history* and with the

life of man. The divorce between spirit and matter began with the philosopher Descartes; today then we have finally arrived at the deification of matter, of technology, of terrestrial reality.... It is the continuing and preoccupying task of the Church to construct bridges for recreating unity in the world and harmony of spirit.... In this constructive effort and in the continual incarnating of spirit in history, she—the Church—meets obstacles and sometimes suffers wounds, but they are obstacles which render her stronger, which make of her a more fruitful and generous mother.

3. It remains, then, for the true follower of Christ *to be loyal to the Church, to love the Church*, the "lighted lamp of the Spirit" for the life and the joy of men. The Holy Father exhorts us further: "In the constant activity with which the Church spends herself to bring redemption to men, she requires our cooperation and help. Let us look up to this holy Mother, this Mother so often grieved, whose sole comfort is the risen Savior. Let us have confidence in her, for in her we shall find our encouragement, sympathy and hope. Let us love her and help her in her colossal work; let us not weaken her, let us not cause division in her members, let us not diminish her unity" (Paul VI, May 13, 1972).

There remains nothing to be added but this: "Oh, give thanks to the Lord, for his...steadfast love endures for ever" (Responsorial Psalm).

THIRTEENTH SUNDAY IN ORDINARY TIME:

Our Resurrection

Readings: Wisdom 1:13-15; 2:23-24
2 Corinthians 8:7, 9, 13-15
Mark 5:21-43

Today the liturgy asks us to meditate upon a rather sad theme: death. The first reading makes it clear that it was not God who wanted us to die; death entered the world because of sin and the envy of Satan. God did not create death, neither does He take pleasure in destroying living beings. "For he fashioned all things that they might have being.... For God formed man to be imperishable; the image of his own nature he made him. But by the envy of the devil, death entered the world, and they who are in his possession experience it" (cf. First Reading). But God knows how to draw good even out of evil. The third reading develops this idea at least in an implicit manner by bringing out the positive aspects of Christian death. Jairus had a lovely daughter of twelve, in the flower of youth; in her eyes he saw the light of paradise. But death claimed her. Jesus, arriving at the house where the dead child lay, said to the people gathered there: "Why do you make a tumult, and weep? The child is not dead but sleeping." They began to ridicule Him, but He sent them all out, taking only the girl's parents and the three disciples to the death chamber. There He took her hand and said, "Little girl, I say to you arise." The child arose immediately and began to walk around. All those who were round about were astonished at this (cf. Mark 5:21-24; 38-43).

We know from the Gospels how Jesus brought back to life some persons who had died, as a proof of His complete dominion over the dead of all times. He said: "I am the resurrection and the life; he who believes in me, though he die, yet shall he live" (John 11:25). Christ, so St. Paul assures us, lived, died and arose again to become the Lord of all the living and the dead (cf. Romans 14:9); He is the one who awakens the dead (cf. 2 Corinthians 1:9), the conqueror of death. With His birth He has sanctified our birth, with His life He has willed to shape our life, with His death He has defeated our death, and with His resurrection He has made our death a point of departure for complete glorification. Death has not lost its tragedy for us but Christ has deprived it of its sting (cf. 1 Corinthians 15:15). It is true that death is still a painful and anguishing experience, but it cannot bring us to ruin. Rather, just as some insects lose their lives in the very act of stinging their victims, so does death find its definitive defeat at the very moment it seeks to destroy our bodies.

The Lord said, "The child is not dead, but asleep." We go to sleep to wake up again, all refreshed with renewed energies. Death is, according to Christ, a rest for a fuller life. It was precisely for this reason that the early Christians used the word "sleep" instead of "death" in their inscriptions on tombs. Furthermore, the word "cemetery" means a sleeping place, a dormitory, that is, a place where "those who lie there are not dead but they sleep and rest in view of an eternal resurrection also of the body" (St. John Chrysostom). Even the word "defunct" (from the Latin "defungi" meaning to complete a work or task) suggests the same idea of one who, after having overcome the trial of life (to live is itself a trial), presents himself to the Master for the reward according to the promise of the Lord: "Well done, good and faithful servant; you have been faithful over a little, I will set you over much; enter into the joy of your master" (Matthew 25:21).

PASTORAL REFLECTIONS

1. *What is our existence?* It is a one-way road leading to death. One day more is always one day less. Death is the final chapter of our lives: we die daily. The Bible uses a very commonplace word to describe our lives: we are wayfarers, each one of us is "on the way" toward the goal. St. Basil makes some interesting comments on our wayfaring through life. He says: "one who travels by ship might just as well be asleep; almost without his wanting it the winds and waves would carry him to port. So for us too: even when we sleep, time passes for us unnoticed. Even sleep is an exactor of its dues. It carries us on to the destination of our lives. Even while we fret, life is consumed all the same.... We are all somewhat like those who race; each one is speeding on toward his goal. It is precisely for this reason that we are alive. This then is the meaning of the 'way.'"

2. *To understand the problem of death means above all to solve the problem of life.* Unless we solve the first, the second forever remains a mystery replete with fears and problems. But only in a religious aspect and in the doctrine of Jesus can we be sure of a true and comforting solution, the one answer in which the biological and physical fear is supplanted by theological and divine hope. The Lord has conquered death not for Himself only; He has done so for us. The resurrection of Christ is also ours. Why? To answer this we must enter into another truth, another mystery: the union existing between the Head of the Mystical Body and the members, whom we are. If the Head be risen, the members too must rise. This victory of resurrection relates not only to the soul which is immortal by nature, but also to the body, mortal and animal, which is now the vital instrument of the soul, functioning like the clock of our earthly existence in time... How can the dead arise, and with what sort of bodies? St. Paul answers that this is the work of the omnipotence of God. He offers the example of the seed, which preserves its essential identity though it undergoes a radical change in its vegetative process. In death, the body that dies is perishable but what is raised is imperishable; what is sown is weak but what is raised is powerful; what is sown is natural but what is raised is spiritual.

3. *"Thus exhilarated with the assurance of the final triumph of our life in Christ,* we bend over the tombs of our dead.... An ineffable consolation enters our grieving hearts! We know in the first place that our dead are still alive. The human soul is immortal. Even if separated from the body, of which it was the living form, it survives. We know that a divine presence envelops our dead. We know more: that some good and beneficial action of ours can be useful to our dead, in the mysterious calculation of merits before God. Prayers, alms, penance, good works can be carried out by us and accredited to our dead.... This is the teaching of the Church. It is the Communion of Saints, operative even

through the celestial cosmos..." (Paul VI, November 2, 1977). We must therefore offer our praise and thanks to the Lord in the responsorial psalm: "I will praise you, Lord, you have rescued me!"

FOURTEENTH SUNDAY IN ORDINARY TIME:

The Characteristics of a Prophet

Readings: Ezekiel 2:2-5
2 Corinthians 12:7-10
Mark 6:1-6

Throughout history there have always been those who presented themselves to their contemporaries as messengers of programs and ideas they had received through inspiration from above. This phenomenon was more characteristic of the Orient, where not a few persons quite openly exercised the art of divining. But prophecy in its classical form was found only among the Hebrew people, among whom the prophet together with the king and the priest constituted the basis of their socio-religious life. From Abraham to John the Baptist, the life and history of this people of God was greatly influenced and even dominated by the voice of the prophets. The coming of Christ, far from eliminating this charism of prophecy, rather gave impetus to its extension as foretold in the Old Testament (cf. Numbers 11:29). With the descent of the Holy Spirit at Pentecost, visions and prophecies became common occurrences among the People of God. It is well known that the gift of prophecy became a dominant note in the primitive Church. St. Paul desired not only that the gift of prophecy be not despised, but much rather that it be preferred to the gift of tongues. He ranked it second in importance, placing only the work of the apostles ahead of it (cf. 1 Corinthians 14:1-5; 12:28). The gift of prophecy was always present in the Church to a greater or lesser degree. Actually it would be hard to understand the mission and the position of many of the Church's saints without reference to this providential and dynamic presence of the Holy Spirit. As we all know, the Second Vatican Council has rediscovered and reaffirmed the prophetic function of the whole Christian people (cf. On the Church, 35; Priestly Ministry, 2).

If we are to consider the characteristics of a prophet, we must indicate in the first place that he is a person chosen by God. He was known by the Hebrews as "nabhî," that is, the one called by the Lord. The Lord said to Ezekiel: "Son of man, I send you to the people of Israel.... You shall say to them: 'Thus says the Lord God!' " (First Reading) On the part of the prophet there must be complete submission to the will of God. Above all, great humility is necessary. Such a calling made Jeremiah realize his own utter weakness, while in Isaiah it awakened a sense of his own sinfulness. In the second reading St. Paul, the great preacher of the Word of God, boasts of his weaknesses as necessary conditions for the power of God to be more manifest in him. In the writing of Hermes entitled "The Shepherd" we find this statement: "The true prophet is without pretense; he is meek and humble, free of all wickedness; he does not speak superficially merely to please others." It is God's way—it is good to remember—to choose the weak to confound the strong.

In regard to the message the prophet is commissioned to give, this must always bear relation to the plan of salvation to be fulfilled and unified in Jesus Christ. Any prophesying which deviates from this soteriological purpose would not merit the name. God inspires words and actions always in view of our salvation, attained through His kingdom, which for us is the Church. The Holy Spirit, who is the soul of this Church, could not authorize a pseudo-prophet to prophesy outside His Church and against her. The decisive sign of authentic prophecy is concordance with apostolic preaching and with obedience. Further, the word of the prophet has not only a constant theme of salvation; it also differs from other proclamations in its method. The prophet speaks and acts against the sinful mentality of the people. The prophet Ezekiel was sent by God to reprove harshly and without mollification the rebel People of God. It would seem that some of the false prophets of today forget this important element of prophecy: they no longer preach about sin; they bypass the truths of judgment and hell, as if these had not been solemnly reconfirmed by the Second Vatican Council itself (cf. Decree on Ecumenism, 7; The Church in the Modern World, 14, 15, 18, 40; On the Church, 48, 49, 51; Non-Christian Religions, 7, etc.). It goes without saying that the prophet must not forget to speak also about the mercy of God. God works not to punish, not to destroy, but to build up and to plant (cf. Jeremiah 1:10).

The stress of this salvific perspective is especially clear in the writings of the prophet Hosea (eighth century B.C.) with the theology of the Covenant developed in the pattern of a marriage: the People of God may be unfaithful to Him, may even play the wanton in the face of His own fidelity; nevertheless the Lord, even though He punishes, will never cancel His covenant of love because the love of the spouse renders any such calculation impossible. The only conceivable calculation—always—is pardon. This thought is developed particularly in the second chapter of Hosea's prophecy. Finally, the mark which distinguishes a true prophet from a false one is his interior moral attitude. The ancient prophets were called "men of God" precisely because of their holy lives. In contrast to those talkers who preached but did not practice, the true prophets made of their own words not only a program for others, but also a duty, an experience for themselves. It is good to note here that many of the prophets, like Samuel, Nathan, the powerful Elijah, and others left us no collection of their teachings, for they had received from God the mission to influence the people more with their attitudes and the testimony of their lives than with their words and counsels.

The one person who eminently sums up in Himself all the characteristics of true prophesying is Christ. He was sent, par excellence, by the Father. All His teachings were directed to the founding of the kingdom of God; He was decisive in His opposition to the sin of intellectual pride even to the point of arousing the hatred of the Scribes and Pharisees. He knew, however, how to embrace all in His infinite mercy in order to give abundant life to all who believed in His divinity. And in this His prophetic mission He was so pure and blameless that no one could reproach Him with any sin at all (cf. John 8:46).

PASTORAL REFLECTIONS

1. There are not a few people in the Church of God *who want to be prophets.* That may be a sign of the continuing action of the Holy Spirit, but it is well to recall that in order to exercise this charism validly, one must observe and put into practice the indispensable conditions thereto. Lacking these conditions, the would-be prophet is merely an exhibitionist wasting the time of the entire People of God.

2. In order that a person be a suitable instrument in the diffusion of the Word of God, he *must necessarily give witness* to a life lived at high spiritual voltage. Only a saint can attract his brethren to follow along in advancing on the way of perfection. "Every soul that rises lifts up the world" (Elizabeth Leseur). What an illusion it is to want to write without knowing how to read, or to work without taking nourishment. Just so, we cannot be true and efficacious prophets if we do not nourish our souls continually at the fonts of divine grace.

3. This *Word of God* is *very necessary* for us. The animals have few problems and many infallible instincts. Men, on the other hand, have many problems and few sure and dependable instincts. Science makes us aware of our problems but it does not always give easy and adequate solutions; rather, sometimes it makes our problems even more complicated. It is only

the Word of God which explains the moral question marks of our existence, rendering it always more noble and worthy to be lived.

FIFTEENTH SUNDAY IN ORDINARY TIME:

Grace, the Exalting Purpose of Christianity

Readings: Amos 7:12-15
Ephesians 1:3-14
Mark 6:7-13

One of the principal aims of prophecy in religion is to manifest to men the design of their salvation. Now, this plan or mystery of salvation is put into effect through the gift of sanctifying grace. The second reading, taken from the letter of St. Paul to the Ephesians, gives us something like a brief theological and biblical synthesis of grace. The Apostle says to the Ephesians: "God chose us in him before the foundations of the world, that we should be holy and blameless before him. He destined us in love to be his sons—according to the purpose of his will, to the praise of his glorious grace which he freely bestowed on us in the Beloved."

In our efforts to express something on this topic we must confess that we are incapable of saying everything, for our poor human intellect cannot grasp such an infinitely vast theme, for the theme of grace is a reality as vast as the life of God Himself. By exclusion we can say that grace is not something like a vague fluid invisibly pervading our whole being; nor is it a philosophical abstraction which appeals to the nobility of our thought. Nor must we imagine that it is something added to our creaturehood as man, in such a way that we could distinguish between body, soul and grace. If this were so, grace would be something quantitative, while we know that it is really and totally immaterial. The sound Catholic and conciliar doctrine tells us that grace is the life of God within us, and conversely, our participation in the divine nature itself. As love is the meeting of two persons, grace is the vital communion between God and man.

Among the effects produced within us by this divine life, freely bestowed upon us by God (hence, the name "grace"), the most sublime is the transformation of our very soul. When two persons love each other they change psychologically. As there can be no change in God, the spiritual metamorphosis effected through grace is realized only and wholly in man. A crystal brought into contact with a source of light acquires an altogether new quality because of the light, though in size and weight it remains the same. So too the creature, man, invested with the invisible gift of grace, is transformed and sublimated ontologically. This is what we ordinarily call the state of grace. This renewal is effected in every dimension of the spirit: grace is ineffable light for the intellect; it is interior strength for the will, a mysterious yearning for supernatural love for the heart, and an urge toward solidarity with the whole universe. It is, in substance, divine life in action through which we, though continuing to remain earthly, become heavenly; though remaining sons of man by nature, become adopted children of God through the gift of supernature.

Another wonderful consequence of this divine life is the right to the glory of heaven. Between grace and glory there is really no difference in quality but only in development. As we are obliged to use comparisons in order to be understood less imperfectly, we might say that as the seed contains the plant, or as the negative film contains the beauty of the final photograph, so also grace is substantially all glory. With this grace "we are heaven and we go to heaven, we are children of God and therefore heirs, even if it is not yet evident in us what we shall eventually become."

Let it be said, finally, that all this transformation takes place through the powerful action of the humanity of Christ. Through His sacrificial human nature He has let us pass from the death of sin to the life of grace, and through His glorious body He will bring this grace to perfect fulfillment in glory. Because of this, Christ is our life and our resurrection.

This is the great truth unique to Christianity. At the beginning of human history the tempter blazed before men this ideal: "You will be like God!" When this project failed because of the sin of our first parents, humanity sought by itself to regain the lost state of perfection. But only with the coming of the Son of God was it possible to reestablish the vital rapport between God and man through the gratuitous gift of divine life. When the Lord created man He could say, "Man is mine!" Now with the possession of grace, man too can triumphantly affirm, "God is mine!"

Substantially, the Christian religion is nothing other than the religion of divine grace. Jesus came to bring us this divine life. The purpose, the soul, the real wealth of the messianic kingdom is the sharing, on the part of men, in the supernatural life of grace. When Holy Scripture speaks of "the end of time" and "the eschatological age" we must think not of the end of the history of salvation but of the time of grace, initiated by the Incarnation.

PASTORAL REFLECTIONS

1. The whole purpose of creation is to make man *live in communion with God.* The Old Testament finds its completion in the New, when the alliance between God and man is fashioned and enriched by this continual presence of God. The Church has reason to exist, to perdure in time in order to be the wellspring of grace and of mercy. A Christian is such only if he lives in the life of Christ, in this life of communion with the Blessed Trinity. Take away grace and everything loses its meaning, everything is reduced to an historical "nonsense," and religion becomes merely philosophy and sociology.

2. With Copernicus, we have lost geographic centrality. Our earth is no more the center of the universe

but only a tiny speck in the immense astronomic panorama. With Freud, we have lost anthropological centrality. With new technological findings we are now having to renounce even the primacy of action. There remains to us now only the *mystical centrality,* living in grace with God, the true deification of man.

3. Man is the perfection of the universe, the spirit is the perfection of man. Love is the perfection of the spirit, and *grace is the perfection of love.* Only the person who is adorned with supernatural grace is a complete success. Just as the fruit is the coronation of the plant, likewise grace—supernatural love freely given to us by God—is the completion of our nature. No one is so wholly man as is the saint.

SIXTEENTH SUNDAY IN ORDINARY TIME:

The Theology of Peace

Readings: Jeremiah 23:1-6
Ephesians 2:13-18
Mark 6:30-34

Nothing nowadays seems really stable and definite. What were believed to be liberations appear now as only new forms of slavery. The solutions of not a few problems are soon followed by other problems of greater magnitude. A civilization of well-being and of technical progress seems to involve ever more evident dangers of spiritual alienation and death. Anxieties and nervous disorders have become the common illnesses of the time. Yet everyone is always striving for peace; we are looking for it everywhere, we call upon it and defend it in every situation.

St. Paul, writing to the Ephesians, calls our attention to the true source of peace. The Apostle assures us: "For he is our peace, who made us both one, and has broken down the dividing wall of hostility, by abolishing in his flesh the law of commandments and ordinances, that he might create in himself one new man in place of the two, so making peace, and might reconcile us both to God in one body through the cross.... He came and preached peace to you who were afar off, and peace to those who were near; for through him we both have access in one Spirit to the Father" (Second Reading).

Let us identify some components of this Christian peace.

Peace can be built only upon the consideration that man is a creature of God, redeemed by Christ. Only in the light of the incarnation and the redemption does man cease to be "a wolf to the other man." Christ in becoming man has made Himself the defense of every other man, even to the point of identification in His statement, "As you did it not to one of the least of these, you did it not to me." With His passion He has thrown down every barrier that divides man from man, every distinction between Greek and Jew, between the circumcised and the uncircumcised, foreign, Scythian, slave and freedman (cf. Colossians 3:11). We are all like unto Him, related to Him. With the dignity and worth thus accruing to him because of Christ, man can flee from the anonymity of the masses as well as from self-exaltation, both of which are hindrances to the acquisition of peace. The very differences existing among men because of their endowments, their intelligence, their office, not infrequently arousing psychological division, antagonism, or jealousies, are overcome by one common denominator: man's worth in himself. Upon each man shines the face of Christ, and if this is once recognized, discord and antagonism will yield to concord and peace.

Every man, though a distinct individual, is at the same time a member of the one social body. Every human act has an inexorable, even if invisible, effect upon society. It follows then that the true followers of Christ, with their virtues, are living and vivifying nourishment within the society, affording it stability, harmony and peace. As a body has need of a spirit to move itself and act harmoniously, thus the state or nation has need of virtuous men to function properly. Furthermore, the grace which makes man the adopted son of God is already a substantial peace which grows and diffuses itself among others; it spreads as if contagious. The man who is at peace in his own spirit is a peace-bearer to society. The intellectual weakness of communism, for example, is that of wanting to achieve a hypothetical universal fraternity with the frail external means of economy. Even the laws of the state are of themselves insufficient for constructing peace; these laws touch only the surface of man and cannot shape him from within. Often too these very laws become occasion for subterfuge, for fear, and therefore are inadequate for the promotion of peace. How true it is that the more laws there are, the less peace there is. It should not be difficult then to convince ourselves that the religion of Christ, well understood and genuinely lived, sanctifies the man from within, making him able to practice the social virtues and consequently also to live in peace. It is with good reason that at the time of Tertullian the Christians, the saints, were always and everywhere considered the true harbingers of peace among men.

Almost without realizing it we have arrived at the consideration of the decisive element of peace, the theological element: Men can attain peace among themselves when "through him we both have access in one Spirit to the Father" (cf. Second Reading). The concept of the common fatherhood of God, together with the filial homage we render to Him, makes us not only companions but also brothers to each other. When Alexander the Great was planning to unite the East and the West, he thought of the universal paternity of God as a valid and essential element for holding the empires in unity. The Hebews called peace "Shalom," that is, rapport between God and His people. The pact of peace meant for them a greater obligation to orientate themselves to the friendship and paternity of God. Let us stress again that only when men decide to glorify God together will they find themselves on the sure path that leads to the enjoyment of peace. "Glory to God and peace to men" are the two correlative and integrating conditions for the progressive development of national and international peace. As if tracing a path to peace the psalmist exclaims, "Happy the people to whom such blessings fall! Happy the people whose God is the Lord!" (Psalm 144:15)

PASTORAL REFLECTIONS

1. Let us not hide the fact that all this *Christian teaching on peace* supposes an *effort and tension* on the part of the men of good will. Jesus Himself, the Prince of Peace, said that His mission was to bring division, not peace. A state of peace is not something that can be acquired once and for always, nor is it a static goal. It is rather an aim ever to be striven for, a road ever to be trod, an ideal ever to be sought after. It is human activity creative and progressive, like the balance of flight which at every instant must be upheld by a propelling dynamism. It is like one brick placed after another in the building up of a house.

2. Since peace is the greatest good for individuals, for families, for nations, for humanity, it is worth all our dedication, *all our collaboration*. It is good on occasion to check on our actions to see that they are directed to interior and exterior peace, to personal and social peace, to the Christian peace "which is beyond all understanding, which will stand guard over our hearts and minds, in Christ Jesus."

3. *The most valiant workers for peace must be the young.* Pope Paul VI, who during his pontificate gave us a valuable and abundant catechesis for youth, very often invited these young people to be constructors of love and of peace. In his discourse of January 1, 1978, the Pontiff reaffirmed the appeal he had already proclaimed earlier (December 22, 1977), by exhorting the great mass of good and Christian youth: "We chose to

conclude our recent Message for Peace Day with an appeal to young people and children all over the world.... You, too, young people and children, have a word, a fresh, new and original word to say and to make adults hear. Say this word of peace.... In your ideals and in your behavior, always give priority to love, that is, to understanding, benevolence, and solidarity with others. Strengthen your conviction about peace in personal and community prayer, in exchanges of views and in meditations...and above all in the sacrament of the Holy Eucharist...: strengthen it finally in filial devotion to the Virgin Mary. You, young people and children, bear within you the future of the world and of history. This world will be a better one, it will be more brotherly and more just, if already, right from the present time, your life is open to grace, to the ideal of love and peace that the Gospel teaches you."

SEVENTEENTH SUNDAY IN ORDINARY TIME:

Christian Sense of Community

Readings: 2 Kings 4:42-44
Ephesians 4:1-6
John 6:1-15

Not seldom have we given thought to the many and interesting components of the Church of God.

As Jesus is true God and true man, having divine nature while being perfectly human, so also is His Mystical Body, the Church. St. Paul and St. John have highlighted the Church as "Koinonia." First of all it indicates having a part in the ineffable life of the Most Holy Trinity. In consequence of this meaning and reflexive to it the term denotes, secondly, existence and life in common with the brethren. In the third place the word signifies also the need to share with others the gifts we have received. In the life of the Mystical Body of Christ there are channels of communication which we can term "vertical" and others which we generally call "horizontal." Vatican Council II also exhorts us to see the Mystical Body in this double dimension, celestial and terrestrial, that is, as a body which receives everything from its Head to give itself to the brethren. This is the dynamic aspect of the cross.

Let us explain further. The true life of the Church is within: she is the very Body of the Lord, fused in the most complete unity. There are various kinds of unity: psychological, that of having the same ideas and sentiments; operative unity, in which the individuals are engaged in the same activity; domestic unity, that of a common dwelling for the members; there is also theological unity, which is realized when the different persons pursue the same goal. Unity as communion of the faithful is far superior to all these in quality and is unattainable by them: it is participation in the Mystical Body, "one faith, one baptism, one God and Father of us all, who is above all and through all and in all" (Second Reading).

But all this perfection must bear fruit externally, in the social context, through the faithful. The vital unity of the Head must permeate the members for the benefit of all mankind. It is at this point that there arises the difference of application of the same divine gifts, when these are received and distributed to others. Man is soul and body; for this reason, even his supernatural activities such as faith, hope, charity and prayer acquire different modulations. The same gifts come to be interpreted in personal and specific ways. Just as in the Trinity there is unity in the nature and distinction in the persons; as the actions of Jesus all had the same dignity as the actions of the Son of God, but were all different and varied as projections of His human nature, so also are the essence and the actions of the Mystical Body of Christ.

From what we have said so far we can conclude that the Mystical Body of Christ is specifically a "community of brothers," in which—except for the diversity of ministries—there exists a true equality of dignity through the possession of divine life, through the vocation to sanctity. It was not for nothing that the Conciliar Constitution on the Church dedicated an entire chapter (the fourth) to this dignity of the People of God, at the same time speaking of the Church as a hierarchy. Another thing to be remembered is this: it would be an error of ecclesial perspective to see the unity in the Church and of the Church as something uniform and monolithic, without the possibility of operative variations, just as it would also be erroneous to canonize as "ecclesial" all the social gestures carried out in the name of the Church but without the distinctive mark of the unity of faith, of hope, of baptism, of communion with the life of the Lord. Finally, it is right to recall that while the parts of the Mystical Body explain their actions in time and in history, they continually and increasingly make us aware of the need of communion with Christ the Head and with the brother members of the same supernatural organism.

PASTORAL REFLECTIONS

1. Our first reflection, taken from the words of Pope Paul VI, is doctrinal. "For a Christian, *renewal is a continuing program.* The Aristotelian principle of the fixed center while the circle around is moving, well reflects the Christian life. Fixity and newness; these terms belong essentially and simultaneously to Christian life.... This combination between fixity in faith, hope and charity, fidelity and authenticity, and of tension towards the inexhaustible exploration of revealed truth, in the lively resourcefulness of the imitation of Christ and of service, always new, always inventive, for the salvation of brothers, should be one of the constant aspirations of the real Christian." And as we remain attached to Christ

and to the riches of the Church, "our capacity of resistance to the revolutionary spirit characteristic of our century, and at the same time of victorious emulation in impressing on our Christian life an agility of movement, a geniality of beneficial operations, a freshness of spiritual, apostolic and artistic expressions, should remind us of the genius of Christianity...." In such a manner we show "fidelity to the risen Christ who will never die again," as well as our solidarity with others, with the world. "And this binomial of fixity and newness should always be present, and provide an answer, both doctrinal and practical, to the great modern question of how to be authentic faithful Christians, free and rooted in truth, in forms of life that cannot undergo variations, and how to be fervent and always straining towards new forms of life always rich in innovations and progress..." (Paul VI, General Audience, April 25, 1972).

2. *Holiness is essentially communitarian.* We are saints, we are saved insofar as we are one and are united in one. Now in this era of profound divisions, of necessary specializations in work and in new forms of apostolate, it is not bad to preserve one's Christian authenticity and one's proper personality in action, at the same time strengthening this union or rather toning it with the manifold life of the Mystical Body of Christ.

3. If we wish to do our part in the building up of the Mystical Body of Christ, let us not disdain the zealous practice of three virtues: *"complete selflessness, gentleness and patience"* (Second Reading). The first is a filial attitude of submission and obligation toward God for the gifts He has bestowed so freely; the second, gentleness, is the indication of our insertion in the spiritual organism which is the Church; and finally patience, which in the biblical sense is gratuity of love and concern for others, makes us suitable instruments for promoting and spreading in the Church the variety of gifts unto the fullness of the total Christ, "Head and members."

EIGHTEENTH SUNDAY IN ORDINARY TIME:

The Vesture of a Christian

Readings: Exodus 16:2-4, 12-15
Ephesians 4:17, 20-24
John 6:24-35

In biblical terminology, one's dress has not only the purpose of protecting and covering the person, but also of revealing his personality and of indicating his interior sentiments, his invisible moral dimension. According to biblical language, for example, to be naked is to be blameworthy before God, as Adam and Eve felt after their fall in the garden of Eden. Nudity is also a sign of depersonalization, for it casts down the person into the chaos of indistinction, from which God has ever been trying to free him. To change one's dress indicates a more profound change, the transformation of one's mentality. The relation between the clothing and the person who wears it is also evident in the fact that for an interior purification the Israelites were told to wash their garments (Exodus 19:10); while growing in spiritual nobility is evinced in the wearing of better clothing. Jesus, absolute perfection, was always irreproachable in His attire, even to the identification of His interior splendor with the radiance of His garment.

To give to another one's own clothing, one's coat, signified, according to the prophets, to give one's own person as a sign of friendship and goodness. The love of God Himself toward His children is taught in the parable of a father who clothed his returned son with festive robes. Nor is it to be forgotten that clothes were the mark of an office received from God. The consecration of a king consisted in the purification, the imposition of the robe, and the anointing; the imposition of the robe was a very important moment, the whole ceremony taking its name from this solemn function of "investiture." As is very well known, the people confirmed the choice of a king by laying their garments along the way he was to pass.

Again, to be invested in a new garment meant in the Scriptures to be admitted to the divine intimacy, as when a woman clothes herself as a bride to enter into the family of her husband. Even the elect of heaven will be clothed in new shining apparel, washed in the blood of the Lamb (Revelation 7:14). And at the end of time, when God will roll up the heaven and the earth like a dress that has finished its function, all the elect vested in a "stole of sanctity" and a "garment of innocence" will make up the new Jerusalem which, adorned like an incomparable bride, will advance toward the Spouse,to be forever illumined by the splendor of the Lamb (Revelation 21:23).

If attire has such importance in biblical thought, it is not surprising that St. Paul uses this terminology to instruct his faithful. He uses especially two verbs: "lay aside" and "put on," to emphasize the negative and the positive aspect of Christian asceticism. This Sunday we read in the letter to the Ephesians: "Now this I affirm and testify in the Lord, that you must no longer live as the Gentiles do, in the futility of their minds; they are darkened.... You did not so learn Christ! ...assuming that you have heard about him and were taught in him, as the truth is in Jesus. Put off your old nature which belongs to your former manner of life and is corrupt through deceitful lusts, and be renewed in the spirit of your minds, and put on the new nature, created after the likeness of God in true righteousness and holiness" (Second Reading).

A follower of Christ is above all one who divests himself of everything purely mundane, of everything that makes up the old man. The true Christian is one who is ever on the watch to free himself from all that could darken or soil his dignity as son of God. Every baptized person, called to walk in newness of life, does not become a slave of human powers and passions, he does not run after idols, nor does he surrender spiritually to worldly compromises, to deception. He does not allow himself to be used as a tool of wicked ideologies, nor does he run after money or use the ethics of "convenience." He does not servilely conform to the dictates of modern fashions in opposition to the dictates of his own conscience, knowing very well that this world passes away.

At the end of this process of purification and tension is the conquest of the real beauty of the new man, as God created him in the beginning in justice and holiness. We all know that the biblical meaning of the word *justice* is the sum of all virtues.

It is again St. Paul who in the same letter to the Ephesians tells us what ought to be the coat of mail of this "armor of God"; he names truth as the belt around the waist, justice as breastplate, zeal as footgear, faith as shield, the word of God as the helmet of salvation and the sword of the spirit. Thus panoplied and armed, the Christian enters decisively into the movement of salvation initiated by Christ, accepted by men of good will.

PASTORAL REFLECTIONS

1. *Life is a gift to be transformed into a conquest, into victory.* Everything in man is fertile tension. He is born a child, but must struggle to become an adult. His life is fundamentally channeled toward virtue, but he himself must direct it toward the happy fulfillment of this purpose. He is immersed in nature, in things, in concupiscence, but he has the power to become free from every earthly conditioning, learning to renounce, to make valid and sublime choices. Man is born with the power of love, intermingled with so many other passions, but it is his duty to become a lover of what has true value. The person who is really alive is the one who has the courage to divest himself continually of all that is secondary, fallible and transitory, to put on what is authentic, necessary and eternal.

2. St. Paul invites us to begin our renewal by acquiring a fresh, spiritual way of thinking (Second Reading). We must not forget that for classical theology, the intellect always signifies *"passage" toward the truth.* Christianity might be defined as a religion of "Unless...." The Lord said, "Unless you turn and become like children, you will never enter the kingdom of heaven"; "Unless you repent you will all likewise perish"; and in our case, "Unless your holiness surpasses that of the scribes and Pharisees, you shall not enter the kingdom of God."

3. The *whole work of redemption is a great work of renewal.* But the new creation, of which the Scripture speaks, begins and is realized with the renewal of man: *only through man can the universe be renewed.*

> Lord, we cannot understand Your love
> in entrusting such serious tasks to us
> despite our weakness.
> We are so filled with calculations and egoism,
> so lacking in confidence and strength.
> If You want us to serve You in some way,
> clothe us with Yourself, O Lord.
> If You desire that we remain
> "salt," "yeast," "light,"
> keep us united to Yourself.
> Lord, let us understand
> that to be Your followers
> means above all to be in the front line
> to free man from egoism and from sin.

NINETEENTH SUNDAY IN ORDINARY TIME:

Fraternal Love

Readings: 1 Kings 19:4-8
Ephesians 4:30—5:2
John 6:41-51

St. Paul the Apostle solemnly reminds us of the great duty of mutual love. In his letter to the Ephesians he writes: "Let all bitterness and wrath, and anger, and clamor, and slander, be put away from you, with all malice, and be kind to one another, tenderhearted, forgiving one another as God in Christ forgave you. Therefore be imitators of God as beloved children. And walk in love, as Christ loved us and gave himself for us, a fragrant offering and sacrifice to God" (Second Reading). The passage is like a brief theological synthesis of the love of neighbor, and it brings into focus the four fundamental characteristics of love: the true essence of love, a model to imitate, the faults which love avoids (negative aspect), and the good it offers instead (positive aspect).

True love is not sentimentalism, it is not mere human sympathy, it is not physiological or romantic emotion. True love does not seek its own advantage, satisfaction or pleasure; it is not egoism or utilitarianism; rather it is essentially the continuing will to give joy to others. It is a going out of oneself to give self to the neighbor; not the giving of some thing, which may be an act of justice, but the giving of self. In biblical language this love is given an unusual name: *agape,* which means effusive goodness, belonging only to God and to those who have been signed by the Holy Spirit.

If a person wishes to be certain of the authenticity of this love, it suffices to compare it with the way Jesus loved. The love of Jesus for men was a total love, full and perfect in a fourfold direction: He gave His whole self as gift; He offered Himself for all creatures, for all time, and in all circumstances. Furthermore, His love was inclined especially toward sinners, it was preferentially abundant for His very enemies.

The program of goodness can be put into practice, taking as first step the exercise of patience with one's neighbor. The virtue of patience is not capitulation, the acceptance of an evil without alternative; it is rather trust. Christian patience is synonymous with hope. The follower of Christ accepts sufferings and social tensions as the farmer sustains the fatigue of the fields, as the sower awaits the fruits of the seed planted in the earth, as the soldier fights for ultimate victory. The truly patient man is not the one who with clenched teeth puts up with his neighbor, but the one who endures the buffets of living together in order to insert himself effectively in the vital flow of the death of Christ, thus to be worthy of resurrection and of life. In actual life, one is truly patient who knows how to wait without getting tired, who does not deceive even though he knows others have been deceiving him, who does not harbor rancor though he is disliked, who permits his statements to be misinterpreted and artfully twisted and put into a bad light, who knows how to say a friendly word to his neighbor after having had to correct a wrong interpretation. One who practices the high ideal of patience in his daily living knows how to lose without lamenting and is able to begin all over again, he knows how to love others without expecting anything in return from them, he remains calm and serene when everything seems to be a failure. He can do all this because for him patience is hope: laboring in love and showing steadfastness of hope (cf. 1 Thessalonians 1:3). And in this sense "his patience is never conquered, but it conquers and always remains the master" (St. Catherine of Siena).

But the most beautiful aspect of the program of charity is positive, the giving of one's own self according to the teaching of the Master: "Greater love has no man than this, that a man lay down his life for his friends." (John 15:13). Sullivan, a 42-year-old man, was working at the Consolidated Edison plant as a maintenance mechanic. One morning while he and his colleagues were inspecting a motor they were struck by the explosion of a heater. The other two died on the spot, while Sullivan offered a piteous spectacle. The explosion and heat had imprisoned the victims and he was literally burned so much that not a single square inch of sound skin could be found. Immediately he was taken to a hospital, but a team of doctors gave him only a few hours to live. Nevertheless they set to work on him and calculated how much good skin he would need if he should survive the crisis. They looked for volunteers to donate good skin for Sullivan.

Thanks to his robust constitution the poor unfortunate man managed to survive the crisis predicted by the doctors, but soon afterwards a second crisis with complications came upon him: he was attacked by asphixiation caused by the lack of respiration of the scorched skin. An immediate skin transplant was urgent. His friends of the Edison plant were alerted. At once seventy of them offered themselves at the office of the hospital to donate some centimeters of skin so that Sullivan could live. The next morning twenty more came. The team of doctors—originally ten but increased to thirty—worked incessantly, taking turns to do the transplants. They effected quite a miracle: they saved Robert Sullivan. This example of heroic love and self-giving happened in 1950.

In our effort to interpret the words "kindness, compassion, forgiveness" (Second Reading) and strike the goldmine of wealth contained therein, we have found St. Paul's words most effective and have therefore formulated a Pauline code of Christian goodness:

1. Live in harmony with one another...associate with the lowly (Romans 12:16).

2. Rejoice with those who rejoice, weep with those who weep (Romans 12:15).

3. "Let each of you look not only to his own interests, but also to the interests of others (Philippians 2:4); bear one another's burdens, and so fulfill the law of Christ (Galatians 6:2).

4. Contribute to the needs of the saints, practice hospitality (Romans 12:13); welcome one another, therefore as Christ has welcomed you, for the glory of God (Romans 15:7).

5. Put on then, as God's chosen ones, holy and beloved, compassion, kindness, lowliness, meekness and patience (Colossians 3:12), forbearing one another... forgiving each other (Colossians 3:13).

6. Bless those who persecute you, bless and do not curse them (Romans 12:14). Repay no one evil for evil, but take thought for what is noble in the sight of all (Romans 12:17).

7. If a man is overtaken in any trespass, you who are spiritual should restore him in a spirit of gentleness (Galatians 6:1).

8. Let love be genuine; hate what is evil, hold fast to what is good (Romans 12:9).

9. Be eager to maintain the unity of the Spirit in the bond of peace. There is one body and one Spirit (Ephesians 4:3-4).

10. May the Lord make you increase and abound in love to one another and to all men (1 Thessalonians 3:12); and so fulfill the law of Christ (Galatians 6:2).

PASTORAL REFLECTIONS

1. In this our civilization when technology and industry give evidence of being able to satisfy so many of our material and pleasurable needs, some exponents of anti-religious—or simply non-religious—mentality think that the Church is something useless for the attainment of the aims of human solidarity. Instead, *it is only the Church which has the operative genius of charity.* The Church has always shown understanding and intuition for all the serious problems of man, more than has any other social organization. Only the Catholic Church has consecrated entire lives to the "sociology of charity"; the Catholic Church has been and will always be the mother who "inspires, guides, sustains, transfigures, sanctifies her children that they may be able to see and serve their neighbor as they would see and serve Jesus, giving themselves as persons to another person."

2. *To love means to be for others.* He loves who makes the sufferings of others his own, who is concerned about the problems of others, who knows how to share the joys of his brethren. He is able to love who knows how to give himself to another even in little things. To *give* may be justice; to *give oneself* is charity.

We shall be judged not according to how many talents we have received, but how we have used them; not only on our vertical relations with heaven, but also on the horizontal plane of the needs of those like ourselves. "How can you love God whom you do not see, if you do not love your brother?" exclaims St. John the Evangelist of charity. The pilgrim way of the human race would certainly be more easy and more beautiful if there were a greater number of "good Samaritans," of Christians who knew how to love in the name of Christ and at His bidding.

3. Borrowing some thoughts from Raoul Follereau, the Apostle of the Lepers, who died in 1977, let us together make *this resolution: Let us love one another!* We must love each other! We must love all, not at a fixed time, but always. Love the poor, love the rich, often very poor in spiritual goods. Love those who are near, love those afar who are unknown. Charity has no limits; it is the immense breath of God whose very essence is charity. Our Holy Father emphasized the same thought: "Love for one's neighbor, social love, if it is to be genuine, strong, inexhaustible, and therefore holy and truly Christian, must have its source in love of God, in religious love" (Paul VI, April 19, 1978).

TWENTIETH SUNDAY IN ORDINARY TIME:

The Food of the Soul

Readings: Proverbs 9:1-6
Ephesians 5:15-20
John 6:51-58

In these Sundays of summer the liturgy invites us to meditate often on the Sacrament of the Eucharist, that is, on Holy Communion. Jesus told the crowds: " 'I am the living bread which came down from heaven; if anyone eats of this bread, he will live forever; and the bread which I shall give for the life of the world is my flesh.'

The Jews then disputed among themselves, saying, 'How can this man give us his flesh to eat?' So Jesus said to them, 'Truly, truly, I say to you, unless you eat the flesh of the Son of Man and drink his blood, you have no life in you; he who eats my flesh and drinks my blood has eternal life, and I will raise him up at the last day. For my flesh is food indeed, and my blood is drink indeed. He who eats my flesh and drinks my blood abides in me, and I in him. As the living Father sent me, and I live because of the Father, so he who eats me will live because of me. This is the bread which came down from heaven, not such as the fathers ate and died; he who eats this bread will live forever'' (John 6:51-58).

Jesus takes us on our weakest point—our desire to eat—and offers us this bread. No less than six times He insists very solemnly on the necessity of eating His flesh and drinking His blood. Why all this preoccupation on His part? The need for this Eucharistic communion arises above all from the fact that through baptism the Christian has received the gift of supernatural life, and to sustain this life he needs corresponding and adequate nourishment. To sustain our bodily life we must have material food; to sustain the life of the spirit (intellect and will) the nutriment of truth and goodness is indispensable; similarly, for the supernatural life of the soul, it cannot do without this heavenly bread. It is easy to see that the desire for Holy Communion is the sign of a healthy and efficient spiritual organism. Just as in our bodily life, if one eats too little or has no desire for food we fear that he is unwell, similarly, if one has no appetite or taste for the Eucharist, we have reason to doubt his supernatural health. If the Lord has given Himself to us under the form of bread, He has surely done so to convince us of the frequency with which we must partake of His great gift. Bread is the most common and familiar type of food; it is the universal nourishment of men, it is a food always palatable and desirable, even if we have it in abundance. And just as our physical life always has need of material bread, so our spiritual life has constant need of nourishment. For this reason the Lord invites us at every Mass: "Take and eat, this is my Body; take and drink, this is my Blood." Not without reason has Vatican Council II defined Christians as "a people journeying toward eternity, led and nourished by Christ" (cf. On the Church, 48), somewhat as the Hebrews journeyed through the desert toward the promised land, providentially sustained by manna.

Not only is the Eucharist a food which develops our spiritual organism and maintains it in vigor, this sacrament is also "divine life, eternal life." In the magnificent discourse of our Lord on the promise of the Eucharist, which we can read in the sixth chapter of the Gospel of St. John, Jesus insists on the qualitative equivalence of Eucharist and Life. In Holy Communion we come to possess physically the very Savior, fountain of life and holiness. He who eats His flesh and drinks His blood "remains in him," lives in Him, is assimilated to Him. Yet more: in receiving Christ, we become mystically and mysteriously in contact with the Father and the Holy Spirit, as they have the same divine nature though they are distinct Persons. It is precisely through Holy Communion that man can harbor the celestial Trinity. This is the very peak of our nobility and our authentic personality.

Certainly we should never succeed in comprehending all the marvel of this donation if we did not know that God is Love. It is this love which seeks to enter into our souls as interior and vital nourishment; it is this love which sacrifices itself, abases itself to our own lowliness, even to the point of taking the form of bread so that we can receive this divine life; it is this divine love which ennobles us, sanctifies us, divinizes us. Thus does Christ love us. He loves us in our lowliness, He descends to our misery, He seeks out our weakness, He makes Himself available to our indolence, amiable to our nature, desirable to our sentiments. In the presence of the Eucharist, every man, woman, youth and child, every person infirm, poor, abandoned, tired, rejected, every sinner can be sure that God loves him even to making him one of His own household, His intimate friend, life of His very life.

If this is so, it is not difficult to believe that Christ Himself awaits us at His banquet table: "Come to me, all who labor and are heavy laden, and I will give you rest" (Matthew 11:28). And there is no point in repeating that Holy Communion is not a reward for the good, but it is a food, a medicine for all who want to remain spiritually healthy and to grow in divine life. It was to make it ever easier to approach the Eucharist that the Church has relaxed the disciplinary rules for the reception of Holy Communion, so that every person can easily "taste and see that the Lord is good" (Responsorial Psalm).

PASTORAL REFLECTIONS

1. We must always think of the *Eucharist* as the *sign of the love of God* for us. In the Incarnation the Invisible has made Himself visible, and in the Eucharist He has made Himself all goodness. The Eucharist is the supreme manifestation of the incomparable love of God for the human race. Christ has instituted the Holy Eucharist and has willed to remain with us even to the end of the world, as a faithful and sacred testimony of all the ineffable divine love in the Most Holy Trinity. St. Thomas Aquinas came so far as to affirm that Jesus loved man so much as if man were his God and he could not be happy without him.

2. *The Eucharist is the reason for the existence of the Church.* The Church and the Eucharist are like two arms of one cross, like two pulsations of one heart. From all eternity the Father presents to the world the image of Himself in the Word, His uncreated Word; the Virgin presents to the world the incarnate Word, and the Church presents to the world the Eucharistic Word. The Church herself has in the Eucharist the source of her own life

and being. The Eucharist is the principal manifestation of the life of the Church. The very perfection of the Church is here, in the Eucharist. At a Wednesday general audience Pope Paul said: "Let us give supreme importance, sons and brothers, to the Eucharist, particularly in holy Mass, the heart of our religion, and in communion with Christ, the Bread of life, which it offers us. Doing so, we will have given to our faith its highest expression, to the Church her genuine vitality, to our souls the school and food of our sanctification, to the world itself the beacon of its unity and peace..." (Pope Paul VI, May 31, 1972).

3. If God is "Emmanuel," that is, "God with us," it is precisely through the *Eucharist that He can remain always with us, to lead us to the Father.* "The true and real sacramental presence of Christ Himself is offered to us...as a sacrificial nourishment for our present pilgrimage towards eternal life" (Paul VI, December 14, 1977). It is this, His real presence, peak point of our meeting with the Divinity in time, which prepares and draws us toward the mysterious ocean of the other life, toward the fullness of joy and glory (cf. Paul VI, June 15, 1977).

TWENTY-FIRST SUNDAY IN ORDINARY TIME:

Conjugal Harmony

Readings: Joshua 24:1-2, 15-17, 18
Ephesians 5:21-32
John 6:60-69

Love is most sublime because God is love, and at the same time it is most abused for it is a reality known to everyone. Today so much is being said about love; there are premarital conferences and meetings on establishing wholesome and happy families, on giving the couples a greater realization of their sublime vocation of living together. We feel, however, that we are not simply being pessimistic when we affirm that this conjugal love has never been so menaced and abused as it is in our time. Among the many reasons that concur for the warping of marital love we can mention the flood of erotic and pornographic literature together with an ever increasing avalanche of other mass media presenting morbid and unseemly aspects of married life. Another reason may be the wholly unscientific pseudo culture which identifies love with sex, as if true love did not embrace, beyond the aspect of sex, affective, rational and supernatural dimensions. The dissolution of the true concept of love has been augmented by not a few socially responsible men who for their own private interests do not hesitate to be accomplices in the break-up of family life, childishly confusing libertinism with liberty, permissiveness with creativity.

There is also, especially in our day, the "plague of divorce." This imposes on the spouses the obligation to preserve their mutual love. The family is the fundamental unit on which society is built, the unit through which other values are tested for validity. Through the authenticity of the family the other social institutions are influenced. Furthermore, in the event of sad calamities, comfort and refuge can be sought and found in the family circle and family love. But, where conjugal love is lacking, all else is inexorably compromised with no way of escape.

St. Paul reminds us on this Sunday, in the name of the Church, that the most beautiful aspect of love is that of the supernatural donation of self. Writing to the Christians of Ephesus he tells them: "As the church is subject to Christ, so let wives be subject in everything to their husbands. Husbands, love your wives, as Christ loved the church, and he gave himself up for her, that he may sanctify her.... Husbands should love their wives as their own bodies. He who loves his wife loves himself..." (Second Reading).

Let us try to understand this Pauline thought as encompassed in this simple reflection: If spouses wish to maintain and further their reciprocal love, they must do so as Christ did for His mystical Spouse, the Church.

First of all, the spouses must regard themselves and give themselves as creatures of God, as beings loved by Christ, as persons for whom the Lord has set a great ideal of sanctity and of eternity. They must love each other, furthermore, seeking in the partner not a person to be used for egotistic ends, but a soul to be completed, to be enriched, to be beautified with the delicate outpouring of fruitful and sacrificial love. To be able to arrive at this supernatural love, it is indispensable that they approach it from the exterior. Love, like the heart, has two motions: to give and to receive. No one can effectively love others unless he continually fills himself with love. No one can give what he does not possess. The fire of love is kept burning only if it is nourished and communicated; otherwise it goes out. The true source of love between spouses is the Lord. Love is tri-personal: he, the husband; she, the wife; and God. Without God and His grace, wedded love can hardly maintain itself perennially diffusive. According to the teaching of the Bible and Christian tradition, it is the Lord who can purify, refresh, invigorate, and make fruitful this human love, when it is united to Him and draws its sustenance from Him through the liturgy and the sacraments. This love, received from the prime source of all love, God, can be bestowed in various ways for the benefit of the partner, in the manner of the sanctifying love of Christ which has produced in His Church the seven sacraments.

Authentic spousal love is humble respect for the specific differences of personality of one's consort; it is ready help in any need, whether physical or psychic; it is smiling indulgence for the inevitable foibles of the one or the other; it is patient anxiety to repair to the full any lack of communication which may have occurred. This Christian love is ever ready to lay aside the fulfillment of one's pleasure in order to give pleasure to the partner; it is a constant desire to offer one's own time and person in order to grow in spiritual affection; it is, finally, mutual love and self-donation in all times and circumstances, with the same heart and enthusiasm with which the two spouses pledged their love and fidelity at the altar. Conjugal accord is, to sum up, fashioned dynamically on the mystical model of the union of Christ with His Church.

PASTORAL REFLECTIONS

1. *To wed is easy, to foster mutual love in this way is to follow the divine pattern.* To live together may be a necessity, but to live together supernaturally means to make of our home the temple of God and the cathedral of true family joy. It is to exclaim with St. Paul: "God's temple is holy, and that temple you are!" (cf. 1 Corinthians 3:17).

2. *The eight beatitudes of the family:*

—Blessed is the family that prays; the Lord will be present in its midst.

—Blessed is the family in which Sundays and holydays are sanctified; it will be like a little heaven on earth.

—Blessed is the family that does not patronize immoral entertainments which disturb the heart and rob it of peace.

—Blessed is the family in which no evil literature enters, no equivocal discussions, to intemperance, no irreverent language, because thus it will be like a garden of God.

—Blessed is the family in which the children receive Baptism as early as possible and are thus initiated into the supernatural life of the Church.

—Blessed is the family in which the priest is welcome, accepted, when he comes to visit the sick, to administer the sacraments, thus making of the home a little church.

—Blessed is the family in which the Gospels are read and meditated upon, and the Holy Bible is the supreme law guiding all thoughts and actions.

—Blessed is the family in which the parents are consoled and obeyed by their children, where the children are lovingly protected and trained by the parents, where the elderly are surrounded by affection and delicate attention, and where all the members emulate the Holy Family of Nazareth.

3. *True love is without limits, even in life.* Most men see in matrimony an event added to life. The truth is, instead, that matrimony is the central event of the whole life. If love is authentic, it lasts beyond death. The great French biologist, Louis Pasteur, discoverer of micro-organisms, died on September 28, 1895, holding in his right hand the crucifix and in his left the hand of his wife. Love is the most powerful force of the world. It needs time, or rather eternity, to be able to flourish and mature completely, in divine joy.

TWENTY-SECOND SUNDAY IN ORDINARY TIME:

The Offering of the Heart: The Right Intention

Readings: Deuteronomy 4:1-2, 6-8
James 1:17-18, 21-22, 27
Mark 7:1-8, 14-15, 21-23

The Jewish religion prescribed many purifications and ablutions for man to be acceptable to God. Christianity centers instead on the interior: purity of heart and the right intention. In biblical understanding the heart is the center of man's interior faculties, the very core of the personality, the volition, the essence of the spiritual ego. To refuse to give the heart to God is to sever the true and profound relation with the divinity. While to offer the heart to the Lord is not only to satisfy the duty of filial submission; it is also to give praise and glory to the Creator, the Father from whom comes "every good endowment, and every perfect gift" (Second Reading).

If this is so, it is no wonder that Christ insisted and urged so much that His followers make a genuine offering of their very heart. He manifested His displeasure when an act of worship offered to God was purely exterior and insincere. " 'This people honors me with their lips, but their heart is far from me; in vain do they worship me....' He called the people to him again and said to them, 'From within, out of the heart of man, come evil thoughts, fornication, theft, murder, adultery, coveting, wickedness, deceit, licentiousness, envy, slander, pride, foolishness. All these evil things come from within and they defile a man' " (Third Reading). Elsewhere Jesus says: "If your eyes are good, your body will be filled with light; if your eyes are bad, your body will be in darkness."

Taking impetus from the gospel of this Sunday, we shall offer some reflections on the delicate theme of the right intention, the projection of a pure and immaculate heart. The intention of a person is extremely important in relation to his moral life; it is like the sap of a tree. According to whether the sap is good or bad, the tree will yield good or bad fruits. The intention is the moral matrix which in a religious sense classifies our actions to be positive or negative, provided these actions are not in themselves morally bad. Every action of ours gets its moral coloring according to the intention with which we do it. Thus if a person gives an alms to a poor man so as to be seen and praised for it, then he is proud. If he gives the alms merely to show his human solidarity, he is merely a gentleman. But if he helps a poor man with alms because he sees Christ in the poor, then he has done an act worthy of a Christian, an act that is meritorious. The blossoms thrown into the air by St. Rose of Lima with the express intention of giving glory to God, formed a luminous cross in the air as a token of divine approbation. The blossoms tossed up by her little brother Ferdinand just fell to the ground in obedience to the normal laws of gravitation, for the little child merely wanted to have some fun. It is not the actions in themselves that have value before the Lord, but the purity of purpose. It is not our actions which really define us, but the intention of our heart which renders us acceptable or less pleasing to God. He looks not so much at the gift but rather at the heart of the giver. In the eyes of the Lord, it does not matter whether one works with a hammer or a pen, with a chisel or a compass. It does not matter whether he thunders great speeches in parliament or in a cathedral, or flies through space at a fantastic speed or does hidden labor in a little corner of his own house. No, the Lord looks into our hearts as into a book and there He measures the true nobility of each soul. To Him an act of love is worth more than the whole universe; the right intention is to the Lord like a heaven of light.

Through the right intention we can overcome the tension between action and prayer; the very work we do becomes a dialogue with God, a prayer. Just as in the Mass, the words of consecration change the substance of the bread and wine, so with our intention we can change and transform all our actions into hymns of praise. Our little round of daily chores can often be so boring and commonplace; but if through the good intention these acts are bound together with the golden thread of love, they become parts of a personal liturgy of glorification to the Creator of heaven and earth. Through the liturgy in the Church, the Christian praises the Lord in the temple. Through the good intention he glorifies Him in the house, in his social environment, in the whole universe. No longer is there a separation between contemplation and action, but rather a link, an integration. Martha works with the heart of Mary, thus prolonging in time the human element of the Incarnation and the divine to the praise of the Most Holy Trinity.

As a final thought, we may not forget that in resolving to do everything for the love of God the Christian derives great peace and serenity. The spring and source of the interior joy of Pope John XXIII was mainly his will to do everything for the greater glory of God and to live at every instant according to the divine pleasure. It is well known that "Good Pope John" lived in the presence of the Lord with the simplicity of a child reposing in the arms of his mother. Because of his right intention he always enjoyed in his heart "a continual feast." It is true that bread, like liberty, is indispensable for man, but the testimony of a good conscience is everything for one who desires to live in joy.

PASTORAL REFLECTIONS

1. A person who travels to a foreign country may be carrying much money with him, but he can buy nothing with it until he exchanges it for local currency. In the spiritual realm: one can have and do so many things, but only through the proper exchange made with the *right intention* can we communicate with the country of God and merit for ourselves not reproof but divine approbation. "O Lord, who shall sojourn in your tent?... He who walks blamelessly, and does what is right" (Responsorial Psalm).

2. *There are two modes of doing one's work:* through fear or through love. The first is that of spiritual slavery, the second, the liberty of the children of God. When we came into the world the Lord placed into the hand of each one of us a packet of bills of exchange. The amounts written are not important; that which validates the sum, whatever it is, is only the authentic signature. In the sight of heaven the one signature that counts consists of these five words: "Done for love of God."

3. *This is the source of our joy.* Not to be understood by our neighbor is surely a cause of sadness and of solitude. However, to know that God observes us, that He understands and loves us; this is the purest joy which annuls all our sadness. The certainty that God understands us to the most intimate recesses of our being is like a reflection and radiance of the joys of paradise.

TWENTY-THIRD SUNDAY IN ORDINARY TIME:

The Use of Riches

Readings: Isaiah 35:4-7
James 2:1-5
Mark 7:31-37

The prophet Isaiah presented the future Messiah as one who would come to save all the unfortunate and poor: "Then the eyes of the blind shall be opened, the ears of the deaf unstopped, then shall the lame man leap like a hart, and the tongue of the dumb sing for joy.... The burning sand shall become a pool, and the thirsty ground springs of water" (First Reading). As we know, when Christ is to present to the Jewish people His credentials as the Messiah, He calls their attention to the fact that He has been sent by the Father to every sort of poor. When He responds to the disciples of St. John the Baptist He quotes almost verbatim the prophecy of Isaiah: "Go and tell John what you hear and see: the blind receive their sight and the lame walk, lepers are cleansed and the deaf hear, and the dead are raised up, and the poor have the good news preached to them" (Matthew 11:4-5).

St. James in the five chapters of his only letter prefers to develop the theme of poverty in the strict and literal sense of economic poverty, stating quite openly that the poor are the favorites of God. "Listen, my beloved brethren. Has not God chosen those who are poor in the world to be rich in faith and heirs of the kingdom which he has promised to those who love him?" (Second Reading)

Following the lead of these scriptural indications, we should like to direct our homily to material poverty, leaving aside for the present many other meanings for the term poverty, even in its biblical use. Immediately the question comes to the mind: Why has such preference for the poor been manifested by God in the Old

Testament, and by Jesus in the New? What could be the real reasons for such a preference?

To give to the poor what is superfluous is an act of justice. God's creation is for all men. He has permitted that there be rich and poor, in order that charity might be practiced in society. Just as He has created man and woman with different potentials for the constitution of a family. Wealth has as its main purpose the benefit of the neighbor and communion with him. On this point it is good to remember that the social doctrine of the Church, from the Gospels to St. Augustine, to St. John Chrysostom, to St. Peter Damian, right up to the *Populorum Progressio* of Paul VI, has always regarded the superabundance of the rich as the patrimony of the poor. Already in the fourth century St. Basil stated: that the superfluity of the rich is the property of the poor, that whatever we possess beyond what is necessary and convenient belongs to the poor, and that the egoism of those who are too well off has been accumulated at the cost of those who are indigent.

To distribute what is excessive to those who through no fault of their own are lacking what is necessary is an effective element in establishing balance and social peace. At the bottom of many economic, political and international problems there lies one particular goad: either the illegitimate acquisition of exaggerated wealth, or the just retaliation to procure normal living conditions. This "mammon" is the god of every war, hidden or open, small or great. And all this permanent social confusion can never be radically healed or lessened until men and nations find proper and just relations to terrestrial realities, regarding them as the means willed by God to promote universal fraternity.

To help the poor is a mark of nobility of soul. Descartes said, "I think, therefore I exist." The modern man paraphrases that in this manner: "I have, I possess, therefore I am, I count." The philosophy of "to be" is substituted by the philosophy of "to have." Truth has been deposed to give place to personal advantage; this is the very thing which has produced such spiritual misery for many individuals. It is wealth sought and desired as a mirage of life. This creates in the soul a haze of moral insensibility, alters the moral balance, and shifts the perspective from a harmonious communitarian life to a closed ghetto of selfishness. The greed for wealth leads men to all sorts of insane things, to unheard-of sacrifices which bar the heart to real goodness and friendship, thus making the victims social misfits, solitaries, misanthropes, suicide victims.

Some years ago a multimillionaire of Texas disappeared without leaving a trace of himself. When all efforts to locate him proved to be in vain, the absence was reported to the police. After another fruitless search, it was decided that as a last resort the house should be combed minutely. The searching party came to his safe, spacious as a small room and fastened with a solid, protecting door. What was their surprise and terror when upon forcing the vault open they discovered the object of their search. The man, clutching a pack of bank notes, was already some days dead. While enjoying the wealth he had amassed, the poor wretch had closed himself into the safe which had now become his coffin.

While selfishness is thus degrading, true nobility of soul lies in our self-giving. It is charity toward the poor which corrects us of our own egoism. Charity is exercised in patience. Goodness protects us from pride and gives us an awareness of limits and relative values. Generosity prevents us from deifying *finite* things. Supernatural love helps us overcome ourselves and raises us above temporalities, letting us exercise responsible mastery over them. To live is to communicate with others; to love is to offer oneself through the offering of the things we call our own. To give and to love is above all to insert ourselves into the mysterious rhythm of the Holy Trinity, which is complete and ineffable donation within itself and outside itself. Because of this, "man bows before genius but kneels before goodness" (Charles Gounod). The Lord who made Himself poor to teach us to give, invites us to help Him execute justice for the oppressed, give food to the hungry, liberty to prisoners. He invites us to help Him "lift up those who are bowed down" so that His message of love and fraternity may be prolonged to all generations" (Responsorial Psalm).

PASTORAL REFLECTIONS

1. *Happiness is an element too necessary to our life to be wasted with an exaggerated attachment to riches.* Unfortunately in our day civilization seems to be in a breakneck race. We seem to be seized with a haste to acquire material things, nor may we lose a moment of time because "time is money." In such a manner of living we keep on being so poor within, so lacking in virtue, though we may be rich in villas, cars and houses. We continue to be restless, nervous, squandering many of those energies which would normally be sufficient to make us more amiable and compatible with those around us.... If we wish to acquire or maintain a little peace of heart, it is essential to "cast out of the heart the greed for temporal things" (St. Augustine). It is very important to be more concerned about what we are rather than about what we have. The spiritual is worth more than the material.

2. *We would have more joy* if we were to use the abundance God has bestowed upon us for the wellbeing of our brothers. St. Paul, making reference to the words of Jesus, reminds us that "there is greater joy in giving than in receiving." Zaccheus learned the truth of this statement when, touched by the grace of the Lord, he gave "half his belongings to the poor and paid back fourfold those he had defrauded" (cf. Luke 19:8). As one candle serves to light another and another, and thus thousands of candles come to be lighted, so in the same way, one self-giving heart ignites another and the flame spreads on and on to thousands of hearts. It is a festivity of love and light!

3. One of the *purest joys* of man is precisely that of *being useful for something,* just as one of the greatest

punishments God can send to a soul is that of depriving him of an occasion to do good. As the allegory has it: It rained all night and the lily filled with water. Its golden pollen was washed to the ground. "The bees will be sad," thought the lily, "when they see that I cannot give them even a drop of nectar." But at that moment a bird passed through the air, lamenting "I am thirsty! I am thirsty!" The sparkle of the water in the lily cup caught his eye, and down he flew straight as an arrow. Balancing himself with his wings he could drink the water held in the petals of the flower. Happy and contented the lily sighed, "That is good! At least I have been useful to someone, even today!"

TWENTY-FOURTH SUNDAY IN ORDINARY TIME:

Faith and Works in the Following of Christ

Readings: Isaiah 50:4-9
James 2:14-18
Mark 8:27-35

On this Sunday we have St. James once again insisting on the practical attitudes proper to the follower of Christ. One of these attitudes, he states unhesitatingly, is that faith without good works is sterile. "What does it profit, my brethren, if a man says he has faith but has not works? Can his faith save him?...So faith by itself if it has no works, is dead" (Second Reading).

In the following of Christ, faith and good works go hand in hand. It is precisely through faith that the Christian is specially fitted to absorb the secular aspects of history, keeping himself attached to the works of God. The need of action is not merely a psychological urge of man, but a positive indication of God's will for him, made known through faith. External works are like the necessary expression of an interior illumination; faith in Christ urges and demands works of charity. The Lord has taught this through many figures. While waiting for His return we must bear spiritual fruit, like good trees. We must trade with the talents given to us. We must keep our lamps lighted; above all we must keep on loving our brethren. The apostles and disciples understood this teaching clearly and well, and followed it to its logical conclusions by engaging in apostolic activities. The first account of the history of the Church, the Acts of the Apostles, describes the works of the first Christians as the Gospel accounts tell us of the works of Jesus.

Intellect and will are constituent elements of man, but the intellect is at the service of the will. Just so, the Christian lives in faith to work in charity. God reveals Himself to us not so much to be known but to be loved through deeds. As the body without the soul is only a corpse, even though the soul can exist without the body; so too a faith without the dynamism of love and action is not a living faith but only a cult. And if Christianity were purely theoretical knowledge, then even the devil himself could be called Christian. On the contrary, genuine Christian life is the happy espousal of faith and good works. After the apostles were powerfully illuminated by the light of the Holy Spirit on Pentecost they went out to conquer the world. St. Paul, struck by the light of Christ on the way to Damascus, humbly asks what the Lord wants him to do. The hero is the person who stakes everything to live up to an ideal; the Christian, the saint, is the one who works in truth and in faith.

How is this struggle to be carried out? In a double line: of contrast and of fruitfulness. Because the believing person must think and act in a manner different from that of one who has no faith, he will always find himself in a perpetual variance with the ideologies and intellectual influences of the world. Unless he is hermetically sealed off from this world, he has no choice but to consistently combat every form of sin and wickedness, every open or hidden threat of paganism. Patterning his thoughts on those of Christ, the Christian believer must place himself as a sign of contradiction for those who will not or cannot believe. This leads to a break and a painful division with the pseudo wise and the worshipers of earthly realities. The believer will be, by definition, "a tried person," "a contradicted person," or even better, a soldier in constant readiness for battle. St. John the Apostle tells us that the Christian is always at variance with the world. The same evangelist says also: "...This is the victory that overcomes the world, our faith" (1 John 5:4). Here we have three key words: victory or conquest, world, faith. The word "conquest" is related to the idea of combat and implies a militant concession. Even St. Paul, the great soldier of faith and action, taught his dear faithful: "An athlete is not crowned unless he competes according to the rules" (2 Timothy 2:5).

In the sixteenth century, philosophy was divorced from life; in the seventeenth, philosophy from religion. In the eighteenth century culture was divorced from the people; and in the nineteenth, religion from the people. And now, in some cases, religion is divorced from life. Far too often God is accepted as if He were someone living in an apartment: it is sufficient that He does not disturb and does not try to influence our actions. Not a few of us Christians have come to the point at which we do as we please. We act quite contrary to what Christ expects of us, contrary to tradition, contrary to the example of the saints, trying to enter heaven and attain the highest sanctity with the least effort. The truth is, though, that sanctity is effected through the grace of God, together with the sincerity of our personal efforts. "God is always sought to be found, and is found to be always sought" (St. Augustine).

All this, however, is to "vivify earthly realities," as Vatican II says. What is the Incarnation? It is God making His dwelling among men in order to save the world. Who is the faithful believer? It is he who, though being in the world, is different from it that he may consecrate it; it is he who takes temporal things seriously in order to charge them with eternal values. From this point of view, it is not difficult to understand that only the person who has clear ideas on the meaning of life can proceed with agility and effectiveness toward a concrete and sublime realization of generous conquests. The persons of deep faith are the very ones who influence history with their dynamic personalities, distinguishing themselves from the anonymous and faceless crowd who lack dynamism and personal enterprise. This is so because he who has more faith sees more, he who sees more loves more, and he who loves more works more. It is through operative faith, the "assurance of things hoped for, the convictions of things not seen" (Hebrews 11:1) that the order of visible things is born and develops. Through a faith made manifest in works, our history of public and private life remains in orderly sequence like the petals of a flower.

Wherever a saint has lived, the earth flourishes. Let us take the example of St. Francis. He was so enamoured because he was illumined by the light of faith. Faith not only assures the permanent youthfulness of the Church, but also it is the reason for her dynamic and explosive vitality.

PASTORAL REFLECTIONS

1. As a first reflection there comes spontaneously to mind the consideration of *the essence of our liberty.* It was the view of the ancient pagans that man was created as a release from an irreversible destiny, like Prometheus chained to a rock, or Oepidus blinded. Liberty is, rather, "a constituent of human nature" (St. Thomas Aquinas). The qualifying acts of the human being are: sensation, knowledge, will, and decision. But the queen of this quartet is the will. Our person can become "personality" only if it uses its own proper liberty to will positive and valid things. As it is said, a person is as good as what he seeks, what he wills. True liberty is not putting on blue

jeans or training dogs. It is evaluating the things that are said, examining the facts and arguments, and then choosing what is good, what is better according to its value, and acting accordingly "not turning aside to the right or to the left" (cf. Deuteronomy 5:32).

2. Christianity, furthermore, has given to *liberty* a great gift in summoning it to the conquest of superior realities *by means of faith:* "It is necessary to draw from faith," our Holy Father tells us, "the normative principle and the operational principle of the good and just life.... Let us always remember St. Paul's words: 'The righteous shall live by faith' (Galatians 3:11)" (Paul VI, July 20, 1978). If we let ourselves be enlightened and guided by faith, we shall be fully exercising our liberty in Christian perfection. If we persevere in this way to the very end, we shall receive the prize of life.

3. The Church desires that her faithful members *let their faith shine in their works.* In this last ecumenical council she—the Church—is manifested to the world in this double beauty of faith and action, as we learn through the two constitutions "On the Church" and "The Church in the Modern World." Therefore, if the faithful believer wants to be a worthy son of the Spouse of Christ he must be illumined by faith to carry on good works, in charity, making the responsorial psalm his program: "I will walk before the Lord in the land of the living."

TWENTY-FIFTH SUNDAY IN ORDINARY TIME:

Christian Witness in Suffering

Readings: Wisdom 2:17-20
James 3:16—4:3
Mark 9:30-37

The good news of salvation had a mysterious dark point, seemingly contrary to everything it offered in promise: the suffering and death of the Redeemer. The passion of Jesus, though predicted by the prophets, was an insurmountable obstacle for the Jews and also for a time for the apostles, for all were awaiting a glorious and powerful Messiah. In St. Mark's Gospel he tells us: "He was teaching his apostles in this vein: 'The Son of man will be delivered into the hands of men, and they will kill him; and when he is killed, after three days he will rise.' But they did not understand the saying, and they were afraid to ask" (Third Reading).

In the face of the problem of pain we too can become almost rigid with fear, we can be thrust by an uncanny human malice into a most acute spiritual doubt in regard to the goodness and power of God. As Christians, we must never surrender the conviction that suffering is the very point of separation between the two economies of the law and of faith, the frontier between the two worlds of the flesh and of the spirit. It is the consecration of our authentic moral life. As Christ by His sufferings has become the key figure in history—the whole of history revolves around His cross—so also the faithful soul can make of his consecrated suffering the condition of his spiritual greatness.

In the First Reading we are invited to reflect on how the trials we have to endure help us give witness to our true attachment to God. Suffering becomes an act of fidelity to our Christian vocation. The wicked said: "Let us lie in wait for the righteous man.... Let us see if his words are true, and let us test what will happen at the end of his life; for if the righteous man is God's son, he will help him, and will deliver him from the hand of his adversaries. Let us test him with insult and torture, that we may find out how gentle he is, and make trial of his forbearance. Let us condemn him to a shameful death, for, according to what he says, he will be protected" (First Reading). This scriptural passage lets us know that already in the Old Testament suffering was looked upon as a test of spiritual fidelity. Let us explain. How often have we protested, "Lord, I love you!" God takes us at our word. He permits all sorts of trials to come our way, not to punish us, not to oppress us, but to give us the possibility of manifesting in deeds what we have professed in words. Without love there is no living; without suffering there is no loving. If we desire to live and love the Lord, we must follow the way of sacrifice and renunciation. The many sufferings and misfortunes we necessarily encounter in life are not signs of failure or of rejection by God. Rather, they can and must be providential occasions to give witness to our genuine love of Christ, guaranteeing our true interior personality. Woodsmen tell us that if a tree stump is cast into the fire it glows with all the colors which had penetrated it in its growth: the black of night, the violet of morning, the red of sunset, the silver of the stars. Particularly in his moments of suffering and pain is a man conditioned to reveal the sentiments he has absorbed: love or hatred, light or darkness, and so on. Holy Scripture assures us: "And because you were acceptable to God, it was necessary that temptation should try you" (Tobit 12:13 *Douay*); and further: "Indeed all who desire to live a godly life in Christ Jesus will be persecuted" (2 Timothy 3:12). Even in the conciliar constitution "On the Church," there are frequent references to this relation of suffering as a testimony of love for Him who suffered for us (cf. On the Church 7, 9, 41, etc.).

The cross of Christ is the heart of the Christian religion, as Paul VI affirms: "Our religious and Christian life finds its focal point in the cross of Christ...it is the key to His doctrine and mission, in such a way that whoever wishes to follow Him must know and must live that cross. Around the cross of Christ gather the new men, converging around Christ crucified as the characteristic sign of the new and finally true religion. First among these is St. Paul, who 'knew nothing except Christ Jesus and him crucified' (cf. Galatians 6:14).... A mysterious fascination emanates from the divine Crucified, which polarizes toward Him all of believing humanity" (Paul VI, March 30, 1977).

At times, however sufferings can be so oppressive that they seem to crush us. What are we to do? Theoretically, we must be convinced that God watches paternally over those who suffer. He will not permit us to be tempted beyond our strength; He always gives His help to overcome the trial. Actually, whenever we seem to be overwhelmed with suffering, at that very time we experience an unusual outpouring of actual grace. It may be some good news, perhaps a person of whom we have never thought offers us some kindness. It may be the happy discovery of an unsuspected opportunity for our wellbeing. When we have just about exhausted our last resources we somehow find ourselves surrounded by a special and unanticipated providence which not only helps us survive but also places us in an atmosphere of interior calm, of spiritual serenity, at times even of a taste for sharing in the cross. God acts somewhat in this way: He sends us many sufferings to wean us away from the pleasures of the world but at the same time He gives us so much strength at the right time that we can joyfully continue our pilgrimage toward Him, in order that we may possess Him more fully and more intimately, which is the goal and premium of every creature.

"I have followed pleasure, I have followed the cross. Come, come to the cross! You will find unsuspected beauty. The first step is hard. Thorns dig deep into the flesh. There is suffering, to be sure; there is full engagement, there is struggle, but then, what a recompense! God Himself comes down, He comes within our very being, and in us He deepens all the treasures of His comforts. He is life, He is love. The wondrous harmony: sacrifice and love, joy and sorrow, is perfected in us through Christ Jesus" (P. Chiaravaggio). The followers of Christ know how to accept suffering for they are convinced that to enter into joy and glory it is necessary to pass through many tribulations (cf. Acts 14:21).

PASTORAL REFLECTIONS

1. Without doubt there is *in everyone's life something hard to accept.* An oriental proverb states: "One

day for you, another day against you." Life is a composite of good and evil, of happiness and sadness, of successes and failures, of hope and of despair. We must make our way through life somewhat like an airplane which skims through limpid skies and then again through cloud banks, or like a car on the highway, now cruising in the bright open air, now threading the darkness of tunnels. In this continuous alternating between what pleases and what brings grief, we may never doubt the presence and the help of the Lord. "He is there when we think we are alone, He is listening when we hear no answer. He loves us when all others abandon us" (St. Augustine).

2. Another way—a human way—of keeping up our spirits in the face of sorrow is *never to surrender an optimistic outlook*. Scientific study in psychology clinics shows us how true it is that a strong psychic disturbance is a great contributing factor in physical illness. It is also true that a strong dose of optimism can effectively neutralize much of our sadness. We can cultivate an optimistic outlook by concentrating our thinking on good and beautiful things. The apostles themselves did so, when in their tribulations they returned in memory to the vision of Tabor where they had contemplated the luminous glory of the Master. Another way to recapture our serenity is to remember that time heals many wounds, and today's pain will seem very little tomorrow. Nor is it without effect to do as the wanderer does: by singing as he strides along, he lightens the weight of his burden and chases away the fears of the night.

3. When we have been touched by sorrow, *it is indispensable to take refuge in prayer*. God gives His help to all, but He has preference for those who call upon Him. It is said that prayer is God's weakness, in the sense that He is moved to dispense His graces to a son who prays. Prayer is man's strength, for through prayer he can obtain even that which seems impossible. It is needless to say that we must pray according to the heart

of God. "You ask and do not receive because you ask wrongly" (Second Reading). The fundamental characteristics of colloquy with God are humility, constancy and trust. We must pray "not to make our life too comfortable, but that we become strong; not that God tailor our duties according to our strength, but that He give us strength matching our duties" (John Kennedy). When sorrows come to us, we must prayerfully reach up to God, for "The Lord is the upholder of my life" (Responsorial Psalm).

TWENTY-SIXTH SUNDAY IN ORDINARY TIME:

Divine Punishments

> Readings: Numbers 11:25-29
> James 5:1-6
> Mark 9:38-43, 45, 47-48

The Gospel is not just any kind of literature: it is a person speaking to the world. If I grasp an individual by the arm, I communicate with the whole person. In a similar way, if I accept one part of the Good News I must accept the entire message. To use another analogy: we might think of the religious truths as "solids." If a solid is touched on any point the touch is felt throughout the body; similarly, if I hold some part of the Gospel, potentially I intend to accept its whole doctrine. If this is so, we are not free to pick and choose from the Gospel truths those parts which we like, and leave out others which do not suit our fancy. If we do not accept all, our choice is fictitious, insincere.

There is no doubt that one of the most disconcerting affirmations of the New Testament is the teaching of Jesus about eternal punishment. Jesus, making use of Judaic representations and traditions, confirms unequivocally the existence of eternal punishment: "...If your hand causes you to sin, cut it off; it is better for you to enter life maimed than with two hands to go to hell, to the unquenchable fire. And if your foot causes you to sin, cut it off; it is better for you to enter life lame than with two feet to be thrown into hell. If your eye causes you to sin, pluck it out! It is better for you to enter the kingdom of God with one eye than with two eyes to be thrown into hell, where 'the worm does not die, and the fire is not quenched' " (Third Reading).

Geographically Gehenna, or the valley of the sons of Hinnom, is a very deep depression to the south of Jerusalem. From very ancient times the place was dedicated to the worship of Moloch, to whom the kings Ahaz and Manasseh sacrificed their own sons. Josiah, the reformer king, made it into a wasteyard where refuse was burned and corpses were cast away. For the prophets, Gehenna became the place reserved for divine punishment. In the New Testament, Gehenna was no longer localized in the valley of Hinnom, but had become a symbol of the type of punishment meted out to the wicked. Often Jesus spoke of this eternal punishment. He will "send his angels to gather all evildoers...and hurl them into the furnace of fire" (cf. Matthew 13:41-42). He will pronounce the terrible sentence of damnation: "Depart from me, you cursed, into the eternal fire prepared for the devil and his angels!" (Matthew 25:41). The Gospels record many other expressions regarding eternal punishment (cf. Matthew 3:10; 5:2; 5:22; 7:19; Mark 9:41; 9:47; Luke 3:9; John 16:11).

The constant tradition of the Church, in consonance with the other religions of the world, has never ceased to teach and preach this terrible truth. Of late, Vatican Council II has quite simply reconfirmed the truth of eternal chastisement (cf. On the Church, 48). Dante, the classical Italian poet, dwells at length on this point. In his epic he traces for his readers a graphic description of hell. Let us briefly try to follow him in his profound theology: God who is infinite justice respects our free choice. In the sad hypothesis in which a soul would want to remain forever separated from Him, this very self-condemnation would produce an unquenchable agony of spirit; for every creature as such is constitutionally drawn toward God who is the supreme source and essential goal of every creature. As a second point, Dante points out that we cannot deny to God what He has decreed in His eternal designs for His own greater glory. St. Paul warns us with the words: "For who has known the mind of the Lord, or who has been his counselor?" (Romans 11:34). The existence of hell does not in the least contradict the wisdom of the Creator. This wisdom demands that divine holiness can never be reconciled with sin: light can never be associated with darkness, nor life with death, "for their opposition is eternal." But if in some way God were forced to pardon one who consciously and deliberately wants to be His enemy, then the master of the situation would be the sinner and not God. The enemy could boast of being able to do anything he pleased in life, while even God Himself could not stop him or do anything about it.

The poet-theologian goes so far as to state that hell itself is a testimony of the love of God. This paradox becomes clear when we realize that the greatest punishment God can impose is to refuse a soul His divine, eternal love. This is the sole and irremediable misfortune which can happen to a person. Through the love of God we were created, through this same love we have become His sons. It is precisely in the placing of oneself against this effusive goodness of the Lord, whose mysterious law is to fashion a vital and perfect communion with men, that the creature is cast into unspeakable torment, clearly perceiving that he has irrevocably failed in the sole purpose of his existence. The condemned soul still retains its essential relation to the source of its life, else it would cease to be, as well as its constituent attraction and nostalgia for its "First Love." But by its own perverse will it has barred forever the way to this divine will. It has decided to remain an implacable enemy of divine Love, and God respects its decision. This is the worm which never dies and the fire which is never extinguished.

PASTORAL REFLECTIONS

1. Furthermore, it is not to be forgotten that above all our wickedness and baseness and our inclination to evil, there is *the perennially salvific power of Christ*, who came not to condemn but to save all who have been given to Him by the Father.

2. Though hell is not a pleasant topic, it is good, however, to meditate now and then on this terrible possibility, as a psychological spur *to live more fully in the love of Christ* who died in order to refashion with men the intimate bonds of spiritual union for all eternity. Living in this love, we can truly experience that "the precepts of the Lord [including those which threaten] gladden the heart" (cf. Responsorial Psalm).

TWENTY-SEVENTH SUNDAY IN ORDINARY TIME:

Negative Effects of Divorce

Readings: Genesis 2:18-24
Hebrews: 2:9-11
Mark 10:2-16

We read in the Gospel: "At the beginning of creation God made them male and female; for this reason a man shall leave his father and mother and the two shall become as one. They are no longer two but one flesh. Therefore let no man separate what God has joined." Mark continues the account: "And in the house, the disciples asked him again about this matter, and he said to them, 'Whoever divorces his wife and marries another, commits adultery against her; and if she divorces her husband and marries another, she commits adultery'" (Third Reading).

This Gospel passage gives us an opportunity to pause a while on the very thorny problem of divorce. Since we cannot speak at length on this very important topic, as it really deserves, we shall limit ourselves to the disadvantages which flow from the breaking of the marriage bond.

First and foremost, divorce negates love. How often in their period of engagement have the young couples sworn mutual love forever: "I shall love you always...I am all yours forever...." Such an exclusive love, a love not limited by time, is true; a love that is provisional and limited by time is not authentic. Let us keep in mind that sex constitutes the point of departure, the call to a higher vocation of self-donation. In the fully matured person there exists an inseparable fusion between sexual impulse and the will to sacrifice. Love has many tones and shades of color, many accents. The first phase is the attraction, pleasure, emotion, sex as is common in lovers. Later there is the esteem, enjoyment of possession as in wedded couples. In a third phase there appears in ever sharper accents the theme of self-donation which culminates in joyful and total oblation of one for the other, even should one have no advantage at all to expect from the other, as can happen in old age. Thus the sexual impulse and the accompanying emotion is only the starting point, which must tend toward maturity in true affection. If we regard love merely as a biological impulse, we would have to renounce the progressive flowering of love, the inner urgency of the ever present need of continual, generous and mutual donation. It would be like starting the motor of a car without wanting to engage the gears to set the car in motion, or like planting a seed without wanting the plant to grow or desiring the fruits the plant should produce. It would be the very negation of true love.

Divorce is contrary to human dignity. A husband, a wife are not things to be used, but they are persons. As such they can never be reduced to objects of pleasure to be exchanged at will. The very charter of human rights approved by the UNO and signed by no less than a hundred nations does not recognize divorce as a fundamental right of the married. A Chinese proverb says: "Marriage was invented so that animals could become men, and divorce was invented so that men could again become animals." Further, the very thought that there could possibly be a separation jeopardizes the conjugal love which tends toward forming "two in one flesh." Uncertainty in such an important relation between man and woman cannot but weigh heavily on them, like the sword of Damocles, and disturb the enjoyment of true happiness. There is yet another thing: Such a divorce law would favor only the rich and the astute; the poor, the simple would, as often as happens, find it too perplexing, laborious and costly to follow through the legal process sanctioning the severance of the marriage bond. It is a strange thing. Precisely in this our present day when there is so much talk about "the dignity of the person, solidarity, understanding" in every assembly, there are also many voices clamoring for divorce and disunion.

Divorce is contrary to good sense. Actually, men marry in order the better to overcome the hardships of life. The defenders of divorce, however, state that the hardships of life, real or imaginary, should be valid reasons for the separation of the married pair.

A fourth argument against divorce is the disadvantage for the children. If education is the continuation of a generation, then that, too, like the birth itself, must be carried out through the cooperation and communal efforts of father and mother. On this point, no one is ignorant of the tremendous affective and psychological harm done to the children when a family is torn apart by the divorce of the parents. For the ego of the child to develop normally and securely it has need of the psychological presence of both parents living together in loving harmony. The child separated from one or other of the parents would be condemned to solitude, insecurity, and, often enough, to vice and delinquency.

Through divorce the whole family structure becomes weakened and tends to disintegration. Only when indissolubility is assured does the family unit become serious, fruitful, secure. But if the stability of matrimony is undermined by law, how can the married couples plan and follow up their vocation to sublime and fruitful ideals? Rather the contrary will happen. For example, is not the phenomenon of juvenile delinquency, of drugs, proportionate to the disrupted families, and is it not perhaps connected with the increase in number of illegitimate children? And the percentage of suicides—is it not three times as great among divorcees as among others? How many social evils are rooted in the psychologically shattered families? It is strange that some people believe society can be improved by the destruction of the very foundations of human society: the family. This is a capital error of method, besides being an unpardonable evil. In a religious vein, finally, it is not without profit to remember that the conjugal fidelity of the spouses is a symbol of the eternal love of God for humanity and the unfailing love of Christ for His Church.

In this our defense of the institution of the family we may be silenced by the ingenious defenders of divorce unless we also mention the so-called "piteous cases." Let us make this observation: Road signals and traffic laws may impede a doctor on his way to a critically ill patient, or they may hinder a businessman from arriving in time to conclude a favorable bargain. But should traffic lights and driving codes be eliminated because of these occasional cases? To do so would be to cause greater loss of life and profit. Following this line of reasoning, it is clear that the removal of the bond of indissolubility only paves the way for more and greater "piteous cases." Certainly, the State must remedy annoying situations and defend the "rights of the family," without, however, promulgating laws which are contrary to the nature of love and contrary to the majority of its citizens. Neither is it valid to argue that the more advanced nations have legalized divorce; such an argument is a puerile confusion of progress and civilization. Civilization always implies the presence of interior and spiritual values. "Civilization does not consist in the quantity of soap used, nor in steam or technical progress; it consists rather in lessening among men the traces of sin."

PASTORAL REFLECTIONS

1. *The Church never ceases to proclaim the indissolubility of the marriage bond,* this great principle inscribed in the very laws of nature, confirmed and strengthened in Christianity by the law of the Gospel in which Christ warns that man may not separate what God Himself has joined together. Constant fidelity to this Christian vocation, however, requires uncommon virtue. "For this reason, strengthened by grace for holiness of life, the couple will painstakingly cultivate and pray for constancy of love, large-heartedness, and the spirit of sacrifice" (*The Church in the Modern World,* 49). God will surely give the spouses sufficient strength to live together if they will give Him, in their home, the place which is His by right—the first place.

2. *The Ten Commandments of Conjugal Harmony.* To marry is easy, but to remain faithful to wedded love is an art. Here are ten little secrets for conjugal harmony:

1) Be convinced that your partner as a person has a right to his or her opinions, preferences, tastes. Love and respect, understand and support the other in the diversities of nature.

2) Remember that it is better to yield in a little thing than to compromise the harmony of hearts. Often with the trivial thing we demand at all costs, our triumph shatters the peace.

3) Never make a decision under pressure of strong emotion, especially when in anger.

4) Even in difficulties maintain a sense of humor.

5) Do not be afraid to admit your own failings, above all when such an acknowledgment will avert or end a quarrel.

6) If one party offers an excuse or asks pardon, have the grace to accept the apology without arrogance and to

make peace immediately with sincere heart, making evident the joy of mutual pardon.

7) Never advertise your family troubles to outsiders. "Wash your soiled linens in your own house," advised Don Bosco. It is a serious error to discuss marital or family misunderstandings with relatives or other people; to do so is only to aggravate and complicate the situations indefinitely.

8) Above all be patient. Harmony under every aspect —sexual, spiritual, professional, social—cannot be realized in a day. But it grows slowly, slowly, as does life itself.

9) Have the prudent technique of knowing how to repair something that has gone wrong, or to strengthen love in little ways: a small gift, a compliment at the opportune moment, a demonstration of affection, some token of your pride and pleasure in the other.

10) Know how to pray together, at least occasionally. In prayer the two souls in love are opened to each other; through prayer they are strengthened in beautifying their love.

3. *A Prayer:*
We thank You, Lord, for having joined our souls in the profound joy of authentic human and Christian love. Make us worthy of this love so that in the indissoluble union of our lives we never lose sight of the ultimate purpose of our marriage.

Grant that throughout life our love may be intense, delicate, serene, and faithful.

A gentle love, at times urgent, but never violent, suffocating.

Make us humble and recollected, so that we may listen to Your voice and go forward, without presumption and without pride, on the way of perfection.

Put into our hearts, O Lord, an ardent desire to please You always, to live for You to know Your truth, to practice Your charity everywhere, despite the inevitable crosses which each one must accept in life.

Make us generous in collaborating in Your designs of love, make us capable and desirous of receiving the children You will entrust to us, of educating them and sacrificing ourselves for them.

Grant us a love which is not closed in the egoistic enjoyment of our own hearth, but open to all in comprehension and service. Help us, Lord, to desire that which is pleasing to You, to be faithful to Your precepts and worthy of Your promises. Let us collaborate in the wonderful design of goodness You have traced for each one of us for Your glory and our joy. Finally, O Lord, grant that we may possess always and everywhere that peace which You Yourself have promised to men of good will, as a prelude to the eternal joys of heaven. Amen.

TWENTY-EIGHTH SUNDAY IN ORDINARY TIME:

Christian Prudence

> Readings: Wisdom 7:7-11
> Hebrews 4:12-13
> Mark 10:17-30

We read in the Book of Wisdom: "Therefore I prayed, and understanding was given me; I called upon God, and the spirit of Wisdom came to me. I preferred her to scepters and thrones, and I accounted wealth as nothing in comparison with her. Neither did I liken to her any priceless gem, because all gold is but a little sand in her sight..." (First Reading).

Some live in the past and they are the old. Others live only in the present and they are the thoughtless. Still others are open exclusively to the future, and these form the good-sized group of anxious and restless persons. The virtue of prudence makes man able to synthesize the modalities of time to the most advantageous point for fruitful and authentic human activity. For solving the problem of life we need meditation which learns from past experiences, decision which masters the present, and the realization of this meditation and decision in the future. For this reason the ancients called the virtue of prudence the "coachman and guide" of every activity. Just as a coach, no matter how beautiful and richly adorned, could bring us to ruin if the driver were not aware and attentive, just so our fine human qualities could produce disfigured and even harmful fruits unless we moderate and regulate these qualities by the virtue of prudence.

The principal office of this cardinal virtue is to assure the good purpose of our every action, which, in order to be a human action, must be conformed to the moral imperatives of the true and the just. The law of the mineral world is gravitation; the law of the vegetal kingdom is affinity; the law of the animal kingdom is sensory response. But the operative law in man is the moral law of good. As error is a defect of the intelligence, so is the doing of evil a negation of liberty and the triumph of imprudence. The virtue of prudence is not a sort of *savoir faire,* a worldly wisdom, nor is it a spineless silence and much less a running with the current or a social craftiness at the expense of others. The truly prudent, on the contrary, is synonymous with the good person, the worker of good.

In the life of each one of us there are times when we must say "yes" and other times when we must say "no." We must then act upon these responses; they are the pillars of our vocation and our profession. It is necessary to speak them decisively and well as a mark of a sane and practiced prudence; otherwise they will invite trouble. Often we have to reflect long and carefully over a certain action we have to perform but once in our lifetime, the consequences of which will affect the whole arc of our existence. *The moral virtue of prudence* may be defined as the ability to know how to find in things and events the sense and the impetus of actualizing the spiritual ideal of our life. This holds particularly for youth, who, despite their love for noise, must learn to find moments for quiet reflection in order to make decisions wisely.

It is good to take cognizance of this our wonderful possibility of setting the standards of our life, as fashioners of our own personality. One moment of peace and of silence shows us better than all the reflections of the philosophers wherein our duty lies. One act of the love and presence of God makes us understand the truth better than all the opinions of men. If we find ourselves in doubt, let us take counsel with the Lord, let us invoke the mercy of God and then decide without anxiety. The perfection of human prudence makes us act even though at times we are not able to achieve fully what we have foreseen in our mediation and reflection. Our response to the conscious decision for good is, in great part, the source of our joy. The unhappiness of many is the result of decisions taken too late. Haste is not necessary; but we must begin in time. The opportunities are slow in coming, quick in passing, and usually never return. And many people would be made happy if we could give them the happiness they have lost by their imprudence. Here, then, is a bit of golden advice: "Youth is not a period of life but a state of the soul, a fruit of one's will, a quality of the imagination, an intensity of emotion, a victory of courage over fear, of zest for adventure, of love for comfort. One does not get old for having lived a number of years; one gets old for having given up one's ideal. Years may carve wrinkles on the skin but the desertion of one's ideals wrinkles the soul. Preoccupations, fears, doubts, and desperations are the enemies that bend one to the earth and reduce one to dust even before death overtakes him. He is young who still has in him the sense of wonder. He challenges the events and plays the game of life. You will remain young if you are open to all that is beautiful, good and great; open to the message of men, of nature and of God. If one day your heart stops, bitten by pessimism and cynicism, then, old man, God have pity on your soul" (General MacArthur).

PASTORAL REFLECTIONS

1. *The inspired books* of Wisdom, of Proverbs and of Sirach abound with words of praise for *the prudent man,* as one who possesses true knowledge of things and of life, as one who is strong and just in the control of his own tongue and his own thoughts. The prudent person—the Sapiential Books often repeat this—stands above others, like the sun above the stars. The Lord Jesus, too, often praised the prudent man (cf. Matthew 10:16; Luke 5:25; *et al*). St. Paul exhorted the Christians of Ephesus to comport themselves prudently, not as foolish persons but as wise.

2. *Human and Christian prudence does not exclude risk.* Risk, adventure, is a mark of spiritual youth. It is the process of doing something with the purpose of accomplishing something. Far from condemning risk, the Lord recommended it in the parable of the talents, condemning rather the servant who, for fear of acting, hid the one talent which was consigned to him (cf. Matthew 25:14-30). The person who lives most is not the one who can count up the greatest number of years, but rather the one who lives with enthusiasm and courage the adventure of life, in hope. The American industrialist Henry Ford carried about with him a little notebook with these reflections written in it: "If you want an easy job to seem difficult, you have only to ask someone else to do it.... Never lament the shortcomings of what you have done; rather find remedies for them.... In the things we do there are no prizes and not even punishments; there are only consequences.... Your compassion is unreal until you give your own self to it.... Even if your action is not perfect, the doing or accomplishing of something is already a sign of human perfection."

3. To be able to see more clearly in the making of our decisions, we have received from the Lord two lights: interiorly, *our conscience,* and exteriorly, *His law.* The

starting point for an action which is to be valid, efficacious and worthy of life, is to judge it in conscience. The conscience which is controlled, illumined and helped by the law of God can make us effectively able to accomplish great actions and sublime programs.

TWENTY-NINTH SUNDAY IN ORDINARY TIME:

The Mystique of Suffering

Readings: Isaiah 53:10-11
Hebrews 4:14-16
Mark 10:35-45

The problem of pain has been the battleground of so many human thoughts and the torment of so many noble souls. In Christ, suffering becomes a problem of election and of transformation, a means of communication, exchange. In the Savior, pain is not mutilation but a victory with which He overcomes absence, separation, time, space. Between God and men, between the world of light and the world of darkness, there is only one bridge of communication: the sacrifice of Jesus, His immolation. "Yet it was the will of the Lord to bruise him; he has put him to grief; when he makes himself an offering for sin, he shall see his offspring, he shall prolong his days; the will of the Lord shall prosper in his hand; he shall see the fruit of the travail of his soul and be satisfied; by his knowledge shall the righteous one, my servant, make many to be accounted righteous, and he shall bear their iniquities" (First Reading). Christ willed to take human nature to suffer as man, to be very close to us. The Son of God came to suffer, to assume into Himself our sufferings, our rebellions, entering within the most mysterious and contradictory heart of our most intimate history. Only he who willed to die upon the cross could fully understand our crosses and help us bear them.

This is a great lesson for us. The believer must have above all an immense trust in the power of the sacrifice of Christ. "For we have not a high priest who is unable to sympathize with our weakness, but one who in every respect has been tempted as we are, yet without sinning. Let us then with confidence draw near to the throne of grace, that we may receive mercy and find grace to help in time of need" (Second Reading). Only this trust in the sacrifice of the Redeemer can free us from our sins. In the desert Moses raised up a brazen serpent which healed all those who looked upon it. That serpent was a symbol, a type of the exaltation of the Son of Man upon the cross, so that all who would look upon Him and believe in His sacrifice might have life. The Lord Himself declared: "And I—when I am lifted up from the earth—will draw all men to myself" (John 12:32).

The sacrifice of Christ with its immense tribute of suffering and of blood should not only arouse in us deep attachment and sentiments of fervent gratitude, but it must also produce within us the dynamic dimension of charity, of service for the life of the brethren. From the Gospel of St. Mark we gather this serious injunction of the Lord: "The Son of Man also came not to be served but to serve—to give His life as a ransom for many" (Third Reading). Actually, suffering and donation are interdependent concepts; they are correlative. The latter is derived from the former as the burning flame from the wood. Love-donation is ecstasy, going out of oneself to live in the service of the other. Whenever we sincerely love another person we have the sensation of a dying and a rebirth. To pass from egoistic self-love to the love of a "you" is like a psychological disintegration, a painful renunciation of self-centeredness to be immersed in the loved one. The Christian accepts suffering to diffuse love, like the trees which absorb carbon dioxide and give off oxygen. In a word, suffering is the powerful means which urges man to transcend his own selfishness in order to communicate more intimately with his brethren, in the way which Christ chose for the salvation and vivification of all men.

PASTORAL REFLECTIONS

1. In the Christian perspective, it is truly a great honor and a precious privilege *to suffer in Christ, for our brothers.* Paul VI confided that his principal mission as Pope was that of suffering for the Church: "Perhaps the Lord has called me to this service not because of any aptitude of mine, not to govern and save the Church from her present difficulties, but to suffer something for the Church, and to make it clear that He, and no one else, guides her and saves her" (General Audience, June 21, 1972). The Holy Father's words to the "Volunteers of Suffering" will also serve as an exhortation to all to welcome the gift of the cross. "Beloved sons and daughters who belong to the great praying family of the volunteers of suffering, we express to you all our satisfaction and deep gratitude. You give a great lesson by the generous acceptance of God's will manifested through your illness. The example of your patience, courage, and the faith that sustains you and which is reflected in the serenity of your countenances, is...a help to discover in suffering itself a fruitful source of spiritual elevation and transcendent redemption.... Accepting willingly for Christ's sake the burden of your infirmities, you remind so many brothers of yours that they are not alone in their sufferings, but have at their side Christ, the divine Model of all men, the only one who not only gives them courage, resignation and peace, but also asks for the offering of these trials in order to carry out His mysterious plans of salvation and the sanctification of souls.... In this way you teach them to give the divine Savior the most precious and beneficial collaboration for the redemption of the world: the collaboration of suffering, by means of which you are called in a quite particular way to complete in your flesh what is lacking in

Christ's afflictions for the sake of His Body, the Church.... And so this is the recommendation we will make to you: remain in closer and closer communion with the whole Body of Christ, the Church. As volunteers of suffering, suffer not only with patience, but also and above all with love. And this you can always do, even when you do not have the strength to recite prayers or do other exercises of devotion..." (Paul VI, April 12, 1972. See also: The Message of the Council to the Sick, Paul VI, December 8, 1965; Constitution On the Church, 11).

2. *But also for the Christians who are not physically ill* there is the *duty to resemble Christ crucified* if we will become His followers and apostles. To be Christ's apostles for our fellowmen it is necessary that we bring our brothers before the Lord and speak to Him about their sufferings; and also to speak to our brothers about the sufferings and passion of the Lord, their true Friend. It is of highest importance that we offer ourselves, together with our never lacking sufferings, to the Lord in view of the continuing passion of Christ for the salvation of the world.

3. When we speak of suffering we must think not only of those physical or moral ills which we can never totally avoid, but also of all the *mortifications and voluntary self-denials* which every authentic Christian should not hesitate to take upon himself if he is to be a preacher of Jesus Crucified, to be made like unto Him, to be His authentic witness. A great mystic confided thus: "When I speak of a mortified life, I do not mean to allude to the great penances of the saints. Far from resembling those beautiful souls who from their very infancy practice every form of mortification,....I make my penances consist only in denying and mortifying my will, in withholding a word of harsh reply, in rendering to those around me little services without letting them be noticed, and a thousand other things of this kind" (Saint Therese of the Child Jesus).

THIRTIETH SUNDAY IN ORDINARY TIME:

Joyous Assurance in Faith

Readings: Jeremiah 31:7-9
Hebrews 5:1-6
Mark 10:46-52

The Gospel for this thirtieth Sunday in ordinary time narrates: "As he was leaving Jericho with his disciples and a great multitude, Bartimaeus, a blind beggar, the son of Timaeus, was sitting by the roadside and when he heard that it was Jesus of Nazareth, he began to cry out and say, 'Jesus, Son of David, have mercy on me!' And many rebuked him, telling him to be silent; but he cried out all the more, 'Son of David, have mercy on me!' And Jesus stopped and said, 'Call him.' And they called the blind man, saying to him, 'Take heart; rise, he is calling you.' And throwing off his mantle he sprang up and came to Jesus. And Jesus said to him, 'What do you want me to do for you?' And the blind man said to him, 'Master, let me receive my sight.' And Jesus said to him, 'Go your way; your faith has made you well.' And immediately he received his sight and followed him on the way."

It is a beautiful lesson. It offers us the occasion to reflect once again on the spiritual paralysis of a person who does not accept faith, to meditate on the vital and joyous dynamism of those who let themselves be illuminated by eternal truth, and to be convinced that the true life of faith is in reality following Jesus Christ as Guide and Master.

Assuredly, without the light of faith we in our life are like the poor Bartimaeus, immobilized, fearful, separated from the world and from the life of others. Without faith, we suffer an existence in which the things surrounding us become a tangled skein we cannot unravel. We enter a labyrinth of ways without an exit.

We face difficulties that seem to have no meaning or solution. We become a prey to sadness and pessimism. Finally there comes a point when he who has no faith, who refuses the light, feels the need to cry aloud for help, for healing. Actually it is more difficult to live in lack of faith than to live by faith. Without faith, St. Paul admonishes us, we are like branches broken off from the stem (cf. Romans 11:20). And St. Peter asks in his turn: "What will be the end of those who do not obey the gospel of God?" (1 Peter 4:17) On the other hand, the man of faith walks securely through life as if he were in his own house, as if he were going through the streets of his native city. Light is given us so that with the eye we can see and enjoy things of nature. Ideas put us in communication with society and with the history of men, but it is the light of faith which puts us in communication with the divine panorama, with divine life itself. Just because of faith the supernatural world, though so distant and mysterious, becomes very close and intimate like a joyous personal experience: "Through faith I see heaven with both my eyes!" exclaimed St. Ignatius of Loyola. Faith reveals in the wonders of infinity!

Faith is most of all a personal rapport with Christ. There is a great difference between culture and faith. The former is a general and abstract relation with ideas, while the latter is a bond—personally and with all the emotion of one's spirit—with the very Person of Jesus. One who lives makes his decisions one after another according to his own will and always attuned to the safeguarding of his own egoistic interests, but one who has faith lives a law of love. He possesses Christ and is possessed by Christ, who has come to illumine and to love every person. The blind man of Jericho who joyfully follows the Savior up the road is an example and an invitation.

We must entrust ourselves to the Light. What we are is a gift God has given us; but what we believe is a gift we can give to God. Now more than ever there is a great need of light, of faith. Scientific theories hold good for a time, but they are not valid forever. Nowadays we give more credence to the opinions of men than to the truths of Christ, more importance to the press than to the Gospel. Technical skills have made more difficult the fruitful exercise of the intellect: the "work"-man has taken precedence over the "wise"-man. The dictatorship of the word, printed or spoken, has complicated the problems of our life rather than resolving them; not rarely the exchange known as dialogue turns out to be obstinate taking of positions to the vantage of egoistic interests and the jeopardizing of charity. It is precisely in this confusion of darkness that he places his trust in the Word of God, he seeks the light of Christ, and finds support in the tenets of his faith. A Christian is a person who has faith as the basis of his action and the criterion of his values.

In the early centuries baptism was called "phòtisma," that is, a sharing in the kingdom of light. The baptized, through faith, became a "child of the light," a "new creature" through the divine splendor bestowed upon him as a gift. For the true Christian, then, faith is not a passing emotional moment of his existence nor is it an occasion of cultural or religious expansion, but it is the very soul of his whole life. This light entering his inmost being and illuminating his activity determines his basic attitudes and beliefs. For the Rationalists, thought is the rule of action; for the esthetics, it is art. For Frederick William Nietzsche, it is man as such. For August Compte, it is progress; for Albert Camus, love; for Freud, pleasure. But for the Christian, the rule of acting and thinking is the Word of God, which he believes absolutely, unquestioningly, constantly, in faith. "The Gospel," affirms Father James Alberione, "has a mysterious power and an intrinsic efficacy upon the mind and the heart. In meditating on the Gospel one feels sentiments similar to what one experiences in contemplating heaven."

It is clear that the faithful cannot but trust in the Church, the depositary of the faith. It is the Church which gathers the new People of God to lead them back to the promised land of the kingdom of God, to make up the assembly of the sons of God. The Second Vatican Council insists very much on this function of the Church to transmit integrally the deposit of faith for the salvation and the happiness of man (cf. Constitution: Revelation 7, 10, 21; On the Church 17, 25, *et al*).

PASTORAL REFLECTIONS

1. *The Church, beacon of light in the faith:* "In our days, as always in the course of the centuries, we hear repeated: The Church, why? What does it do? What use is it? Well, let us make the supposition—fortunately, after Christ, an unreal one—that the apostolic Church was no longer on earth. What would happen? What would happen would be what happens on a dark night, in a closed room where the light has gone out: a great confusion about the prospect of vital space, an interminable irrational struggle, a time without hope" (Paul VI, September 7, 1977).

2. *Difference between the dogmas of God and those of men.* There is a very great difference between the dogmas of God and the political, artistic, scientific dogmas imposed by men. Human dogmas are stopping points not to be bypassed. Particularly if they are political they must be observed, not discussed. They are imposed rather than proposed; at least this is so in the intention of the lawmaker. The Church, on the contrary, fixes or proposes dogmas, the mysteries of which cannot be wholly comprehended, but permits and even invites the faithful to reflect, to investigate, to discover new applications. Thus the dogma is a starting-point for research, a joy for the intellect. Here the believer is one who loves.

3. *The global dimension of faith.* Actually, before all else our faith consists in entrusting ourselves to God, in

having confidence in His word and His promises. Secondly, it is sensing His presence in all the vicissitudes of life as the silent and invisible artist and architect of the world. In the third place, the man of faith has the conviction that the whole of history, though unfolding as it is through the free will of men, is not rushing headlong toward its annihilation or ruin, but rather moving toward a fullness of glory, toward "new heavens and a new earth" (Revelation 21:1).

THIRTY-FIRST SUNDAY IN ORDINARY TIME:

Why and How We Must Love God

Readings: Deuteronomy 6:2-6
Hebrews 7:23-28
Mark 12:28-34

Two things are necessary to go forward well in life: humor and religion. The decisive and qualifying element of our life is to have a religious vision, a *Weltanschauung* inspired and upheld by divine love.

Unfortunately, even now there is a lack of this religious perspective in the lives of many. Alban Stolz, an esteemed German professor and a great Christian of the last century, stated, "On the tombs of the majority of men who die, one could well write this epitaph: 'Here lies one who did not know why he lived.'" Sadly, this is only too true of our times also. As the prophet Isaiah complained in his own day, we too can say that man is moving away from God, the only source of every good. Man has lost the sense of a spiritual orientation.

Among the many reasons that can be adduced to explain this loss of the sense of God, one can be proposed as the foremost: the deification of earthly values. The expanse of the visible has become so voluminous that there is no more room for the vista of the Invisible. The

Hebrews failed to recognize Christ because they absolutized their Law. The Romans remained pagans because they believed only in strength and rule. The Greeks were constrained to adore the Unknown God for they looked upon human wisdom as their absolute queen. Thus we, too, have lapsed into idolatry by worshiping technology, pleasure, matter, and human experience; for this reason we cannot easily encounter the Lord. Our presumed self-sufficiency has turned out to be something like a psychological density which does not permit the entrance of God into our souls, just as a dense cloud prevents the light of the sun from illuminating the things of this created world.

But God wants us to be with Him. He commands it. We read in the book of Deuteronomy: "Hear, O Israel: The Lord our God is one Lord; and you shall love the Lord your God with all your heart, and with all your soul, and with all your might. And these words which I command you this day shall be upon your heart; and you shall teach them to your children, and you shall talk of them when you sit in your house, and when you walk by the way, and when you lie down, and when you rise. And you shall bind them as a sign upon your hand, and they shall be as frontlets between your eyes. And you shall write them on the doorposts of your house and on your gates.... Hear, therefore, O Israel, and be careful to do them; that it may go well with you, and that you may multiply greatly, as the Lord, the God of your fathers, has promised you, in a land flowing with milk and honey" (First Reading).

But why must we surrender ourselves to God? We must not forget that God is our Creator. To God we owe everything: our being, our life, our liberty, our conscience and therefore our obedience, our human dignity and all our true well-being. We ought to learn from the Orientals, from the Hebrews to learn of the great transcendence of God, His absolute dominion and supremacy over the whole earth, over every creature. These people did not discuss about God, they simply adored Him; for them, God had no need of defense or justification. He was supreme, the source of all reality: to Him they attributed their lives, totally.

For us Christians, there is a second reason for our attachment to God: the reason of the Incarnation. Through the Incarnation God entered into history, into our very life. The earlier visits of God to man were occasional, peripheral; now, through the Incarnation, the dwelling of the Lord among us is definitive, profound, vital and permanent. Now, everything gravitates around Christ: the past has prepared for His coming, the present has received Him, and the future is dedicated to the realization of His kingdom. Even the Church is "a gift" of the continuing presence of God among us. To ignore God, therefore, voluntarily and sinfully, is to cast oneself outside the pale of history; to lose faith in Him is, practically, to lose one's head. It is this very communion with God which sustains us in our very humanity, while the loss of the concept of God takes away even our concept of creaturehood, our individualism. The Lord uses appealing words to assure us that attachment to Him will make us happy.

The love of God for us and ours for Him must not, however, remain theoretical and platonic; it must rather be actual and dynamic. Love needs to act. When love is authentic, it leaves the realm of words and launches into deeds. It is on the lookout for occasions to prove itself concretely. It is no wonder then that the Lord, enjoining us to love Him totally, completes the exposition of His command by exhorting us to "hear and be careful to observe" His will (First Reading). The commandments of God are the classical means of practicing love of God, of manifesting love for Him in a practical way. At the same time they are the bulwarks for safeguarding our Christian life and making it fruitful. It is to be noted further the exercise of divine love in the life of the faithful Christian will make even the difficulties of life vanish; "love renders everything easy. Nothing is difficult for one who loves, while everything is difficult for one who does not love."

But the most opportune and practical means of loving God is that of loving our neighbor. Love of God and love of neighbor are, in fact, similar. They are like two triangles with the same angular formation, though they are of different sizes; or two concentric circles, one inside the other, which though differing in size have the same geometric properties. It is especially in the New Testament, with St. John in the lead, that this dynamic interdependence of the two commandments of the Lord is emphasized. Actually this apostle of love always speaks of love of neighbor as an effect of the supernatural love of God within us. It is well to recall here that in Christianity, God penetrates humanity so that man can find God through his fellowman. God is not only the Transcendent; He is also the Incarnate One in human nature. Every mystical ascent toward God has necessarily, therefore, its point of reference and qualification in the neighbor. Just as in Christ the divine and the human nature are united, so there must be a bond of union between the divine plan and the plan of man. As the love of God becomes mercy when it touches our misery, so His love for us and ours for Him must be transformed into effective and generous love for our neighbor. The inseparability of these two loves is the root of Christian spirituality.

PASTORAL REFLECTIONS

1. *We all have need of returning to God.* "As man gets to know himself, and realizes that there is something irregular, unfinished, unhappy, bad in his existence, he feels the unsatisfied need of confessing his own imperfection; a need that documents an unfulfilled greatness, a betrayed duty, an inevitable remorse.... We

all know the wisdom of a saying on which human psychology is based: 'Man's greatness is great in that he recognizes he is wretched' (Pascal, *Pensees*, 397). These considerations, which recognize a painful, dramatic and even tragic condition of human existence, have a precise echo in the Gospel. They are like a voice which not only reawakens sad consciousness of our congenital infirmity, but which at once announces a remedy: 'The time is fulfilled, and the kingdom of God is at hand; repent, and believe in the gospel' (Mark 1:15); 'Repent, for the kingdom of heaven is at hand' (Matthew 3:2; 4:17)." Thus did our Holy Father, Paul VI, exhort the faithful on March 8, 1978.

2. *The profound significance of conversion:* To be converted—as is suggested by the Hebrew word "gher"—is to make an about-face from the streets of the world and go to dwell in the country of God. In plain terms, it is to respond to the thoughts and desires of God, observing and practicing His commandments. It is to our advantage to take inventory of our spiritual state in relation to what God expects of us. The strong man does not say, "I would like," he says, rather, "I will, now." The converted man is like repentant Peter, the man of "right away." Once a talkative man came up to George Bernard Shaw and said, "I would like to go around the whole world and tell everybody to observe the ten commandments." The famous author replied: "Do you want some advice? First begin to practice them yourself!"

3. The two commandments of love of God and of neighbor are bound together, first of all, because when all is said and done it is *the very same love* which God pours out upon us and then through us is diffused among our brethren. It is not our love we are bestowing upon the neighbor but—at the level of Christian revelation—it is God who continues to love men through that love which He Himself has poured into our hearts through the Holy Spirit (cf. Romans 5:5).

THIRTY-SECOND SUNDAY IN ORDINARY TIME:

The Positive Aspect of Our Death

Readings: 1 Kings 17:10-16
Hebrews 9:24-28
Mark 12:38-44

In the past we have shed far too many tears weeping in quite a pagan way over death, seeing in it only a decomposition, an irreparable separation. Though it is tremendously true that death is inherent in our very life, we are all hastening toward it; it is also quite true that in death is the burgeoning of our true life. Life and death are interchangeable terms; they are correlative and bipolar concepts like the two scales of a balance. The binomial life-death is present everywhere in creation. The pulp of a fruit loses itself to give life to the seed. The seed dies to produce the plant. The flower withers and dies to yield the fruit. The bay tree and many other plants are ever green, in winter and in summer, for as soon as the leaves die away and fall they are immediately replaced by others. Thus it is also in human life. Infancy dies to yield place to youth. This in turn disappears to give rise to maturity. Maturity vanishes as old age sets in, and so it goes. What we call existence, therefore, is an alternation of living and dying. Our time is like a week of seven days: it is a continual dying to be reborn until the earthly span is over. Life and death are always in conflict, but the final victory belongs to life.

The birth and the fructifying of life from death is a reality of our very being. The awareness of death gives us a better understanding of ourselves. Death drastically gives us a measure of our limited and finite lives. Death is the eternal satire on human follies. Death is also the knowledge of things. Though we may not be experts in religious philosophy we can share the common experience of understanding that things seen and loved with a certain detachment are viewed in a better light. "Enveloped in the present way of living and acquainted only with the immediate present and its destiny, man loses the true sense of the values of time itself; he exalts these values as if they were the only ones, definitive in themselves. Later then he despairs on discovering that they are ephemeral and fleeting, and he no longer sees the purpose these values should ultimately serve" (Paul VI, October 31, 1971).

Death convinces us that we ought to be good, or at least that we ought not deviate too far from the right path. God knows how much worse we would have been had it not been for the thought of death. The grim thought that man is destined to die is a potent urge to be good. As we are all destined to die one day, or rather, as we are already dying daily, we ought to have a kinder attitude to our neighbor who has the sentence of death written on his forehead. Our life is a one-way traffic: we are all bound for eternity, our common destiny. If at the end of the road we are all going to be stopped by time, why not be friendly to each other along the way? In life we should vie for only one thing: to outdo the others in benevolence.

Our souls, too, are given powerful impetus in the thought of death. As Pope John Paul II stated, "At whatever moment death may come, it will always be accepted as an alternative to life, as a dimension which completes its whole meaning. 'For to me to live is Christ, and to die is gain' (Philippians 1:20). If Christ gives life all its meaning, then man can think of death in this way. He can await it in this way! And he can accept it in this way!" (October 31, 1979)

The most consoling and precious fruit of our corporal death is that of divine union. "But a deep instinct leads him rightly to shrink from and to reject the utter ruin and total loss of his personality. Because he bears in himself the seed of eternity, which cannot be reduced to mere matter, he rebels against death. All the aids made available by technology, however useful they may be, cannot set his anguished mind at rest. They may prolong his life-span; but this does not satisfy his heartfelt longing, one that can never be stifled, for a life to come" (The Church in the Modern World, 18). To this tormenting question we can and we must give a firm and sure answer: our soul is immortal. Hence, for a Christian, death is not the end but the beginning, the beginning of true life; it is the gate opening into eternity. It is like the announcement behind the barbed-wire enclosure of a concentration camp, "We are going home!" To die is to open the door of our real and permanent home and say, "Home at last!"

PASTORAL REFLECTIONS

1. *To die serenely is the most beautiful thing we can do in life.* But we must prepare ourselves for it. At the end of life all the fruits of our good works are gathered together. The good things we possess, death takes all away, but the good deeds we have done, death gives back to us. Our final and definitive lot is determined by what we have done. Let us recall the parable of the talents. We must regard these gifts of life as our fortune, but at the same time as our responsibility. The use we have made of them will decide our salvation.

2. *To live well means, actually, to be and to remain united to Christ,* to accept entirely His Person, His efficacious redemption. The turning point of history is the death and resurrection of Christ; he who dies with Him, who unites himself vitally with the Savior, will assuredly be worthy of resurrection with Him. This is the leit motif and the recurrent promise of the New Testament.

3. *We find Christ specifically in the Church.* Christ merited salvation and resurrection for us through His human nature; He applies salvation and resurrection to us through His social or mystical nature, the Church. The Church is none other than the "powerful arm" with

seven fingers (the sacraments) which, receiving from Christ the efficacious strength of salvation, seeks to bring this saving grace to every single one of the sons of men.

THIRTY-THIRD SUNDAY IN ORDINARY TIME:

The Last Judgment

Readings: Daniel 12:1-3
Hebrews 10:11-14, 18
Mark 13:24-32

The whole of history moves toward three spiritual moments: the resurrection of Christ, His second coming, and finally life eternal.

In the Gospel of today St. Mark briefly dwells on the end of the world and the final judgment of men by Christ.

Rather than developing in this homily the certainty and propriety of this final judgment, it may be more opportune and beneficial to enlarge upon the encounter of each individual soul with its Creator and supreme Judge. In the middle ages, the final judgment was prevalently interpreted as the moment of God's vengeance, the victory of the inexorable justice of God. We must not forget, however, that the attributes of God are inseparable, therefore His justice is always interlocked with His mercy and the other divine characteristics. There is another factor: the Hebrews did not possess a very large vocabulary, and the word "justice" could mean a host of things. It could mean distributive justice on the part of God in that He rewards each one according to his merits; it could mean divine fidelity, the sanctity of God, the mercy of God, and so on. One clear instance of divine justice manfiested as mercy is the parable of the judge and the widow, narrated by St. Luke, the evangelist of divine benevolence (cf. Luke 18:1-9).

Not a few passages of the New Testament present to us the day of judgment as an encounter of love. St. Paul says: "The Lord will be a righteous judge for those who wait with eager longing for his appearing" (cf. 2 Timothy 4:9). "Christ, having been offered once to bear the sins of many, will appear a second time, not to deal with sin but to save those who are eagerly waiting for him" (Hebrews 9:28), as the author of Hebrews tells us. St. James reminds us, "Listen, my beloved brethren. Has not God chosen those who are poor in the world to be rich in faith and heirs of the kingdom which he has promised to those who love him?" (James 2:5) In St. Peter's first encyclical he exclaims: "Blessed be the God and Father of our Lord Jesus Christ! By his great mercy we have been born anew to a living hope through the resurrection of Jesus Christ from the dead, and to an inheritance which is imperishable, undefiled, and unfading, kept in heaven for you, who by God's power are guarded through faith for a salvation ready to be revealed in the last time" (1 Peter 1:3-5). The apostle St. John states with utter certainty: "In this is love perfected with us, that we may have confidence for the day of judgment" (1 John 4:17). St. Jude's only letter, consisting of only one chapter, is wholly concentrated on the theme of judgment. Among other things he says: "But you, beloved, build yourselves up on your most holy faith; pray in the Holy Spirit; keep yourselves in the love of God; wait for the mercy of our Lord Jesus Christ unto eternal life" (Jude 1:20-21). It is beyond doubt that the most beautiful canticle of confidence for the day of final reckoning is that of the famous eighth chapter of the letter to the Romans. St. Paul foretells and preaches in words weighted with exultant Christian optimism the great triumph of love of all those who remain faithful to Christ the Lord.

Likewise, not a few saints have regarded the day of judgment as a meeting of lovers. St. Angela of Foligno (+ 1309) tells us of a vision she was granted: "Christ the Son of God presented me to His Father and I heard Him say: 'O my spouse, my beloved whom I have loved with a great and true love, I desire that you come to me not sad but rejoicing, filled with joy and clothed in royal apparel such as is fitting for the bride of a king.' So saying, He showed me a magnificent bridal gown. It was neither purple nor scarlet, nor was it made of costly silk or fur, but it was all woven of brilliance especially suited for a garment of the soul. A mantle prepared by the bridegroom for His long-loved bride. Then the Incarnate Word of God showed me in an ever more vivid manner the true meaning of the Word and all it stood for. Calling me to Himself He told me tenderly, 'Come, my beloved, my bride, come. All the saints await your coming in glory!' Thus He concluded, 'I have not sent angels or saints to call you, but I have come myself to accompany you because you are so deserving and so dear to me.' " Reason does not contradict this at all, for "God is Love." The whole grand plan of salvation is realized in this divine and infinite mercy. There is surely no reason to doubt that the final great moment, the decisive moment of this history of love, will be the culminating act of God's merciful love. Truly, according to the inspired words of St. Paul, it will be precisely on the day of judgment that Christ will present to the Father the fruits of the redemption, which He has freely accomplished in loving kindness.

If a teacher were to recruit students and teach them gratuitously, supplying them with books and everything else necessary for their studies at his own expense, if with his own free initiative he were to take care that they had all the time they needed to master their studies, all this out of pure love and mercy, certainly he would not look forward to the day of examinations to make these students fail. Rather, would he not do everything in his power to make them pass, and even brilliantly? Does not our Christian religion present us with a God who goes out in search of men, to educate them to holiness, to save them? So we should think of God as looking forward to the day of judgment as a day of the glorious epilogue to crown His word, as the occasion when He will seal His friendship with man forever in an unending and inseparable union of love and beatific vision.

PASTORAL REFLECTIONS

1. *We ourselves prepare our own judgment.* At the end of our life we shall be that which we have chosen to be. Our single actions are like the individual frames of a film: the beauty of the whole film or the lack of it will depend on the units which make it up. As in an illuminated aquarium all the little fishes are seen darting about, so will all our moral twistings and turnings be evident. All our actions will appear as dancing around the central nucleus of our spiritual ego; all forming one whole, all the tiny parts making up our interior personality. God with His light and His love will penetrate all, He will see clearly what we are. If we have lived and been enriched with a fullness of light and love, we shall be worthy, through spiritual affinity, to communicate eternally with God. If on the contrary we are darkness, sin, we will condemn ourselves to an eternal separation from God, eternal Light, eternal Love, our prize and true destiny.

2. If such is the case, it is most important that as we move on toward our journey's end, we *trade diligently with the talents we have received from the Lord and for the Lord.* We must always live in love and in divine grace, the vitalizing lymph of our own life and of all mankind. Living thus in the comforting grace of God, which supernaturally supports our whole being as creatures, we cannot but live in complete conformity to our dignity as children of God. Through the dynamic radiance of the virtues of poverty in spirit, of meekness, of patience, of sanctified sorrow, we shall be the messengers and the witnesses of the beatitudes.

3. *All these virtues,* however, will have their *center and queen: faith.* The various scriptural allusions relative to the final judgment convey a moral exhortation for the happy outcome of this final examination of the soul:

faith in Jesus Christ. It is, in fact, this faith which saves us in time and in eternity: "He who believes in Christ has life everlasting."

THIRTY-FOURTH SUNDAY IN ORDINARY TIME
SOLEMNITY OF CHRIST THE KING:

The Kingship of Christ

Readings: Daniel 7:13-14
Revelation 1:5-8
John 18:33-37

The liturgical year of Cycle B closes with the glorious vision of Christ as highest Ruler and supreme Master of history.

Christ our Savior has ultimately confirmed and established His kingship in virtue of His passion, death and resurrection. These three moments of the life of Jesus not only are historical fact, but they also constitute the essential fabric of history. History no longer has a linear movement, as a material succession of facts and of persons, but it has acquired its epicenter, its focal point, around the Son of God. The centuries no longer flee away fearfully, without hope; they rotate fecundly around the cross of Christ. St. John the apostle reflects this thought when he calls Christ the "alpha and omega" of human events. This is to say that just as all words and names are comprised of the vowels and consonants of the alphabet, so all the events in human life depend upon and are influenced by the salvific presence of the Savior.

A second characteristic of the kingdom of Christ is its interiority. Jesus said to Pilate: "My kingship is not of this world; if my kingship were of this world, my servants would fight, that I might not be handed over to the Jews" (Third Reading). It is a kingdom whose army is composed of the virtues of humility, patience, mutual love, simplicity, in a word, everything which makes up the message of Christian truth. As opposed to the purely external facts which form the chronicle of events, the divine kingdom of the Savior impregnates life with an interior ethic, the vital lymph of all true progress and all authentic history.

Of this kingdom there shall be no end, but in an irresistible manner it shall move onward toward its fullness, its complete victory. As the so-called geological epochs, narrated in the Bible, culminated in the creation of man, so also the various stages of the future of history are mysteriously channeled toward the second coming and final triumph of Christ, when all will proclaim His divine kingship. This is not to say that everything will be easy and smooth. Rather, at the end of time, after other sorts of disturbances, the kings of the earth will attempt the last and most severe attack against the Lamb, who, however, will be the Conqueror of all, including death (cf. Revelation 17:13). The prophet Daniel, too, assures us of this final victory: "I saw in the night visions, and behold with the clouds of heaven there came one like a son of man, and he came to the Ancient of Days and was presented before him. And to him was given dominion, and glory, and kingdom, that all peoples, nations, and languages should serve him; his dominion is an everlasting dominion, which shall not pass away, his kingdom one that shall not be destroyed" (First Reading).

PASTORAL REFLECTIONS

1. The catechesis of the first centuries included this teaching: The Father constituted *the Son the King of history and the Lord of the universe* because He suffered and was crucified. The first Christians were also convinced that, participating in the sufferings of Jesus, they not only rendered their own interior life more authentic, but also acquired the right of divine kingship for all the People of God. Each one of us has to suffer, more or less, in one way or another. Why, then, should

we not look upon and accept our sufferings as having redeeming value, as an interior dominion for the increase of the kingdom of God?

2. To be worthy of this spiritual dominion it is necessary: to *let ourselves be dominated by the Person of Christ*, to be docile to the mysterious action of His grace and His truth, to be fortified with all those virtues which are proper to the kingdom of Christ. Let us remember: The chronicle of history is determined by facts, but civilization is the fruit of virtue.

3. *All our history, placed as it is between the two comings of Christ*, marches relentlessly toward its culmination, toward the "victory day" of the Supreme Judge. All the present disturbances, all the battles of ideas, all these conflicts of contrary principles, this universal flood of errors which drowns the intelligence, dries up the heart, all will come to die at the feet of Christ, just as after a great tempest, the waves come to die calmly on the seashore. We are not to look at the march of events with fearful eye trying to save ourselves by hiding away from earthly realities. We must rather maintain a serene and confident optimism anchored in the victorious power of Christ. He who does not walk along this way, or worse still, who purposely puts himself out of this way of the sweet reign of Christ puts himself out of the very margins of history. In other words, he fights in vain against Him who holds in His hands the fate of our existence.

Also available from St. Paul Editions

Reading the Bible—a Guide to the Word of God for Everyone
J. Kingsley Dalpadado, OMI

Each chapter offers an introduction to a book of the Bible, giving background, setting and explanation, select passages for reading and thoughtful applications. Charts, quizzes, answer keys, suggested hymns and prayers make this an ideal text for school, adult study, or individuals desirous of understanding Scripture better.

cloth $5.95; paper $4.95   SC0430

Reading the Gospels
J. Kingsley Dalpadado, OMI

This book serves as a guide to enter, as it were, into the real world of the Gospels, and see them as the Word of God to be believed and lived in our daily lives.

cloth $5.00; paper $4.00   SC0432

Reading the Acts, Epistles and Revelation
J. Kingsley Dalpadado, O.M.I.

Anyone interested in Scripture will find, along with hours of enjoyable reading, the results of the latest exegetical studies.

"The Gospels present to us what Paul calls 'the mystery of Christ.' The *Acts* and *Epistles* proclaim it, explain it and apply it to our daily lives. The book of

Revelation written in a time of crisis and persecution, is a magnificent declaration of faith in this mystery which dominates history and transcends time."

cloth $6.95; paper $5.95   SC0431

Gospels for Sundays and Feasts—The Biblical Message

Rev. Manuel Miguens, OFM

Commentaries on the Sunday and feast day Gospels with a sound, positive approach. "A constructive and positive approach seems to answer best the needs of the religious audience in today's world. It is not debate and doubt, but religious truth and firmness that can be meaningful today and bring home a message of faith, hope, and love." (From the Foreword)

B cycle
cloth $7.50; paper $6.00 — SP0203
C cycle
cloth $7.50; paper $6.00 — SP0206

Spiritual Life in the Bible

Daughters of St. Paul

A volume which pursues the truth about a wealth of timely and fundamental subjects.

Written in a form of dialogue, the author continually draws from the book of books—the Bible—whose author is God, the Author of Truth and the true Light of the world.

A book which will be of interest to both those who believe in objective truth, and those who honestly seek to pursue the truth.
cloth $5.95; paper $4.00 — SC0445

Morality Today—The Bible in My Life

Daughters of St. Paul
A unique way to study the Ten Commandments!

In simple and clear language, but with a very personal approach, each commandment is explained in all its aspects, negative and positive. We are invited to ponder...adore...and speak to God so that through instruction, reflection and prayer we may understand and love His holy Law.

All will find this book both informative and inspirational.
cloth $3.00; paper $1.95 — SC0088

In the Light of the Bible (Vol. I & II)
Sr. Concetta, D.S.P.

"These little books present basic teachings for Catholic living in Christ and (as their title indicates) present them in the clear light of the written Word. Anyone interested in studying or teaching the Christ-life will find these books helpful and authoritative, because their authority rests on God's inspired Scripture."

Most Rev. John F. Whealon
Archbishop of Hartford

Vol. I – 141 pages; $1.25 — SC0060
Vol. II – 117 pages; $1.00 — SC0061

Introductions to the Books of the New Testament
Daughters of St. Paul

Crystal-like insights that are both brief yet comprehensive give an immediate grasp of the content, style and message of the sacred books.
80 pages; paper $1.00 — SC0080

My Daily Gospel
Compiled by Rev. J. Robaldo, S.S.P.

A Gospel passage for every day explained simply and applied to practical life situations by the Fathers and Doctors of the Church.
495 pages; cloth $4.00; paper $3.00 — **SC0090**

Please order from any of the addresses at the end of this book, specifying title and item number.

Daughters of St. Paul

IN MASSACHUSETTS
   50 St. Paul's Ave. Jamaica Plain, Boston, MA 02130;
      617-522-8911; 617-522-0872;
   172 Tremont Street, Boston, MA 02111; **617-426-5464;**
      617-426-4230
IN NEW YORK
   78 Fort Place, Staten Island, NY 10301; **212-447-5071**
   59 East 43rd Street, New York, NY 10017; **212-986-7580**
   7 State Street, New York, NY 10004; **212-447-5071**
   625 East 187th Street, Bronx, NY 10458; **212-584-0440**
   525 Main Street, Buffalo, NY 14203; **716-847-6044**
IN NEW JERSEY
   Hudson Mall — Route 440 and Communipaw Ave.,
      Jersey City, NJ 07304; **201-433-7740**
IN CONNECTICUT
   202 Fairfield Ave., Bridgeport, CT 06604; **203-335-9913**
IN OHIO
   2105 Ontario St. (at Prospect Ave.), Cleveland, OH 44115; **216-621-9427**
   25 E. Eighth Street, Cincinnati, OH 45202; **513-721-4838**
IN PENNSYLVANIA
   1719 Chestnut Street, Philadelphia, PA 19103; **215-568-2638**
IN FLORIDA
   2700 Biscayne Blvd., Miami, FL 33137; **305-573-1618**
IN LOUISIANA
   4403 Veterans Memorial Blvd., Metairie, LA 70002; **504-887-7631;**
      504-887-0113
   1800 South Acadian Thruway, P.O. Box 2028, Baton Rouge, LA 70821
      504-343-4057; 504-343-3814
IN MISSOURI
   1001 Pine Street (at North 10th), St. Louis, MO 63101; **314-621-0346;**
      314-231-5522
IN ILLINOIS
   172 North Michigan Ave., Chicago, IL 60601; **312-346-4228**
IN TEXAS
   114 Main Plaza, San Antonio, TX 78205; **512-224-8101**
IN CALIFORNIA
   1570 Fifth Avenue, San Diego, CA 92101; **714-232-1442**
   46 Geary Street, San Francisco, CA 94108; **415-781-5180**
IN HAWAII
   1143 Bishop Street, Honolulu, HI 96813; **808-521-2731**
IN ALASKA
   750 West 5th Avenue, Anchorage AK 99501; **907-272-8183**
IN CANADA
   3022 Dufferin Street, Toronto 395, Ontario, Canada
IN ENGLAND
   57, Kensington Church Street, London W. 8, England
IN AUSTRALIA
   58 Abbotsford Rd., Homebush, N.S.W., Sydney 2140, Australia